AF291282

HISTORIC NORFOLK

FROM THE AIR

Mike Page and Pauline Young

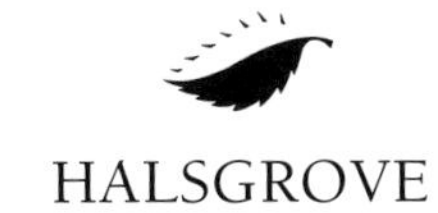

HALSGROVE

HISTORIC NORFOLK
FROM THE AIR

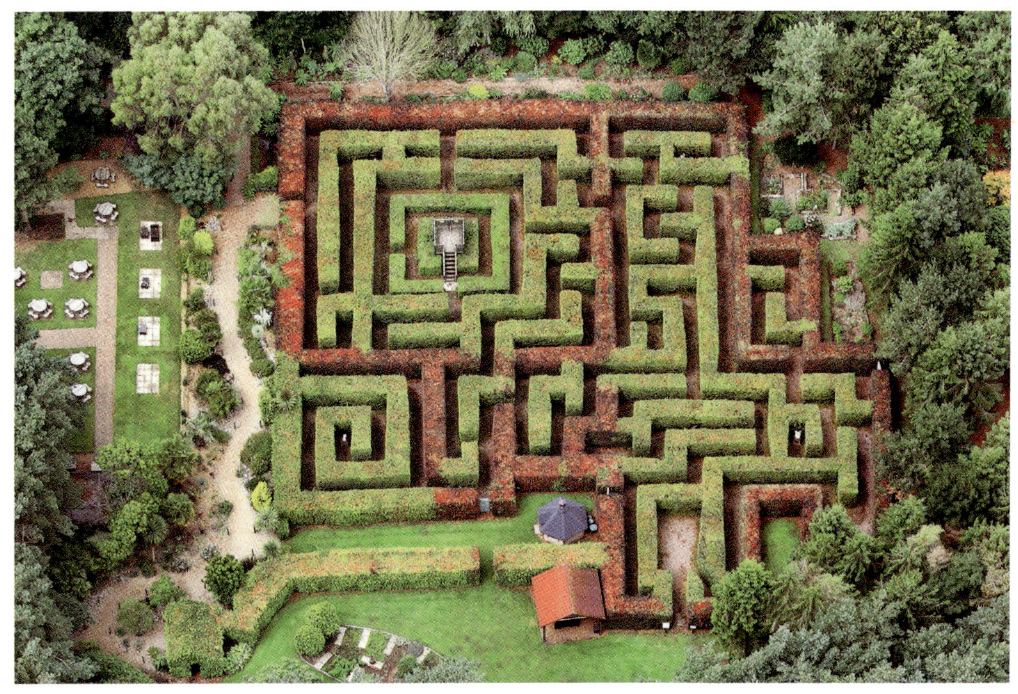

Mike Page and Pauline Young

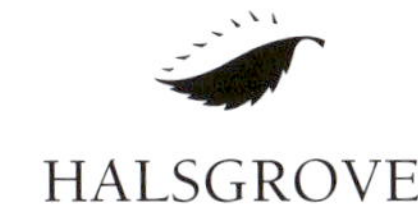

HALSGROVE

First published in Great Britain in 2022

British Library Cataloguing-in-Publication Data
A CIP record for this title is available from the British Library

ISBN 978 0 85704 350 4

Halsgrove
Halsgrove House,
Ryelands Business Park,
Bagley Road, Wellington, Somerset TA21 9PZ
Tel: 01823 653777   Fax: 01823 216796
email: sales@halsgrove.com

Part of the Halsgrove group of companies
Information on all Halsgrove titles is available at:
www.halsgrove.com

Printed and bound in India by Parksons Graphics Pvt. Ltd.

Front cover: Whitlingham Country Park (main image); Great Bircham Windmill (bottom left); Norwich Castle (centre); Cow Tower (bottom right).
Back cover image: Mrs Elizabeth Woodhouse of Breckles Hall.

Contents

Introduction 6

Chapter 1 Norfolk Industries 8

Chapter 2 Roads and Lanes, Trains and Planes, Ferries and Wherries 22

Chapter 3 All Work and No Play Makes Jack a Dull Boy
(In Norfolk there are plenty of play opportunities for Jack and Jill) 32

Chapter 4 Murder Most Foul and Other Nasty Happenings 52

Chapter 5 Metamorphosis; A Change of Character
(How familiar objects are put to alternative uses) 63

Chapter 6 War 80

Chapter 7 Norfolk Connections 100

Chapter 8 Do Different (an old Norfolk saying)
(People who put Norfolk on the map by doing just that) 118

Bibliography 144

Acknowledgements 144

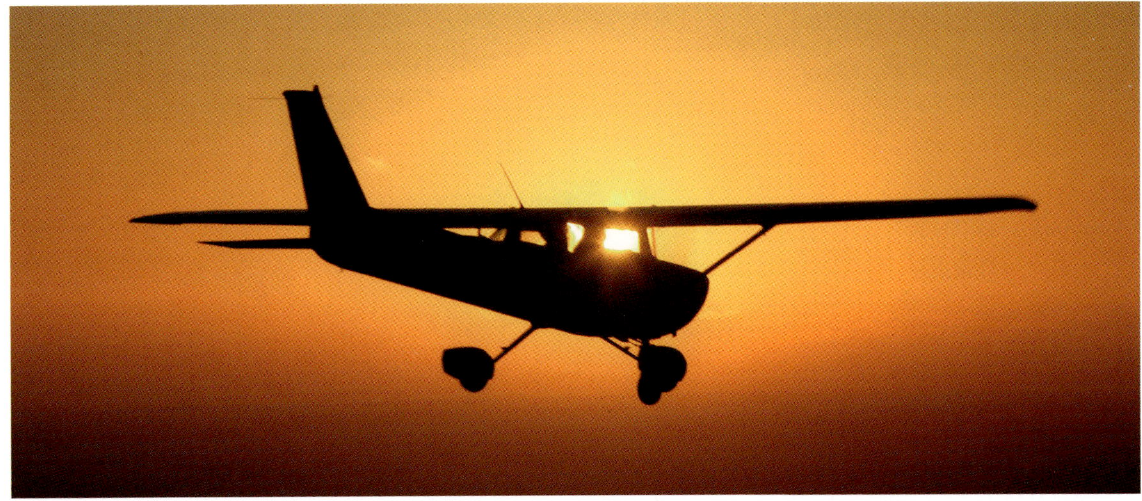

Introduction

As recently as twelve thousand years ago, Doggerland, a glacial expanse linking much of Europe to landmasses further distant began to experience climate change. Around 9000 BC temperatures rose and rain fell. The population began to emerge as hunters who fashioned primitive tools and sea levels rose to create the North Sea thereby separating Britain from the continent. From this isolation developed an independence of spirit which remains to this day. This is especially true of the generations of Norfolk-born men and women, the North folk, who take pride in being 'out on a limb' on the eastern edge of England. Most consider it a great blessing that no motorways venture into Norfolk. The aim of this book is to illustrate the many facets of Norfolk life which have emerged over the centuries and of the people who made Norfolk famous or sometimes infamous.

Aerial photography, fittingly in the context of this book, has helped greatly in the discovery of diverse subjects such as flint workings, ancient tracks and long-gone buildings. The aerial photographer has, among many other subjects, charted the building of Great Yarmouth's new harbour, the installation of North Sea wind turbines, the continual erosion of the coastline and the effects of sea defences. What a triumph it will be when some young pilot, possibly still at Primary School today, takes aerial pictures of the dualling of the Acle Straight!

This book is a tribute to all who made Norfolk the very special place it is today.

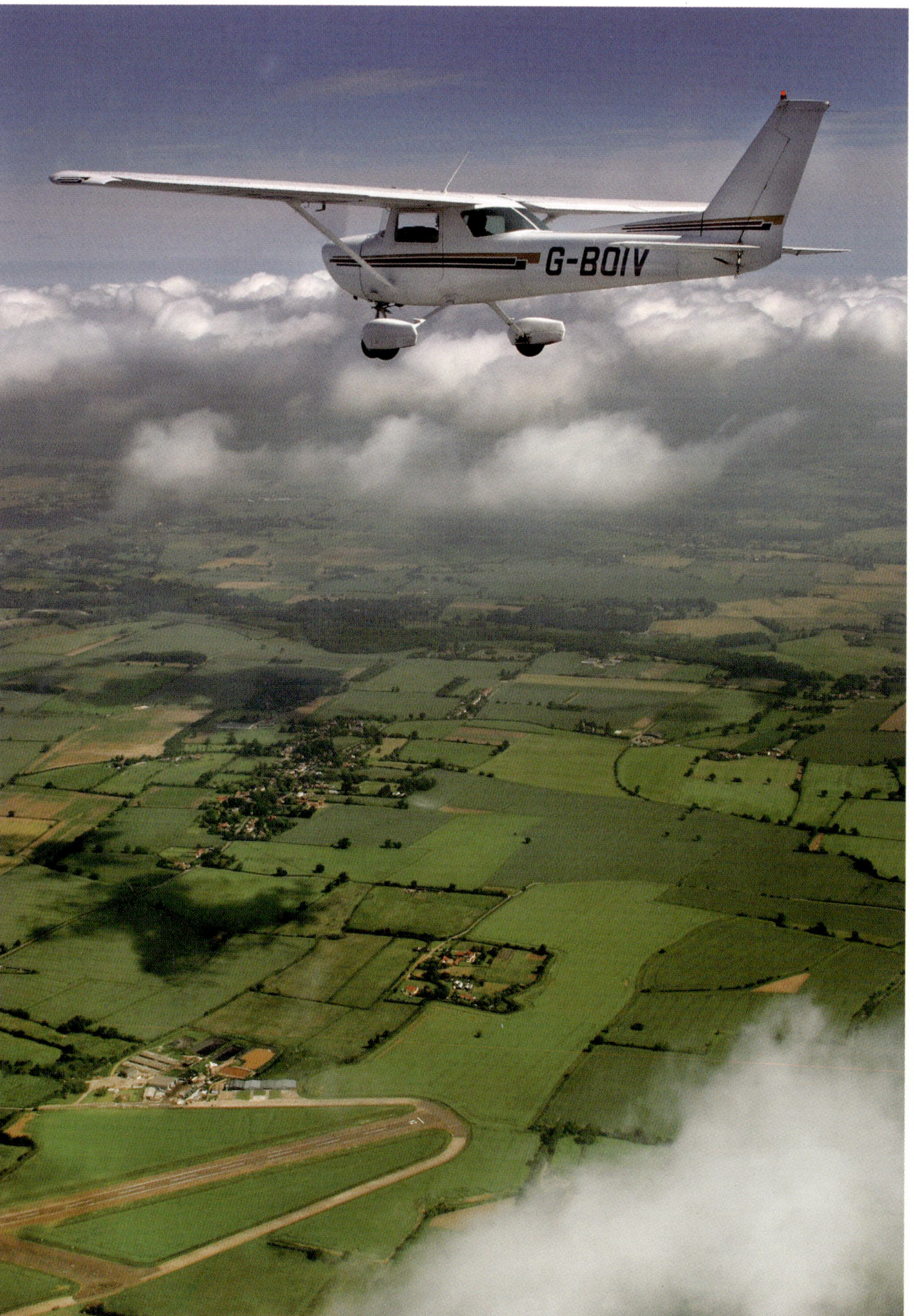

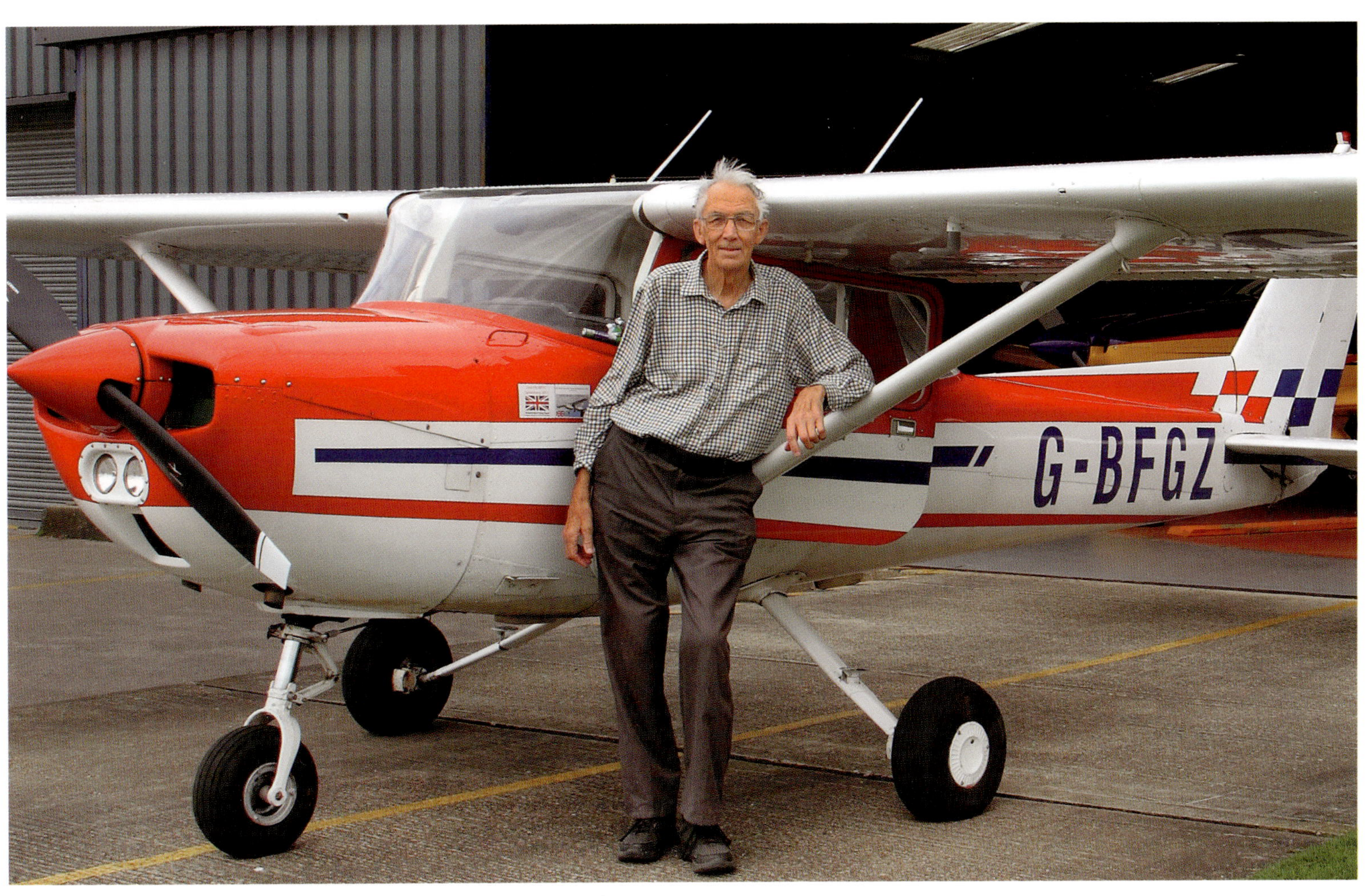

G·BFGZ

Chapter 1

Norfolk Industries

Some of the most picturesque scenes in the county are the result of very hard labour by a workforce not necessarily all that willing. The industrial aspect may be overlooked when admiring the view.

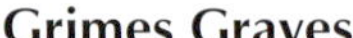

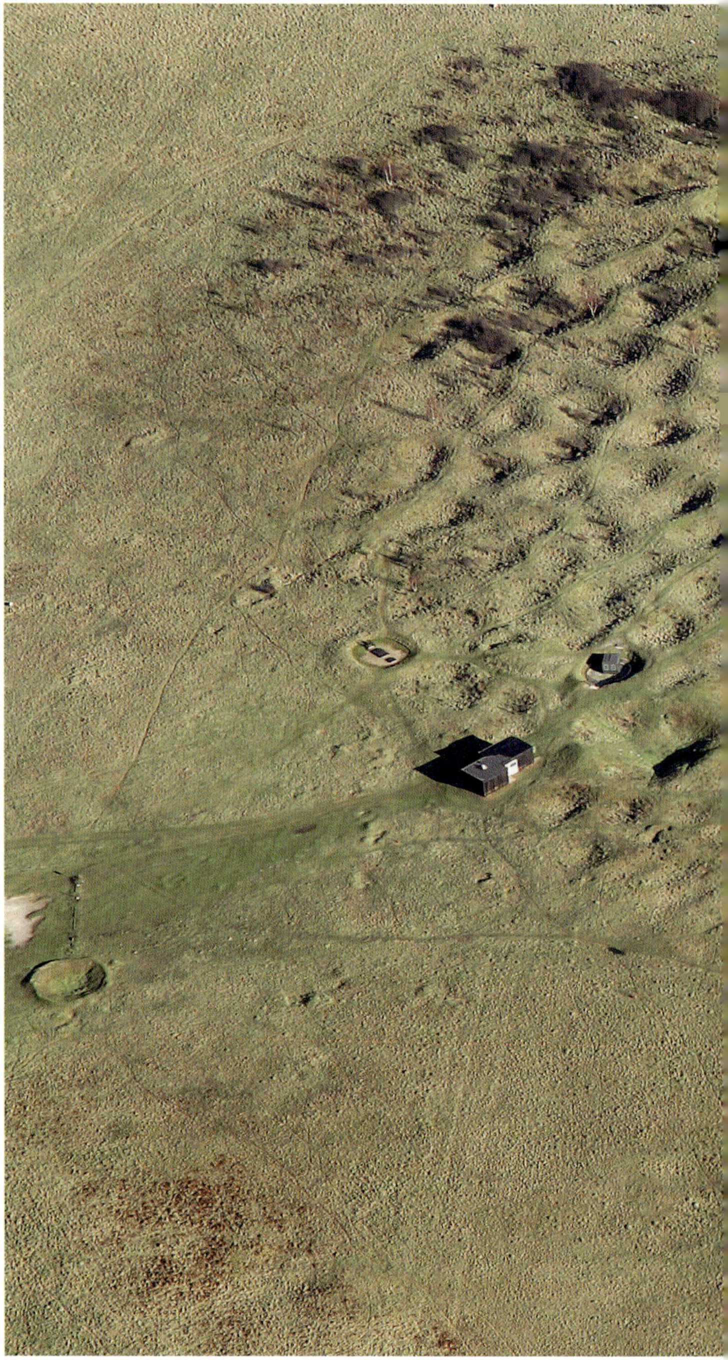

Grimes Graves

A field of mounds and hollows was excavated in 1897. It was then that they were discovered to be Neolithic flint mines. Shafts 30ft (9m) deep were revealed. There were interconnecting passages whose walls were of black flint. The field was named after Norse god Grim and dated back to 10,000 BC. Red deer antlers had been used as primitive tools to fashion the stone into tools and weapons. As late as the Napoleonic Wars, flint provided the spark for flintlock pistols. Today there's ladder access to one chamber. The site is administered by English Heritage.

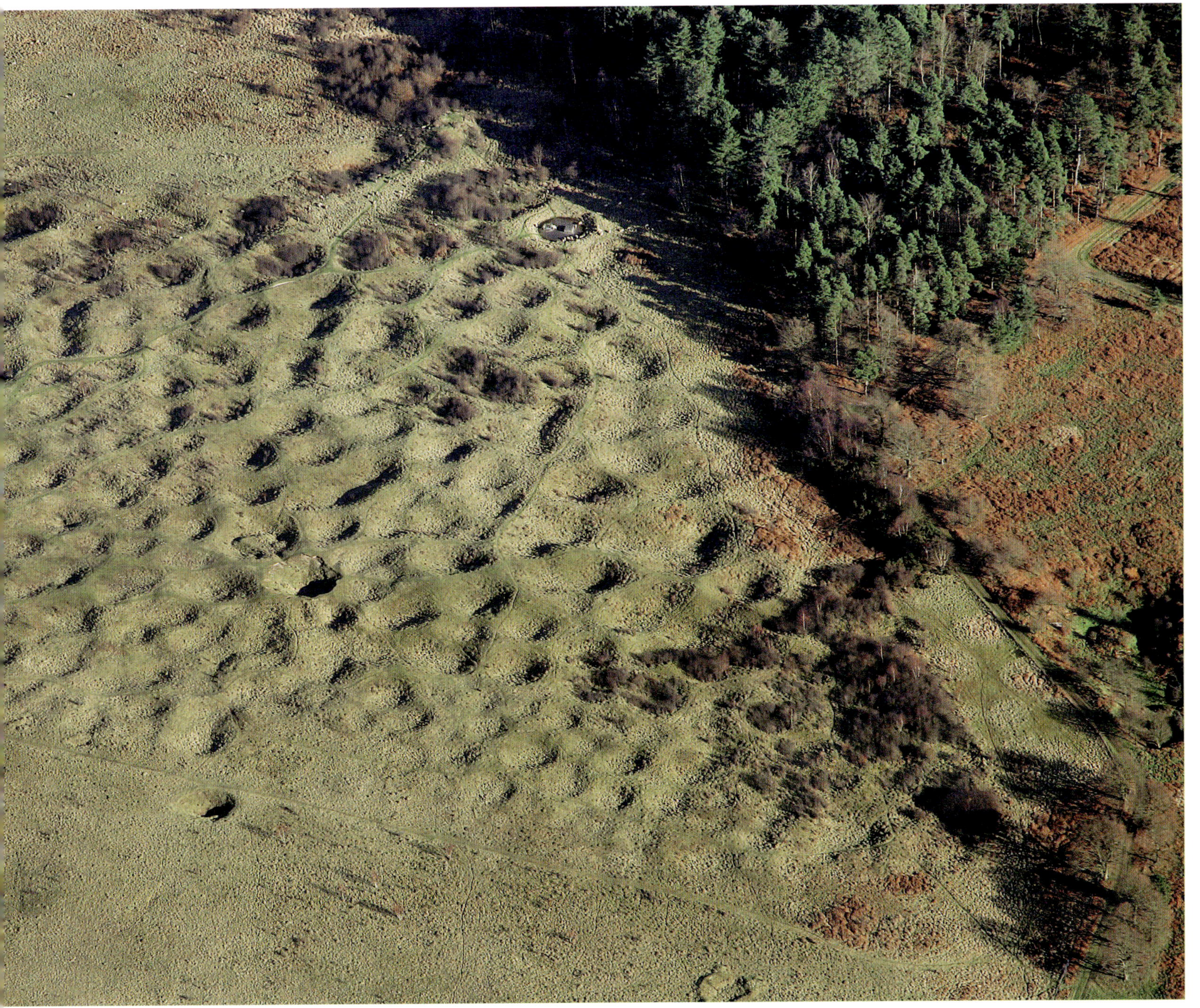

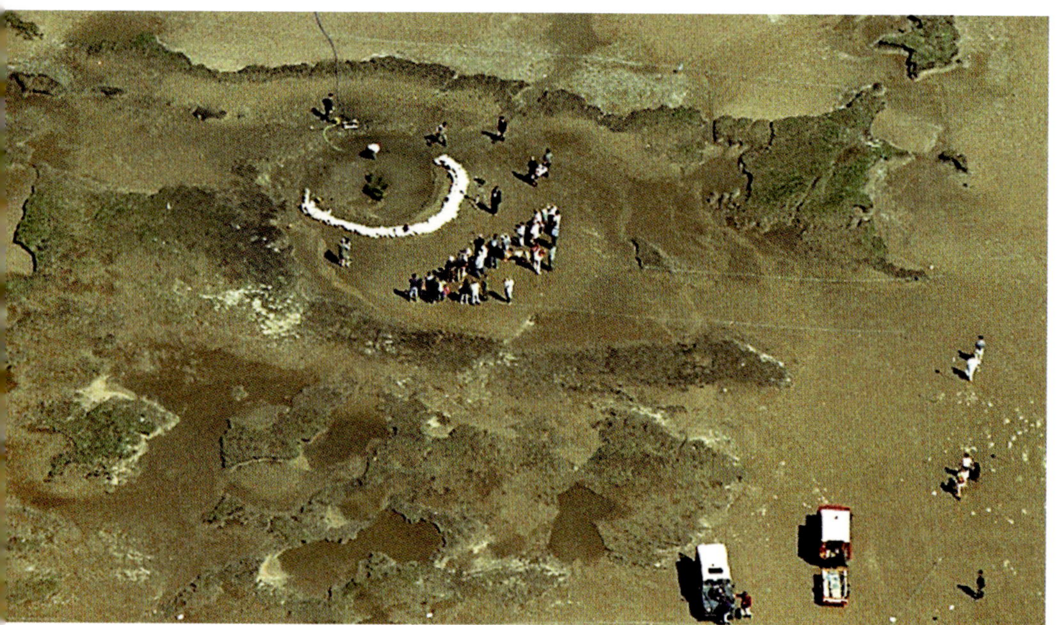

Seahenge

In 1998 at Holme next the Sea near Hunstanton an extra ordinary sight appeared. Low tide revealed a circular henge (purpose uncertain) dating from the Bronze Age (about 2000 BC). The 55 felled oak timbers were excavated and taken to Flag Fen near Peterborough to the Fenland Archaeological Trust for examination. The upturned roots at the centre of the circle may have been a sacrificial area. Slowly, over subsequent centuries the forest in which the trees had been growing had died, soil was washed away revealing the present beach (coastal erosion is nothing new). Salt in the surrounding marsh had preserved the timbers. They're now on view in Kings Lynn Museum.

The archaeological team from Flag Fen plus onlookers.

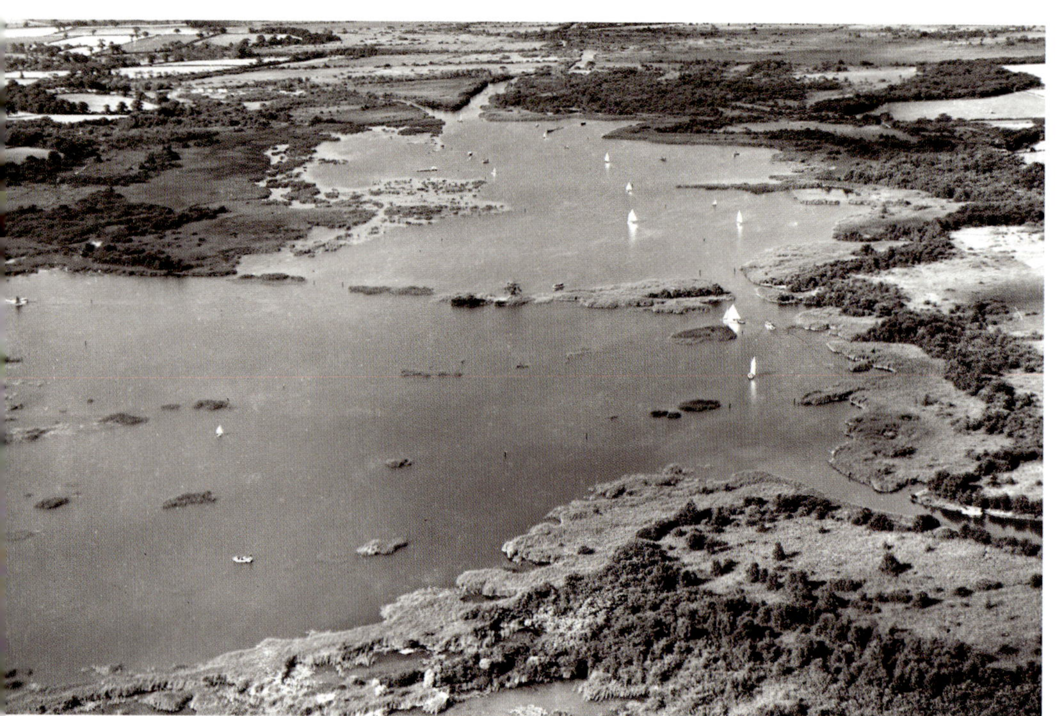

The Broads

1954 The straight line of the causeway across Barton Broad separates the parishes of Irstead and Barton Turf.

1954: to the right of picture (lower half) is the entry of the River Ant. It exits the Broad middle top, as a channel on the right hand side of the green triangle of 'The Heater' so named because it's said to resemble a flat iron – aka a 'heater'.

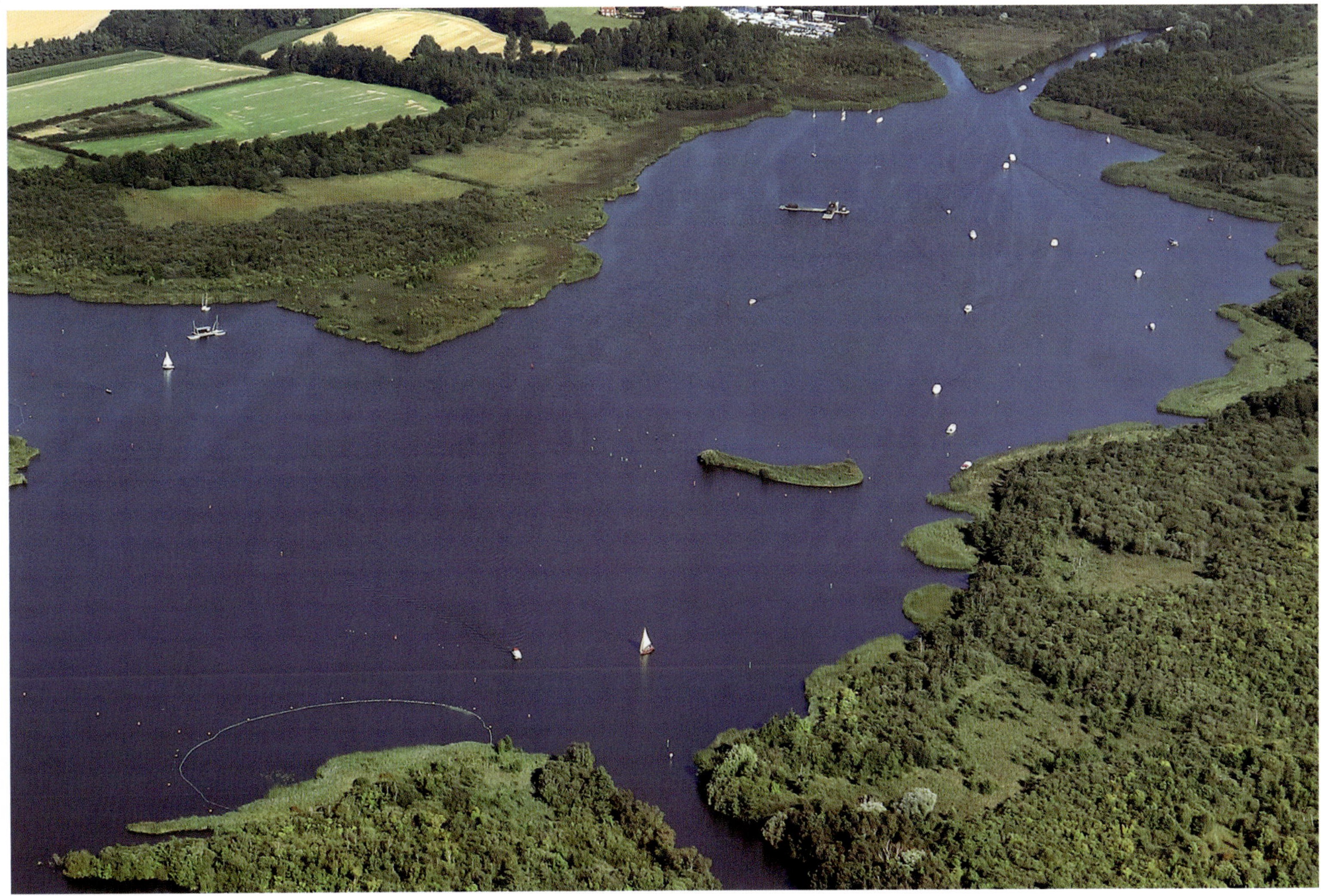

It's difficult to imagine the peaceful waters of The Broads as an industrial site but in the 1960s, and contrary to the then current belief, a group of scientists including Dr Joyce Lambert demonstrated that what had been assumed to be natural lakes were flooded workings of previous peat extraction. This was based on the discovery that the sides of the diggings were vertical rather than sloping as they would have been in a naturally-formed lake. Consisting of compressed vegetation the extracted peat turves were left on the banks to dry out before burning. Accounts for Norwich Cathedral until the fifteenth century show receipts for thousands of turves used for cooking and heating. A reminder of the industry's existence lives on in place names such as Barton Turf and Turf Fen. Dr Lambert's peat-sampling tool (looking much like a giant apple corer) is on display in the Museum of The Broads at Stalham.

A similar view of Barton Broad in 2019. The causeway has eroded leaving only the island known as Pleasure Hill.

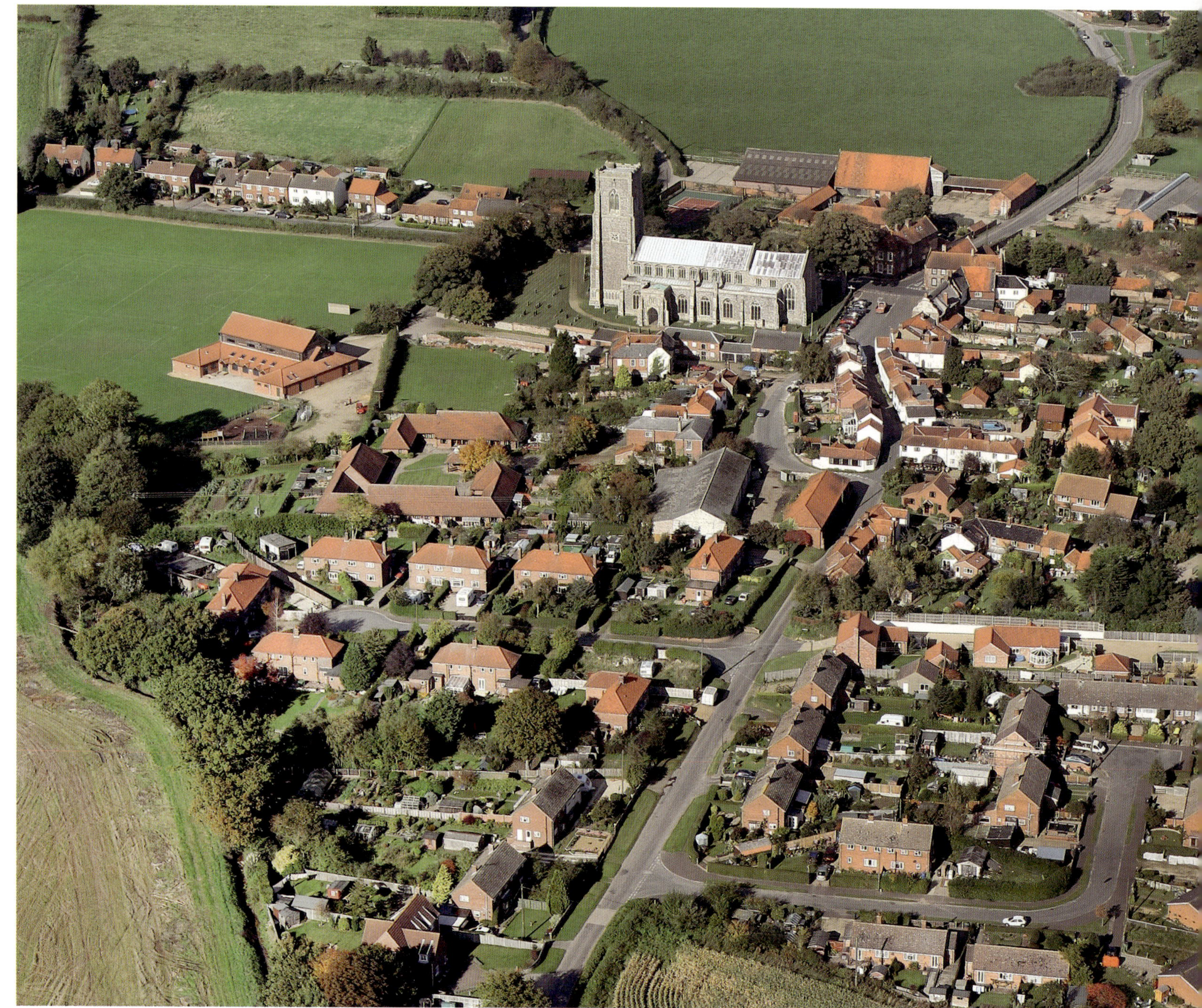

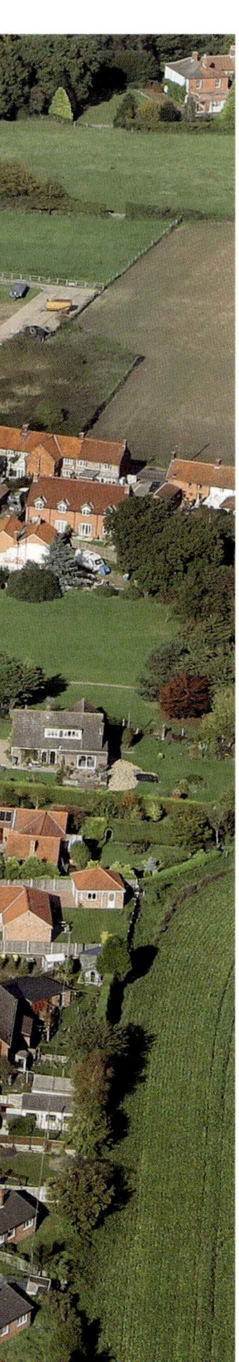

Worstead

Worstead gave its name to the type of yarn spun and cloth woven there until the seventeenth century. The dry Norfolk and Suffolk soils were well suited to sheep husbandry. The wool 'staple' was long and strong, spinning and weaving were well suited to be cottage industries. The prosperity of East Anglia was founded on the wool trade. The tradition of the Lord Speaker in the House of Lords sitting on a wool sack remains to this day. The magnificent churches of Lavenham and Long Melford were built or restored with fortunes made in the wool industry, as was Worstead's to a less grand degree. Spinning wheels and weaving looms stand in an aisle of Worstead church. The skills were introduced into East Anglia by Flemish weavers also known as 'Strangers' who fled to East Anglia to escape religious persecution on the other side of the Channel.

Worstead Saint Mary the Virgin begun 1379 and, unusually, it was constructed in one continuous build.

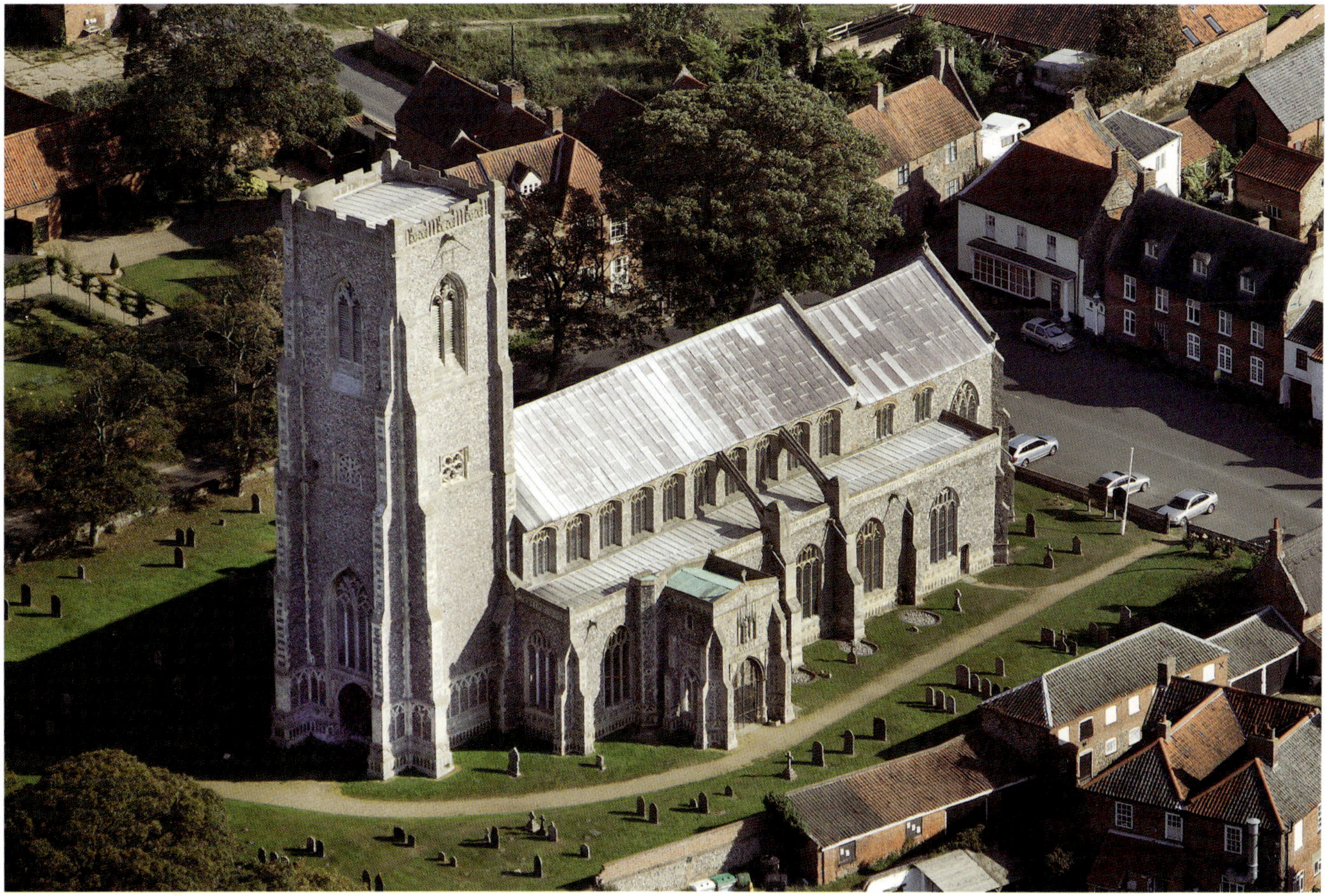

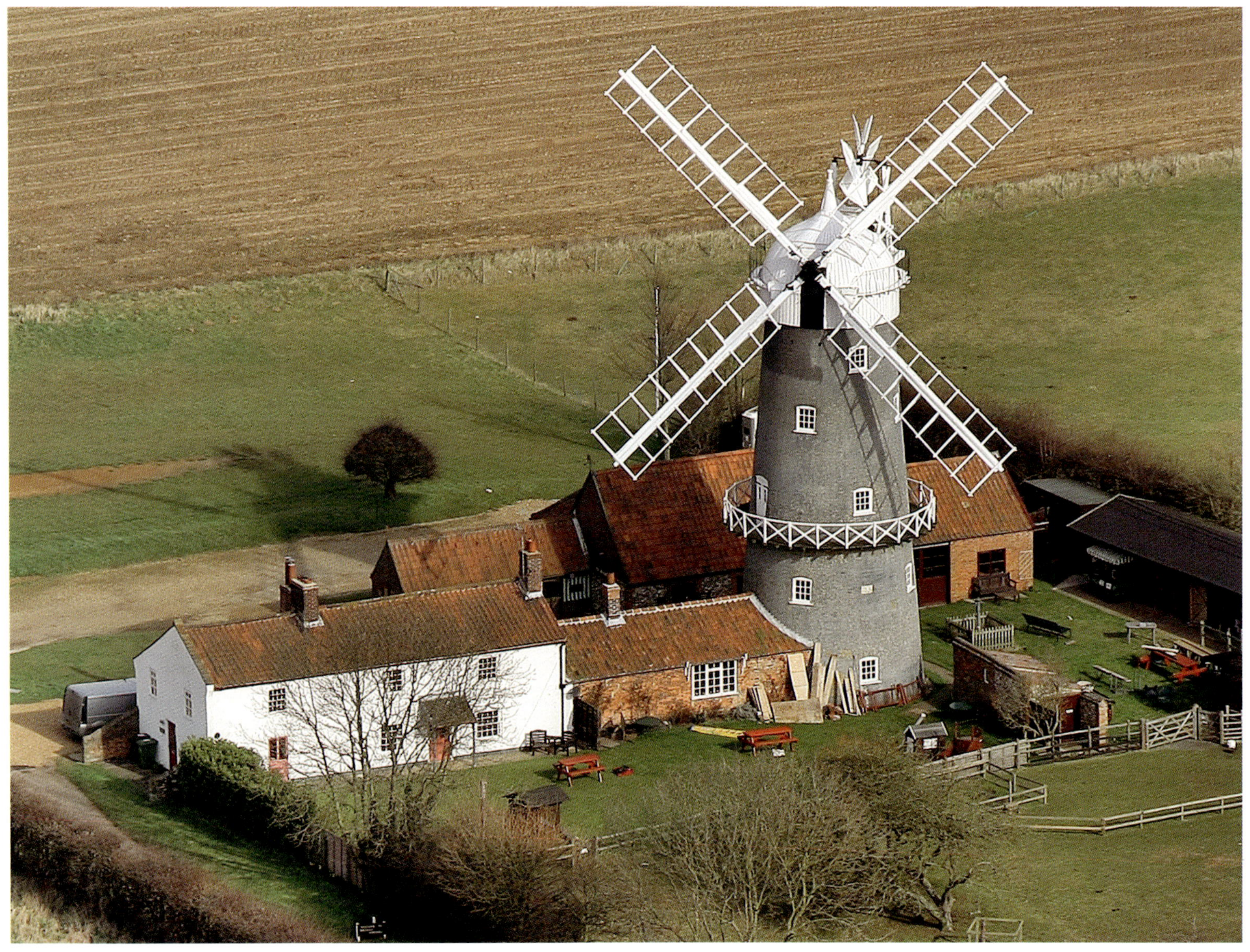

Great Bircham Windmill

A county of grain-growing fields plus dykes needing draining is natural windmill country. Sadly, as with so many other enterprises, technology overtook it and the picturesque windmills were abandoned – except in a few instances. Great Bircham's corn grinding windmill has been renovated, returned to its original purpose and along with a bakery has a tea shop selling bread flour ground on the premises. How's that for vertical integration?

Norwich Castle

The first Norman castle was timber built but was replaced within fifty years by the structure we have today. The massive artificial mound must have required much (possibly unwilling) labour. Recent excavations have revealed a Saxon cemetery within the mound.

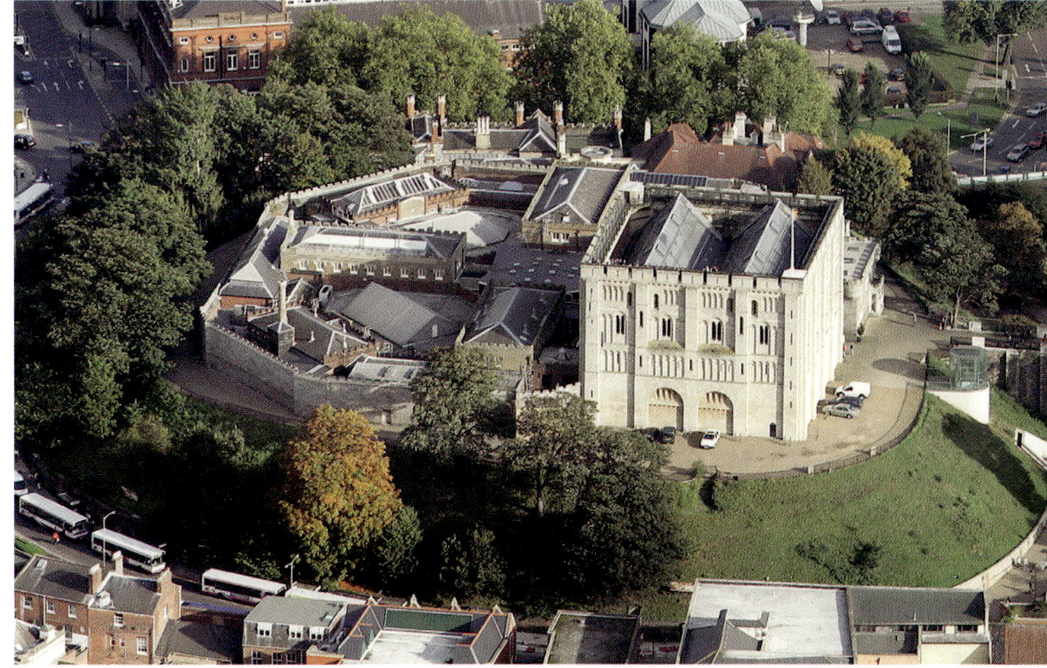

Castle Rising

Building the castle (c 1130) must have required much imported material for the artificial mound, probably brought in using the Babingley River. Built of Barnack (Northamptonshire) and Caen (Normandy) stone, for twenty-six years from 1332 to 1358 it became the prison of the hugely unpopular Queen Isabella (nicknamed the 'She Wolf of France'). She was the widow of the Edward II (whom she murdered) and mother of Edward III (he was the one who locked her up).

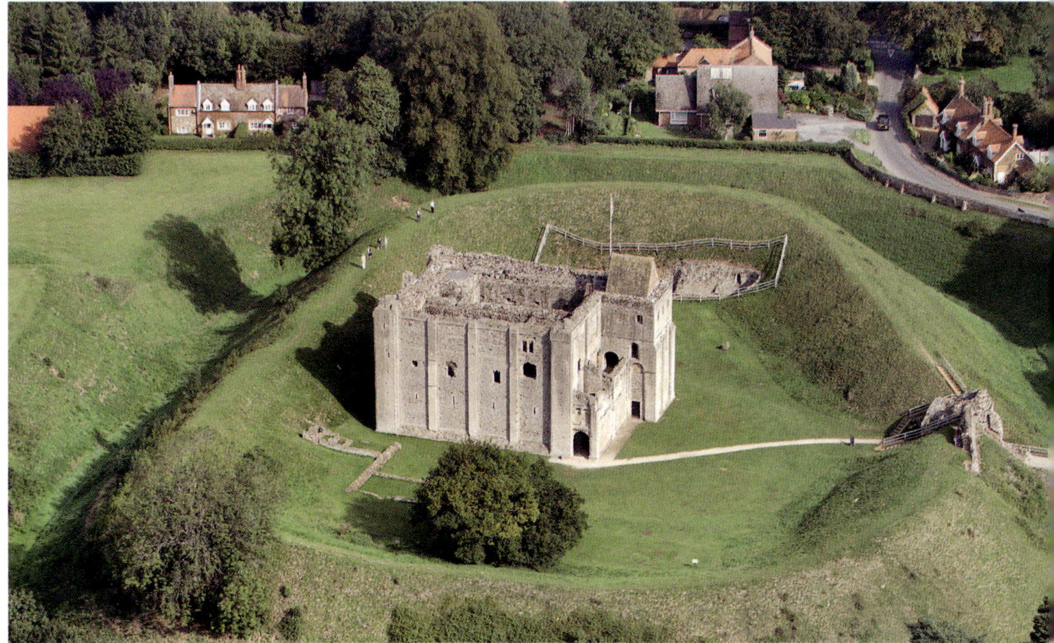

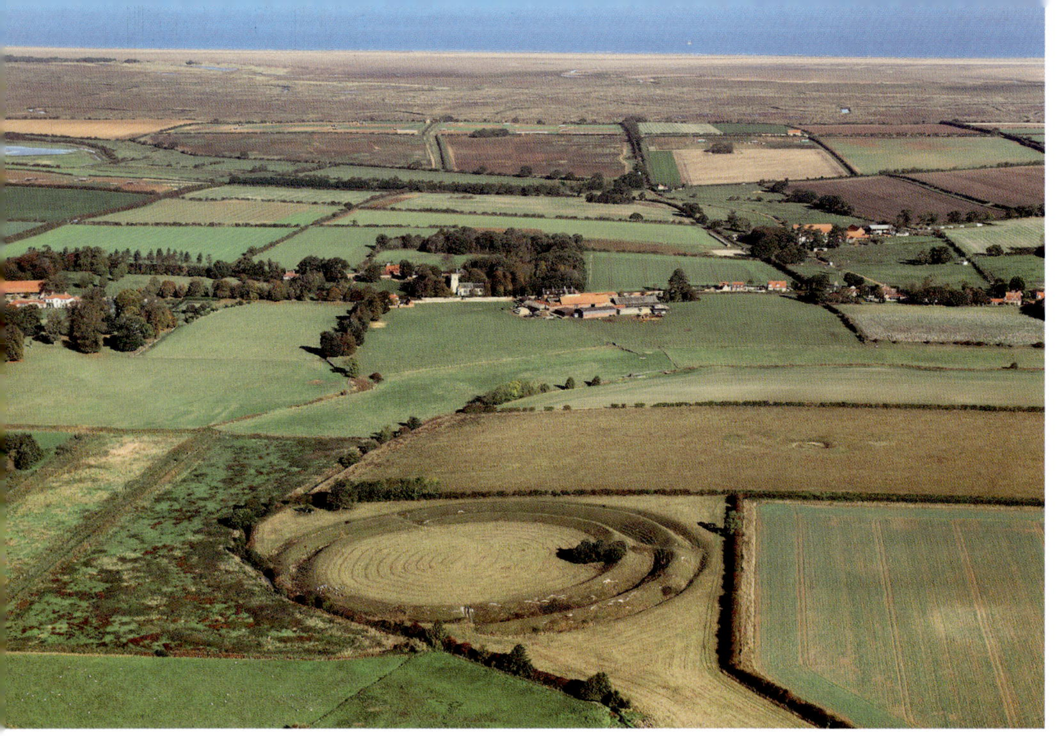

Warham Hill Fort

An Iron Age (700 BC–400 BC) hill defence and in a site of almost 4 acres, it's the largest preserved hill fort in East Anglia. It is sited next to the River Stiffkey. Others nearby include Narborough and South Creake.

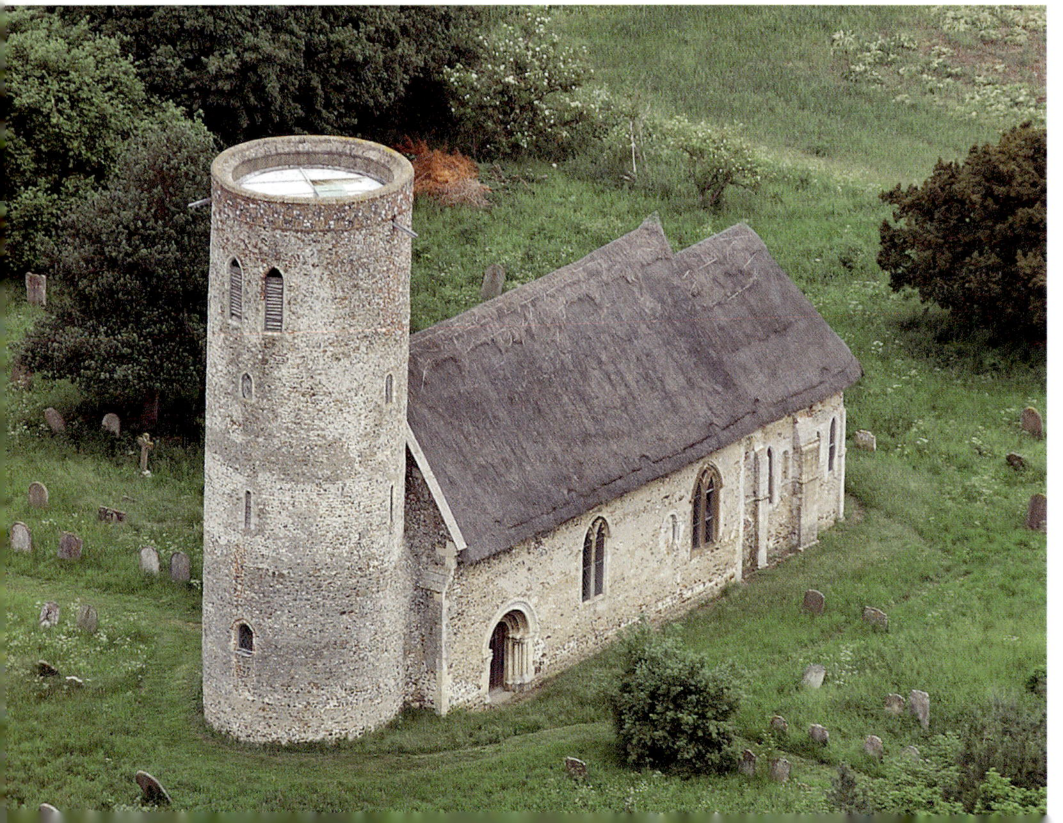

Churches

Hales Saint Margaret. Norfolk has over 600 churches and this thatched one is a little gem. Its rounded door, window arches and round tower all point to Norman origins. The 'layers' of flint in the tower indicate the progress made each winter and also the different fields from which the stone had been collected. Building took place only in the winter, in the summer all hands were needed in the fields. The taller the layer of stones, the milder the winter.

Reed Cutting

Reed cutting is a winter activity, when the reed has died and there is no sap left in the stem. The enterprise tends now to be carried out by something resembling a combine harvester where previously a scythe was used. Traditionally the reed was bundled into stooks of 60cm (24 inches) circumference which were transported from the marshes by water. It was loaded into a reed lighter and punted across the river to await collection by the thatcher.

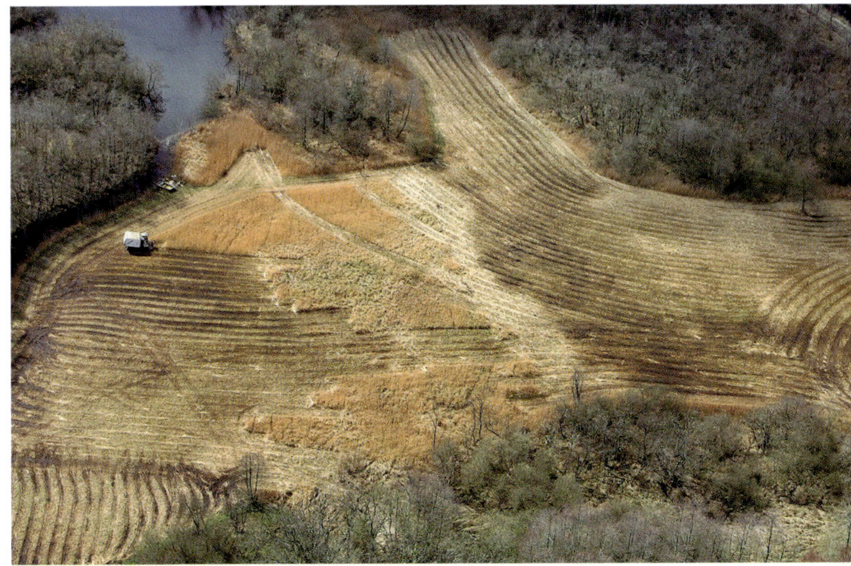

This reed has been cut by a purpose-built machine – a recent innovation.

Thatching

Reed has a straight hollow stem in which air is trapped thereby making it an excellent roof insulation. When the thatch has been pegged down the ridge is covered with sedge which bends. Both reed and sedge are pegged down with hazel 'brotches' and the whole is covered with wire netting to prevent it being used as a nesting material. The pattern on the sedge ridge is the thatcher's own trade mark. A thatched roof lasts about eighty years.

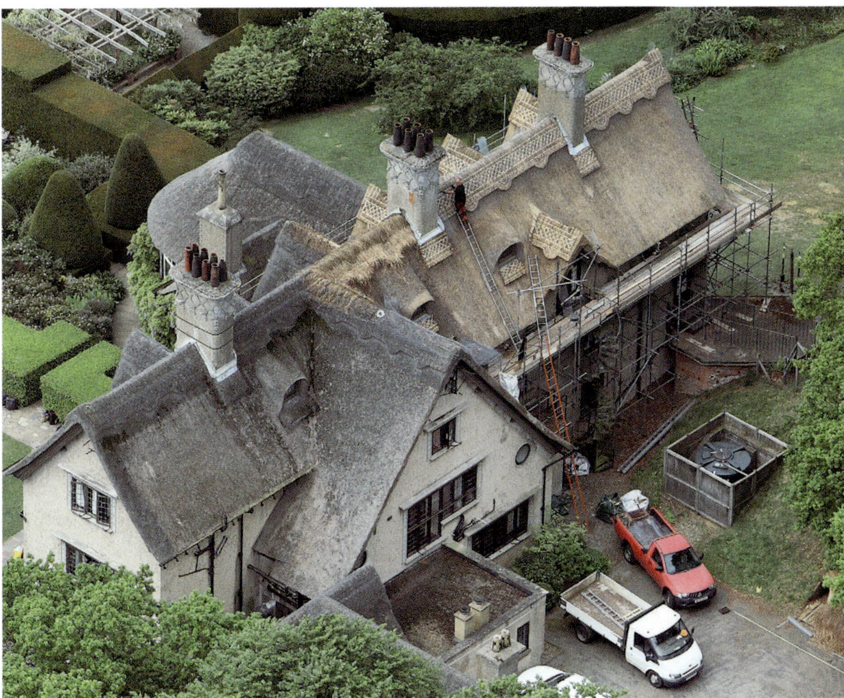

Rethatching How Hill House. Note the patterns of the hazel brotches (pegs) and the sedge ridge.

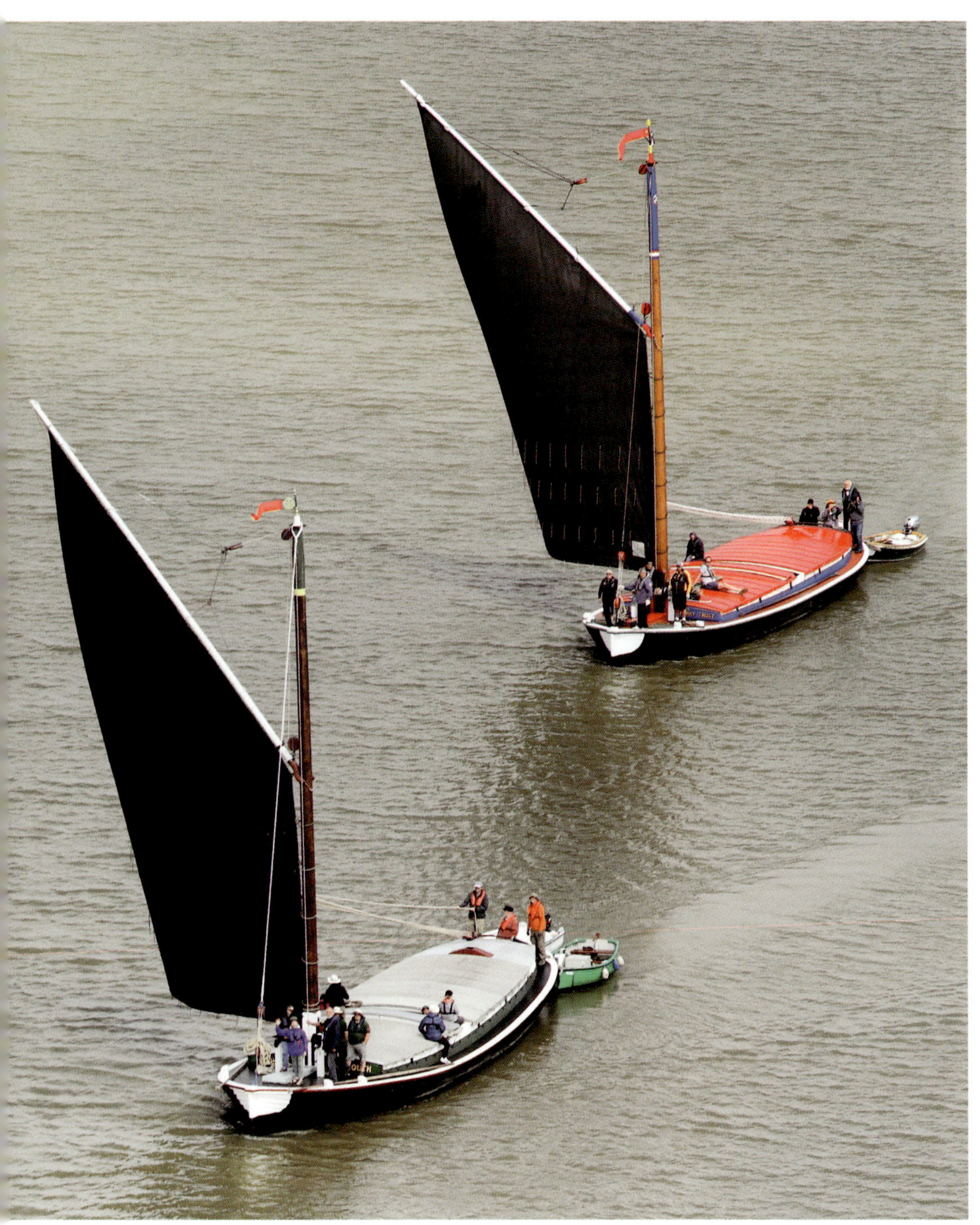

Wherries Maud (fore) and Albion.

Boat Building

In a county of rivers and broads such as Norfolk boat building is one of the oldest traditions. Trading wherries, of which *Maud* and *Albion* are the sole survivors, were built for the shallow Norfolk rivers. Such was the wherryman's skill that he could whilst under way 'shoot' a bridge by lowering the mast with sail still attached, pass under the bridge, raise the mast and continue his journey. Wherries loaded and unloaded their cargoes at village 'staithes'. There's a replica of a wherryman's cuddy (cabin) in the Museum of The Broads at Stalham. The distinctive black sail was coated with soot, tar and fish oil to lengthen its life. Wherry *Albion* (originally *Plane*) was preserved by the Wherry Trust, an initiative begun by Humphrey Boardman and Lady Mayhew after WW2. Wherry *Maud* was rescued by Essex millwright Vincent Pargeter in the 1990s using parts salvaged from other wherries which had, deliberately, been sunk on Rockland and Surlingham Broads for preservation.

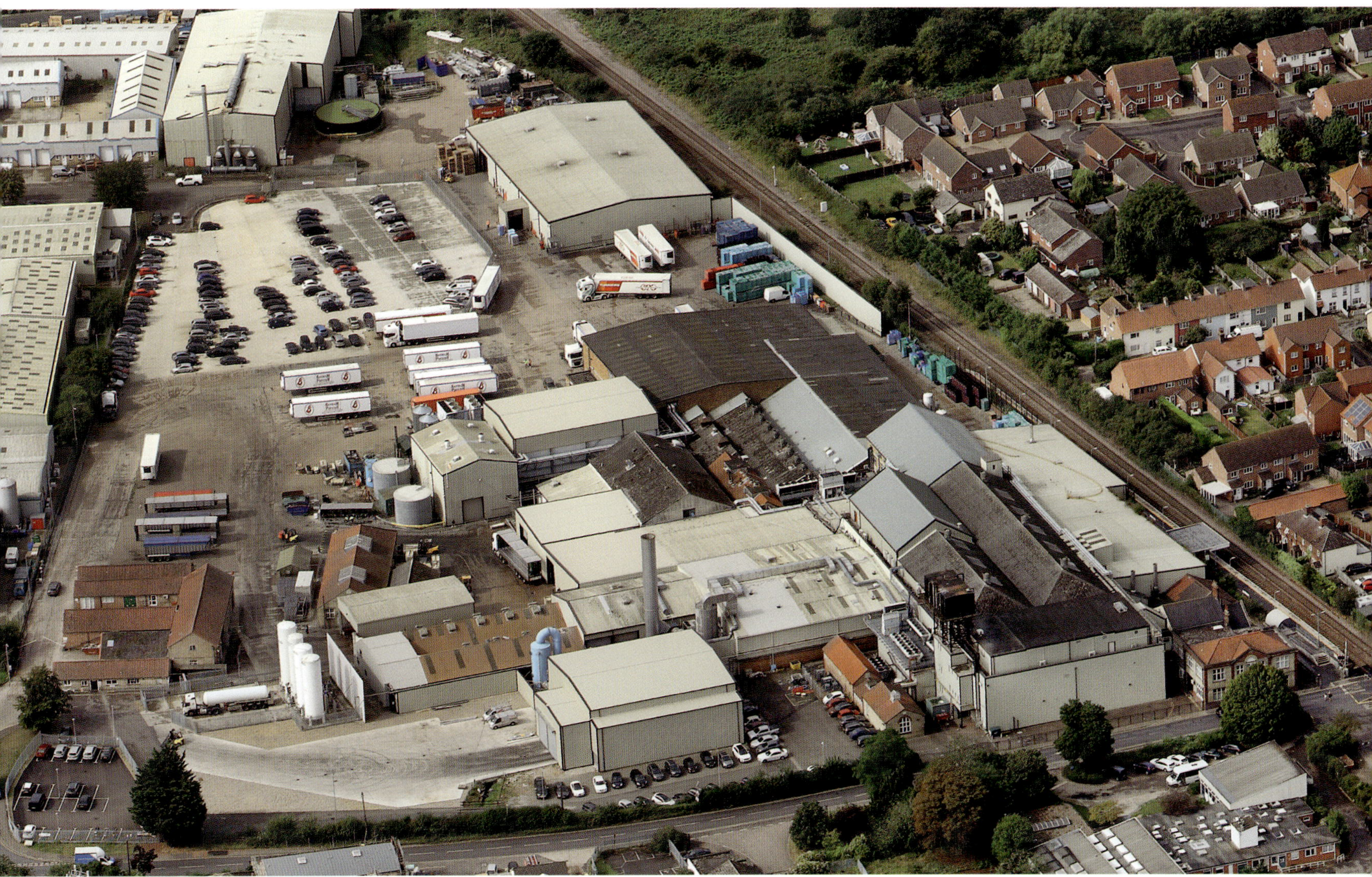

Gaymers Cider

Alongside Colman's mustard and Caley's chocolate, Gaymers Cider had the distinction of being a well-known Norfolk product. Sadly all three are now made elsewhere. For two centuries the Gaymer family had been producing cider in Norfolk. In 1896 the works was moved to Attleborough to take advantage of the adjacent railway line. Production continued there until 1995 when the business transferred to the West Country. The factory is currently used in the food industry by Banham Poultry.

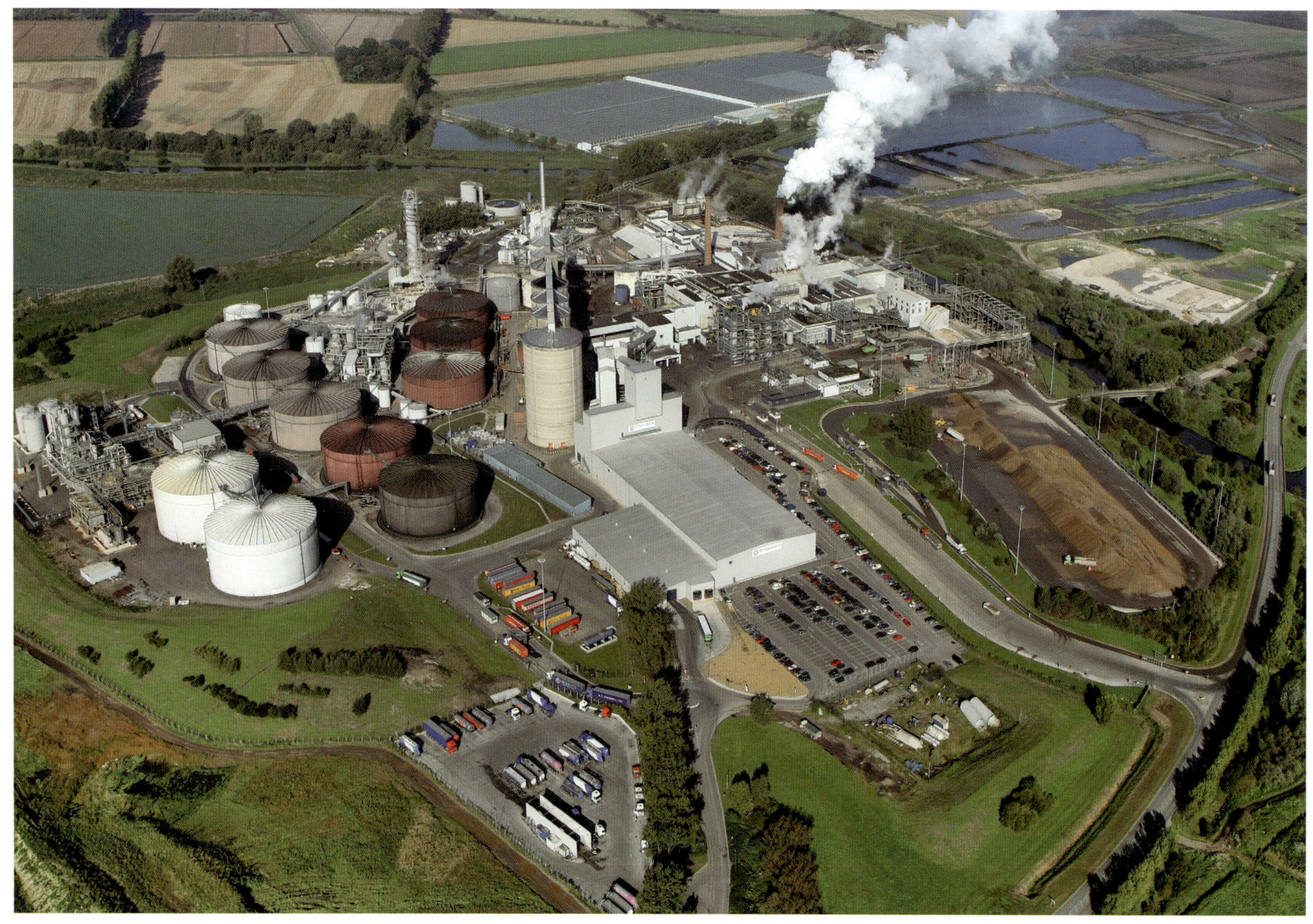

Sugar Beet Production

The plant at Wissington in West Norfolk is the largest of the four factories in England, the others are at Bury St Edmunds, Cantley and Newark, all on the eastern side of the county. The initiative came from Holland and the essential factor apart from suitable soil conditions in which to grow the crop is the availability of water both for processing and transporting. The Wissington factory was established in 1925. The River Wissey carried beet traffic between Wissington and Kings Lynn until 1943 when road transport took over. At Cantley (established 1912) the River Yare had the same role. The Wissington site now has a bio-ethanol plant (used in road transport fuel) and also grows hemp for the pharmaceutical industry. During the winter 'campaign' (processing of sugar beet) there's a distinctive semi-sweet smell wafting over the fields.

Engineering Excellence

Lotus Cars was the brainchild of Colin Chapman, a structural engineering graduate. In 1952 the Lotus engineering firm was created and was based on the former RAF airfield at Hethel. From the outset Colin Chapman worked on the principle that 'light weight is best'. The firm continues to produce some of the most successful high performance cars on the market – incidentally putting Norfolk on the map in yet another direction.

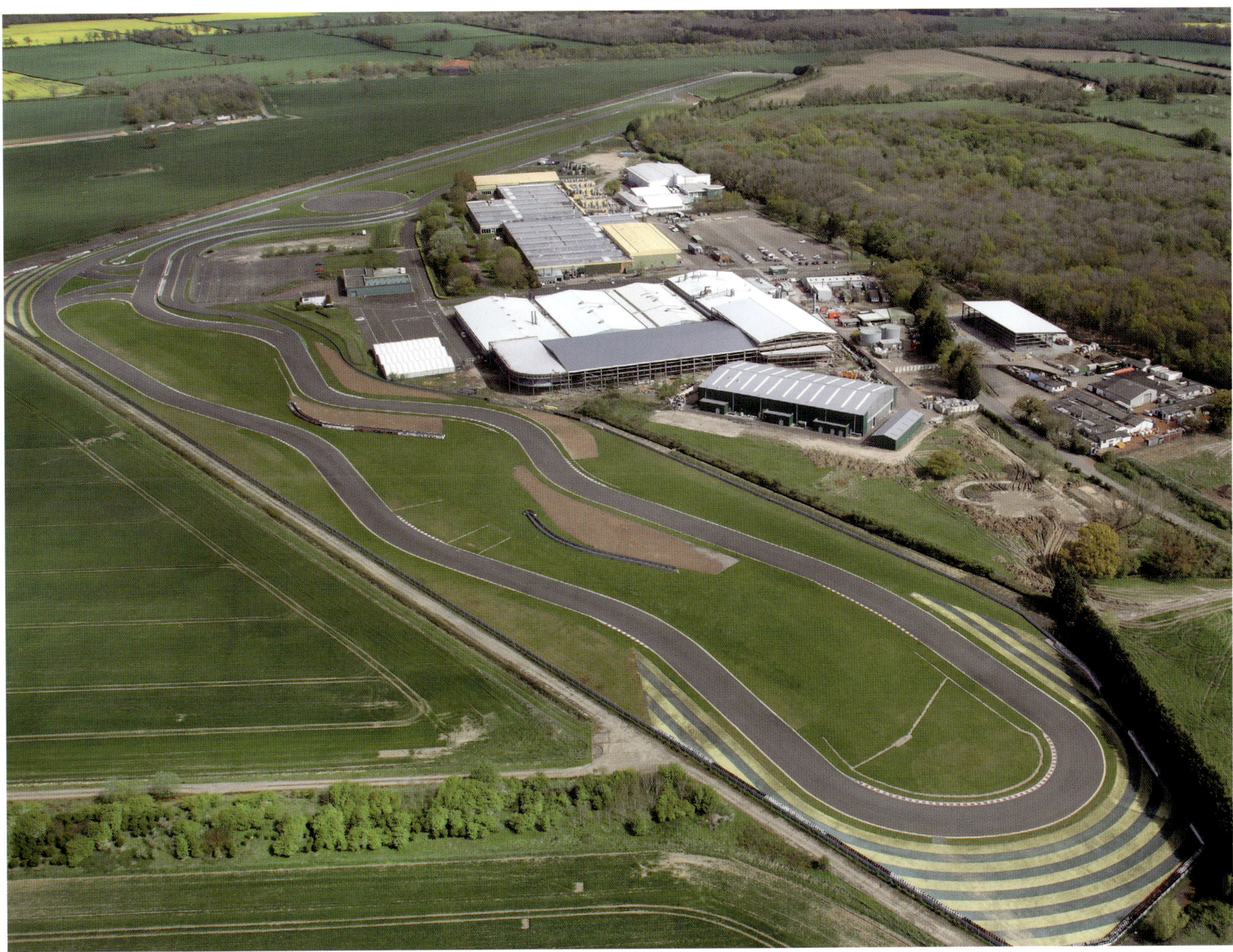

Chapter 2

Roads and Lanes, Trains and Planes, Ferries and Wherries

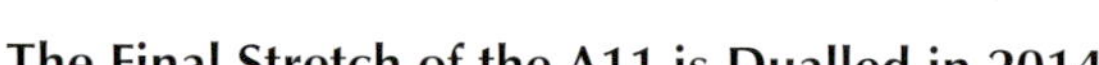

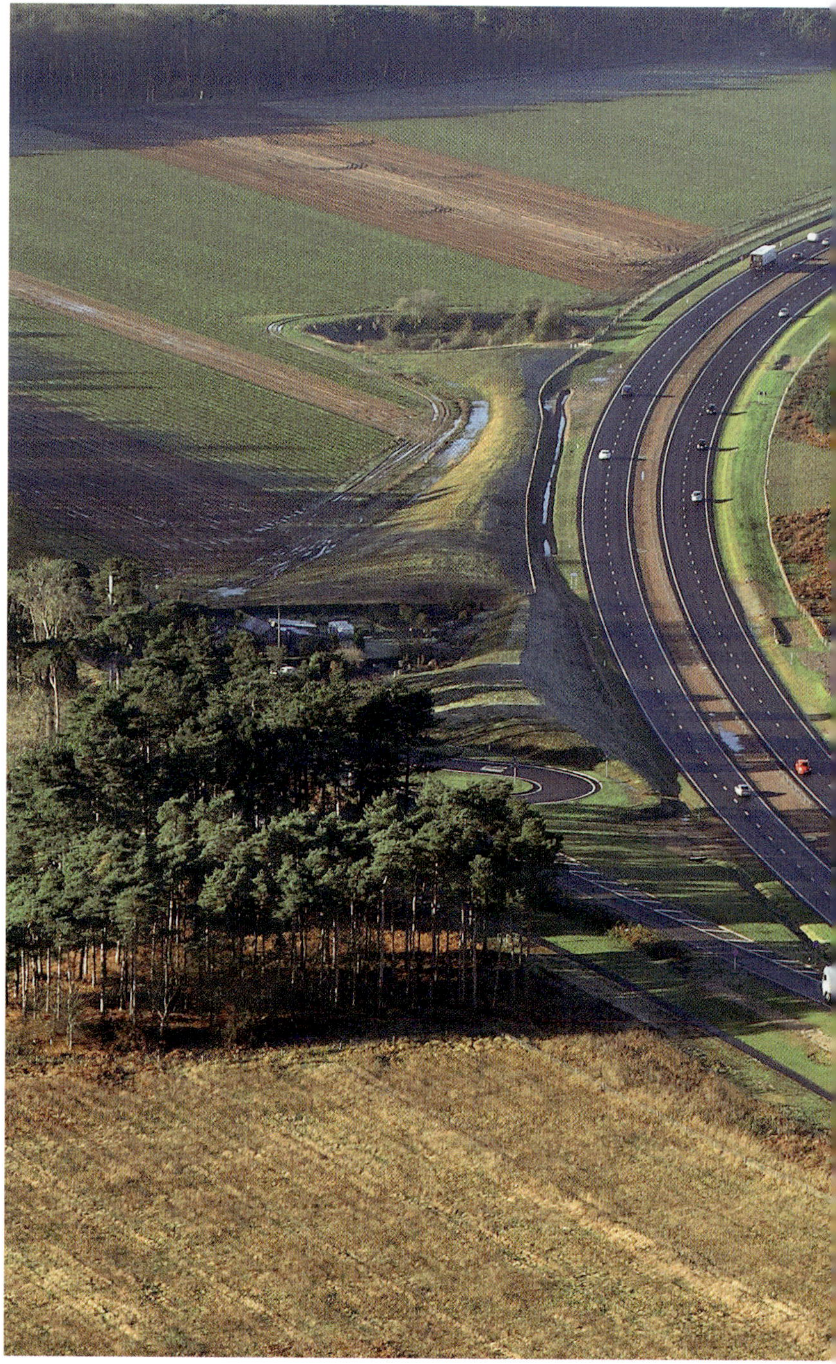

The Final Stretch of the A11 is Dualled in 2014

Celebrations all round but especially for the bat population for whom special bat bridges to guide them across the Elveden Bypass have been installed. Stretched between telegraph poles the mesh 'bridge' guides bats over and above the cars – if they use it!

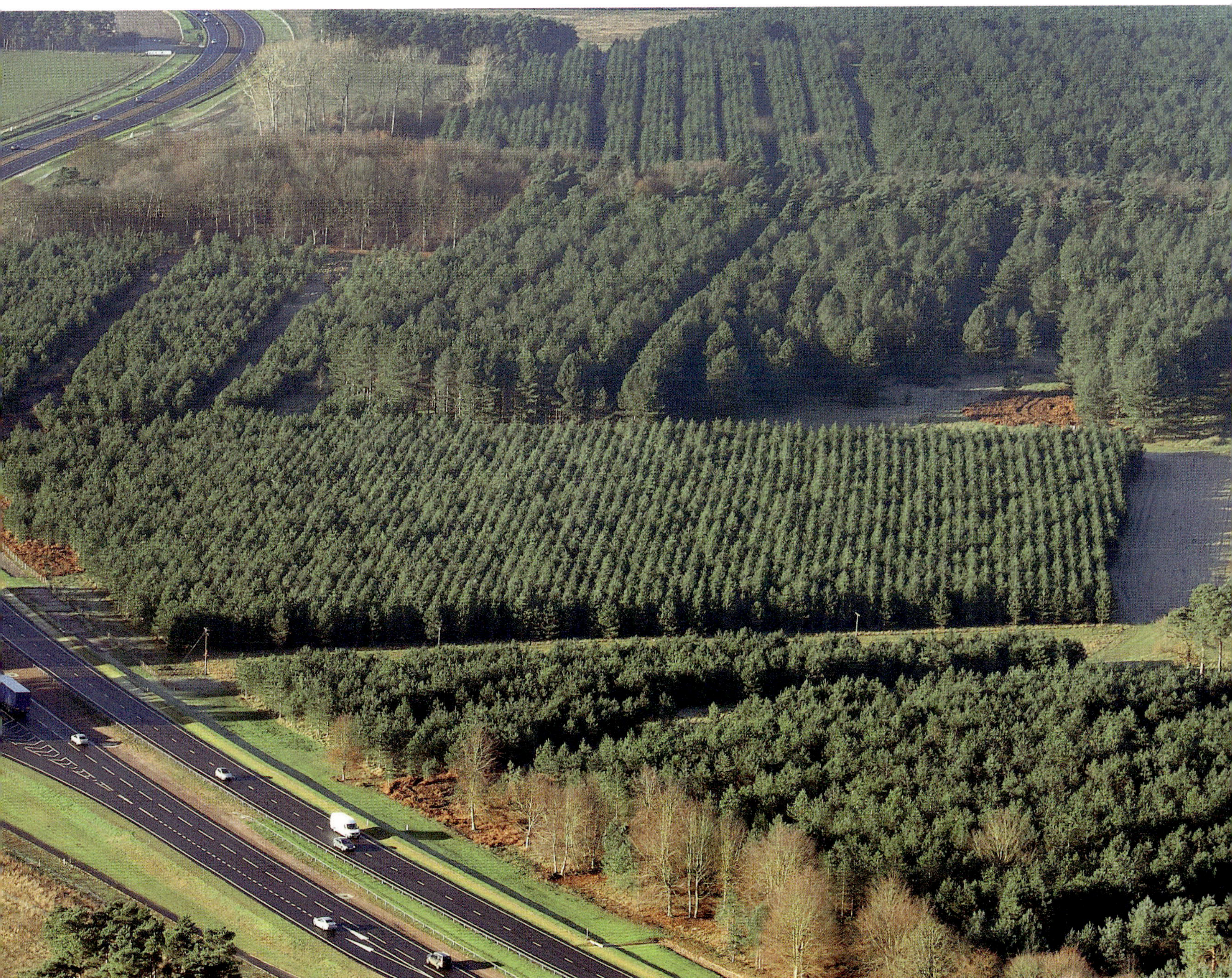

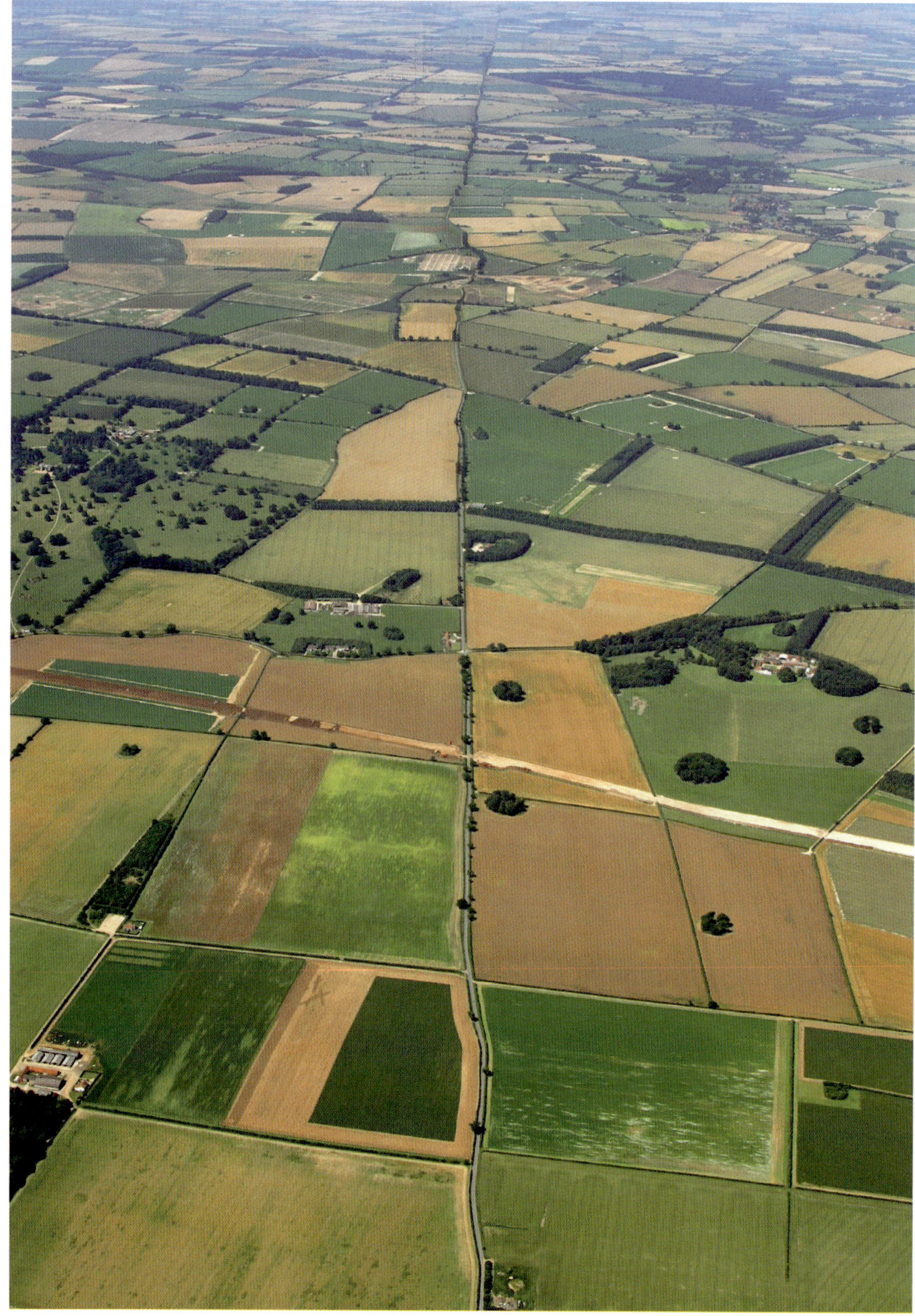

Peddars Way

Contrary to popular belief the mainly dead straight Neolithic (c2500 BC) Peddars Way predates what was assumed to be a Roman road. It begins as a trackway near Knettishall (Suffolk) and ends at Holme next the Sea. The Romans used it for marching troops up to the coast to ferry them across The Wash to Lincoln and beyond. The name is derived from *pedester*, on foot.

This pre Roman road is more or less dead straight apart from the kink in it around Castle Acre.

The Acle Straight

Built in 1831 the 'Acle New Road' quickly became 'The Acle Straight' because that's what it is. Its busy 9 miles contains only one bend and carries single lane traffic between Acle and Great Yarmouth amid constant calls for dualling. Building a road across marshland such as this is tricky because of unstable ground but this was achieved nearly two hundred years ago.

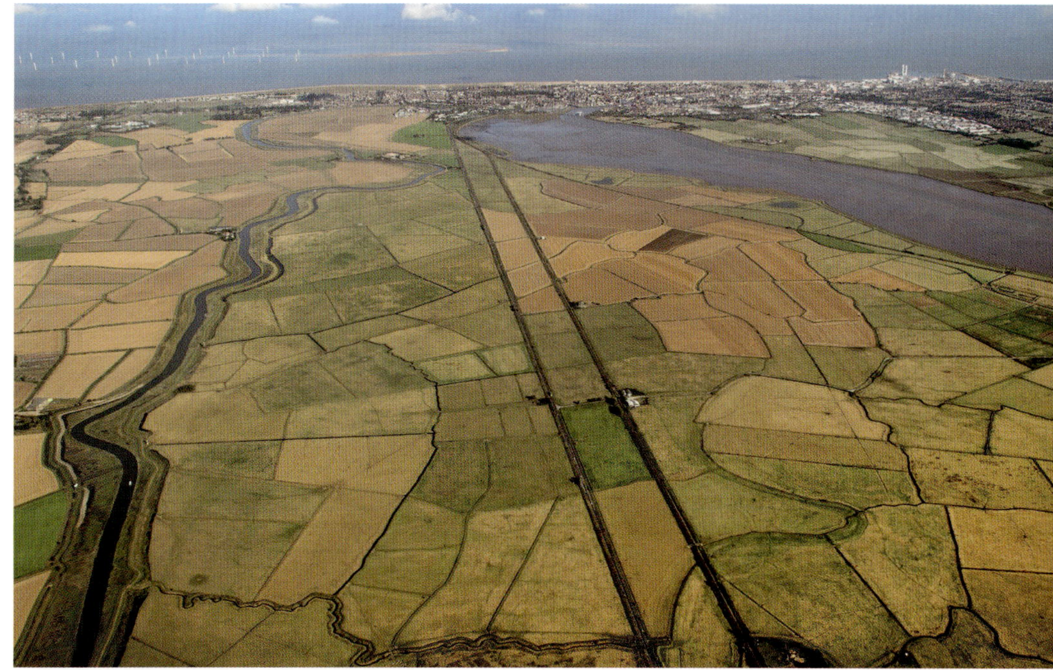

The Norwich NDR

The Northern Distributor's aim is to relieve congestion on the roads closer to the city centre and facilitate movement around the industrial areas including Norwich Airport. Recently its name was changed to the Broadland Northway.

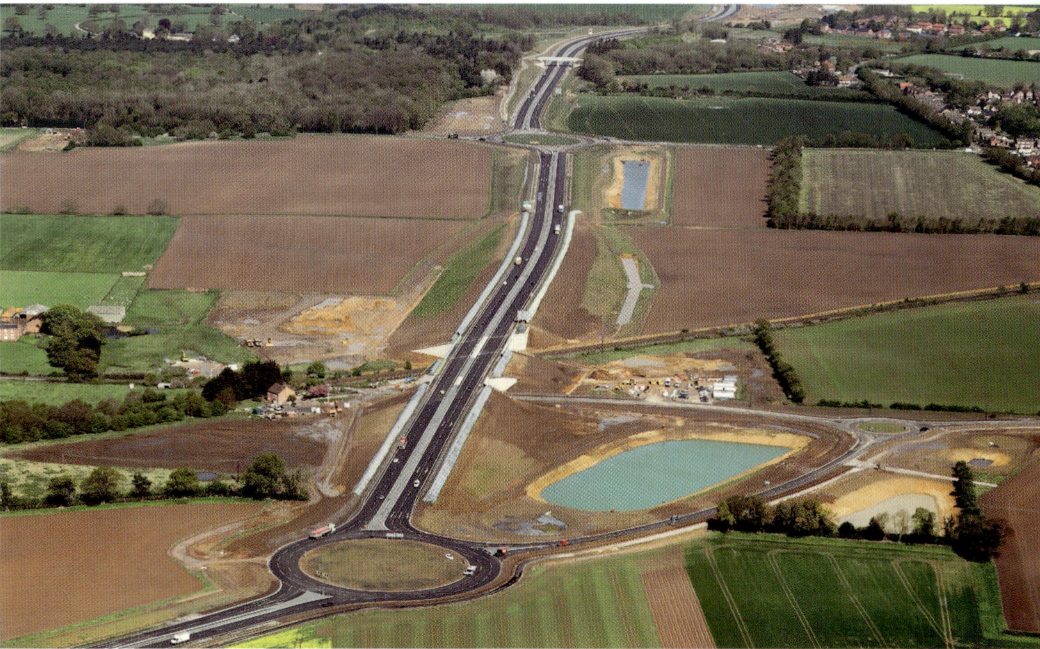

The blue lagoons are drainage ponds and the rainwater entering them was very clean during the initial construction of the road.

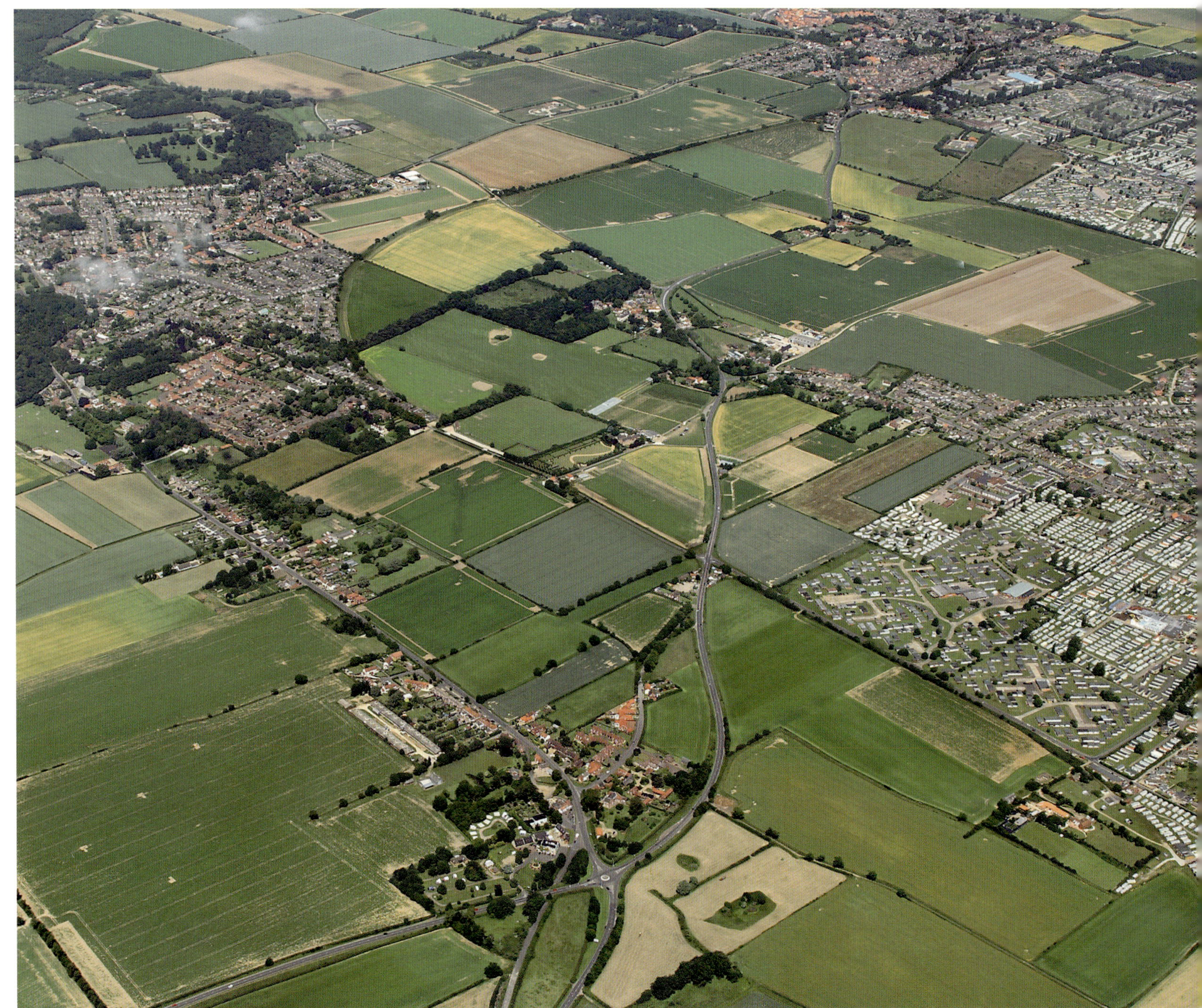

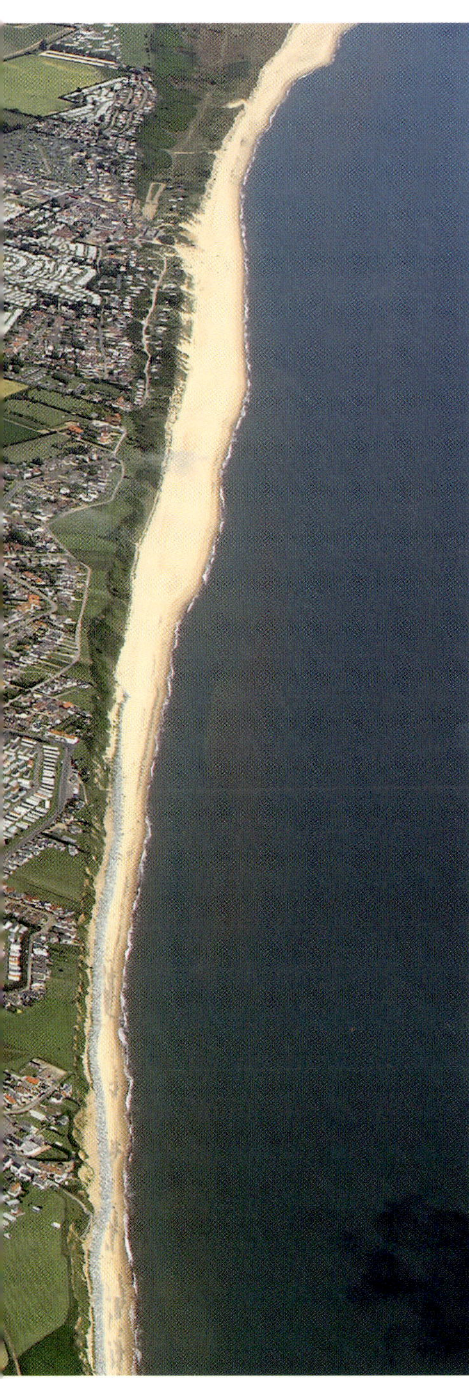

Trains

The track of the Midland & Great Northern Railway, closed in February 1959, is still visible as it curves inland past the holiday villages of California and Scratby, then on to Ormesby and distant Hemsby. This line ran from Great Yarmouth's Beach Station to the junction at Melton Constable and ultimately gave access to the Midlands and the North. The railway served all four places shown in the picture, although the halts at California and Scratby operated only in the summer months from 1933 onwards.

It was in industrial areas of the country where railways originated and several lines to the Norfolk coast were built to encourage the development of tourism in these areas from the 1860s onwards. Today many of the lines which brought holidaymakers flocking from the industrial Midlands to Great Yarmouth, Cromer, Sheringham and Hunstanton are long gone. With changing holiday patterns and the development of road transport it was inevitable that lines would have to be closed. A few lines live on as 'heritage railways'. The Poppy Line runs between Sheringham and Holt while the Mid Norfolk Railway runs between Wymondham and East Dereham, hopefully to extend northwards to County School one day. By road you can see reminders of former lines, such as dead straight stretches of highway where the carriageway has been built over former trackbed, and evidence of dismantled bridges.

Planes

From the late 1800s Boulton and Paul were successful general engineers. They became involved in aircraft manufacture in 1915. The factory and airfield on Mousehold Heath produced many different types of aircraft and sub assemblies. They also built and modified aircraft for many other manufacturers. In 1934 the aviation side of the business was sold and the airfield ceased to exist. Remaining aircraft production was transferred to Wolverhampton and continued under a different trading name. The hangars in the picture survived and are still in use today surrounded by an industrial estate and retail park.

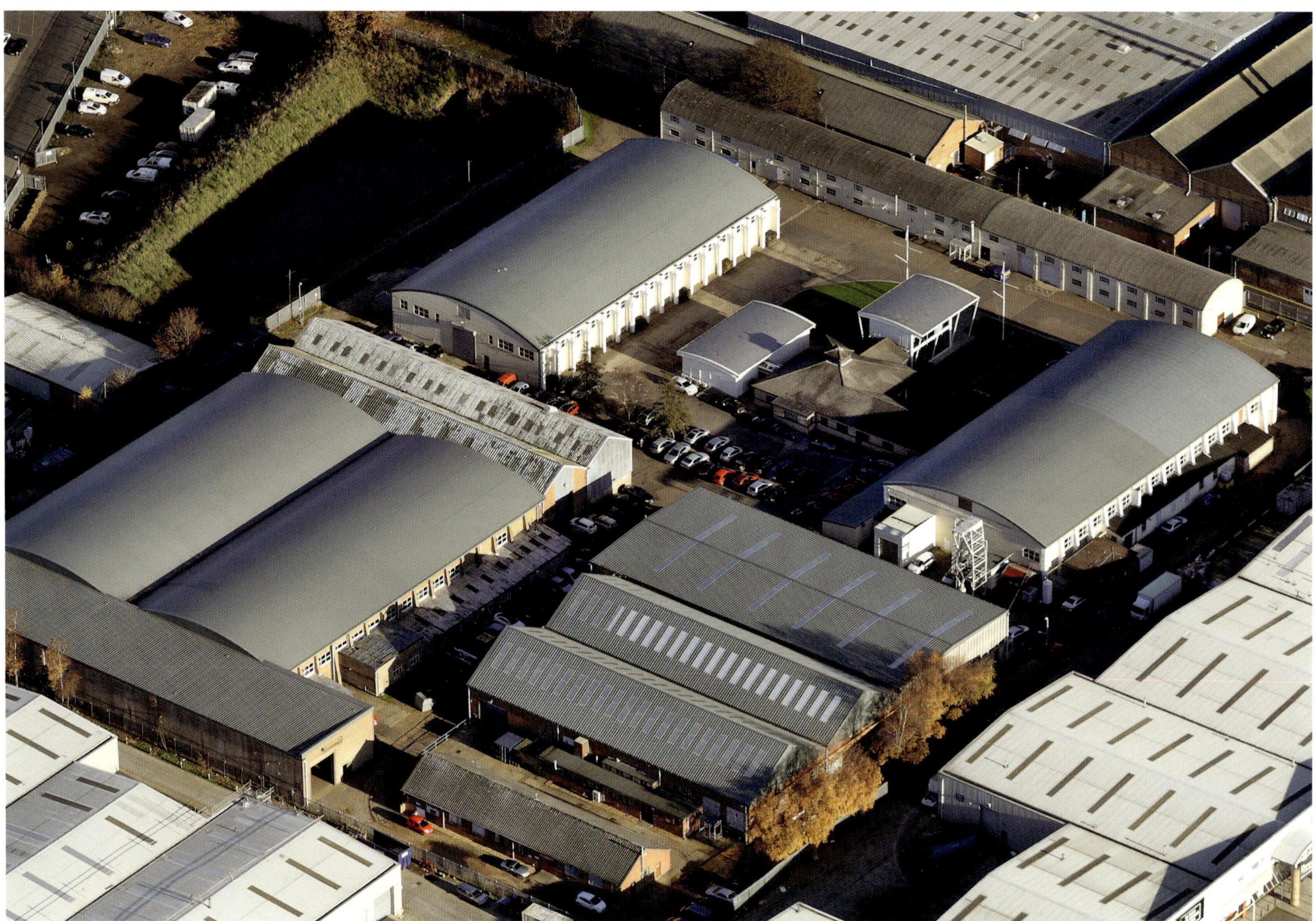

The original hangars of Boulton and Paul.

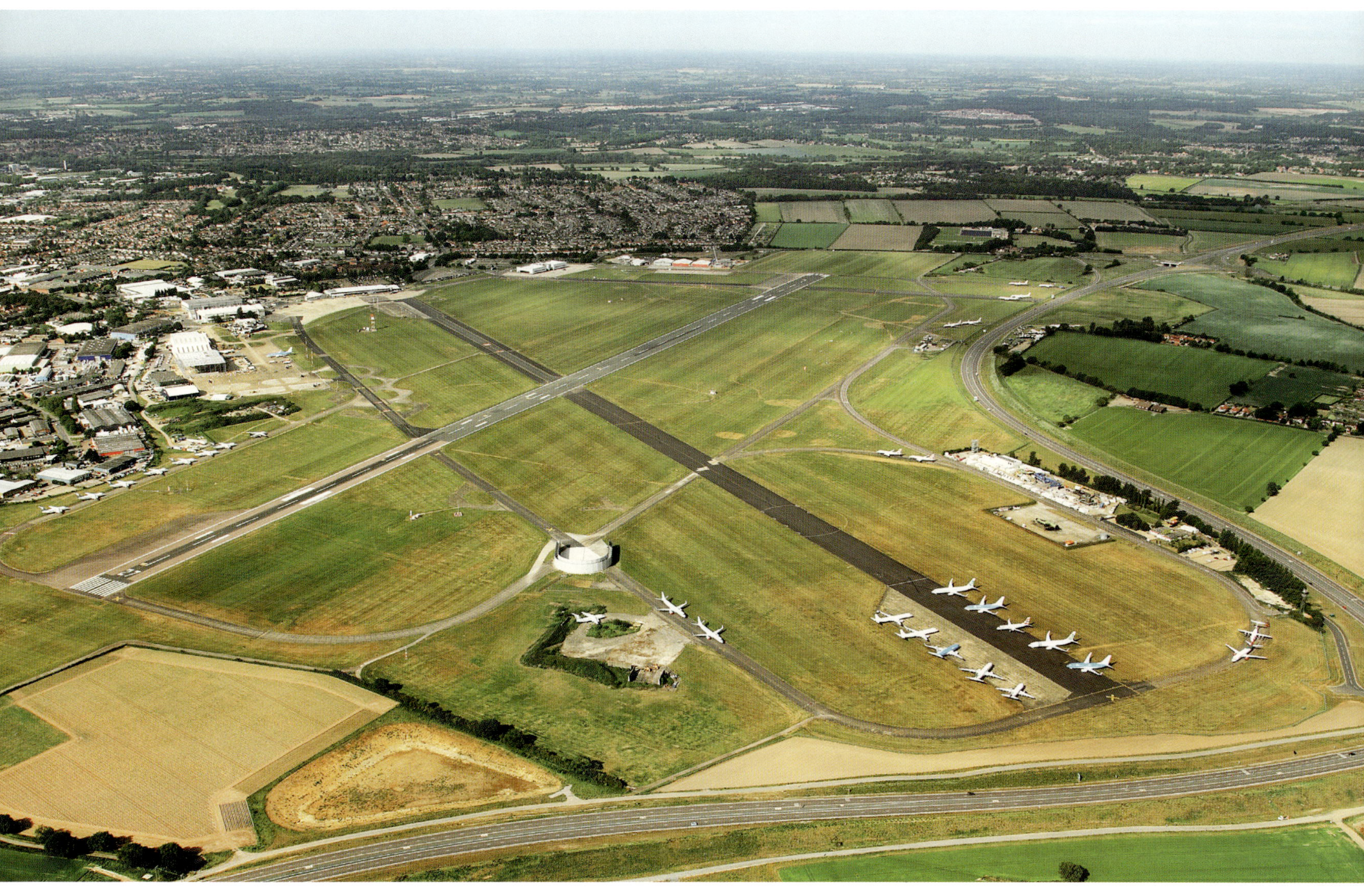

RAF station Horsham St Faith was built on the north-west edge of Norwich at the start of WW2 in 1939. It was from here that an aircraft en route to a German bombing raid dropped over France a box containing a replacement pair of artificial legs for Wing Commander Douglas Bader.

The wartime airfield closed in 1963 and became Norwich Airport in 1968. Norwich Airport's prosperity has come from changing requirements. In the 1970s much of its demand came from the high volume of business generated by the North Sea (oil and gas) industry. In the 1990s demand was led by the convenience of Norfolk's proximity to the international flight hub of Amsterdam. Norwich is closer to the Dutch coast than it is to London.

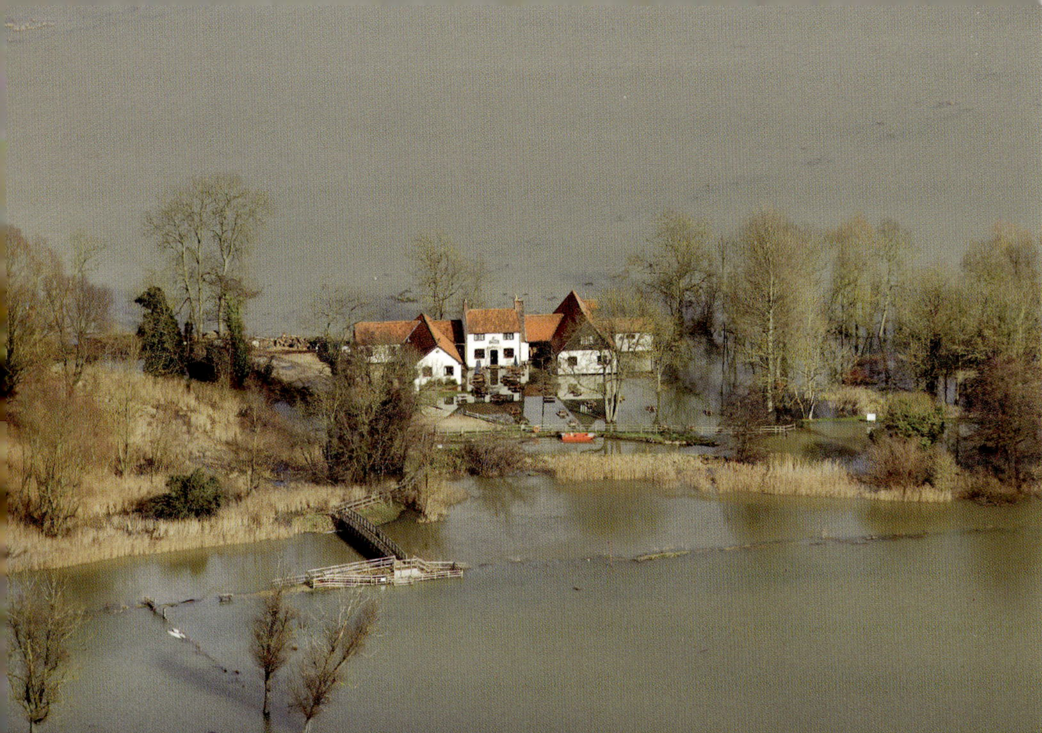

All Terrain

The Locks pub at Geldeston floods fairly regularly when the River Waveney overflows its banks and if one of these vehicles parked near the pub isn't an amphibious DUKW (aka 'duck') then it would have been useful if it had been. The pub takes its name from Geldeston Lock which was part of the now disused navigation up to Bungay.

The DUKW was made by the General Motor Corporation (USA) where their models were referred to by the letters of their type. D=date of design (1942), U=utility, K=all-wheel drive, W = dual tandem rear axles. Try pronouncing that.

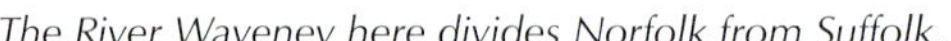

The River Waveney here divides Norfolk from Suffolk.

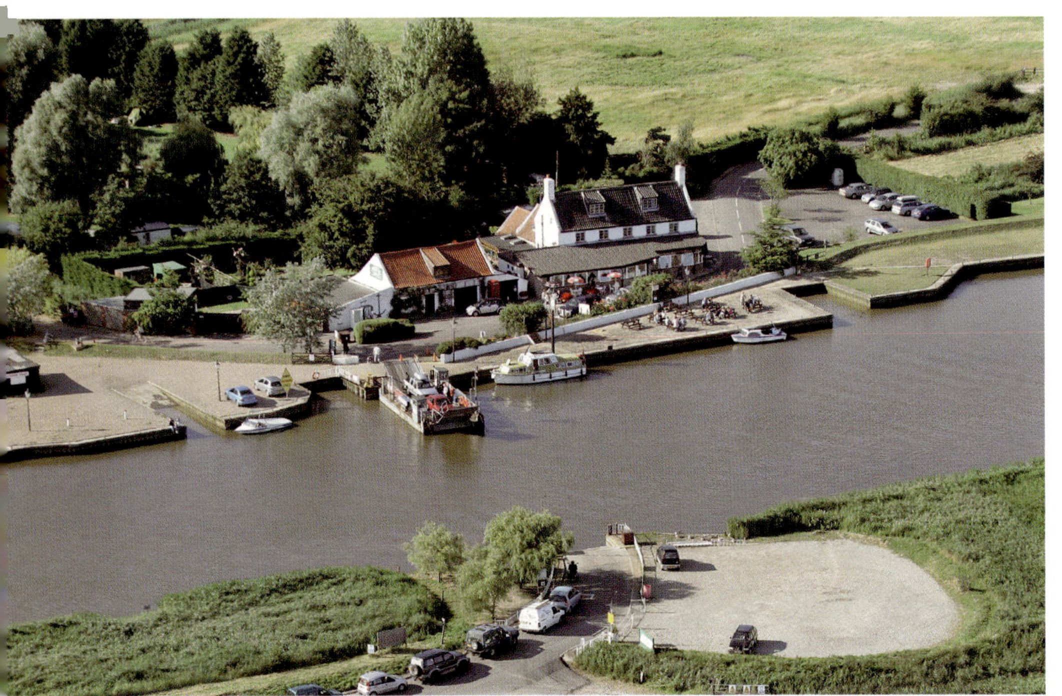

Ferries

Long before Norfolk roads evolved from mere tracks there were ferries. One of the few working ferries remaining is at Reedham, motor driven and guided by chains across the River Yare. And there has been a foot ferry across the River Great Ouse at Kings Lynn to West Lynn since the thirteenth century.

The Reedham Ferry and pub of the same name.

Wherries

Pleasure wherries were a development of the trading wherry. Best known perhaps is *Hathor* (pronounced 'Hartor') and named after the sun god. The panelling inside the cabin is superb. At the turn of the last century it was common for working wherries to be converted to holiday use (the wherryman as crew) in the summer months. ET and Mrs Boardman had booked the wherry *Gaviota* for such a holiday but at Wroxham their boat was missing – there had been a mix up with the bookings. Instead a wherryman with the *John Henry* working up the River Ant offered to take them along. Afterwards they discovered that only the *John Henry* was small enough to pass under the old Ludham Bridge. Had they gone on the other boat they would never have seen How Hill and the site on which subsequently they built their house.

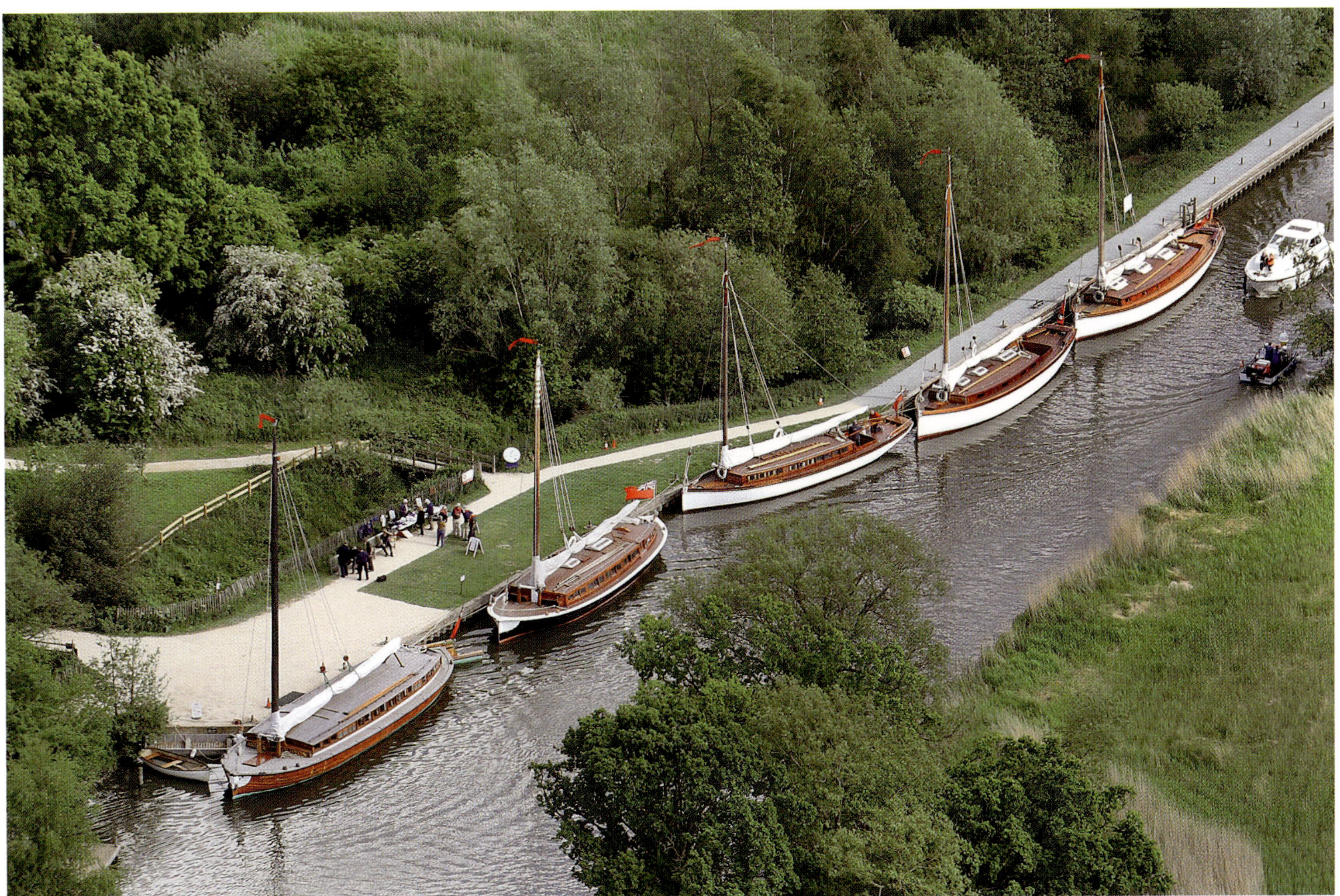

Wherries Ardea, Hathor *and wherry yachts* Norada, Olive *and* White Moth.

Chapter 3

All Work and No Play Makes Jack a Dull Boy.
(In Norfolk there are plenty of play opportunities for Jack and Jill)

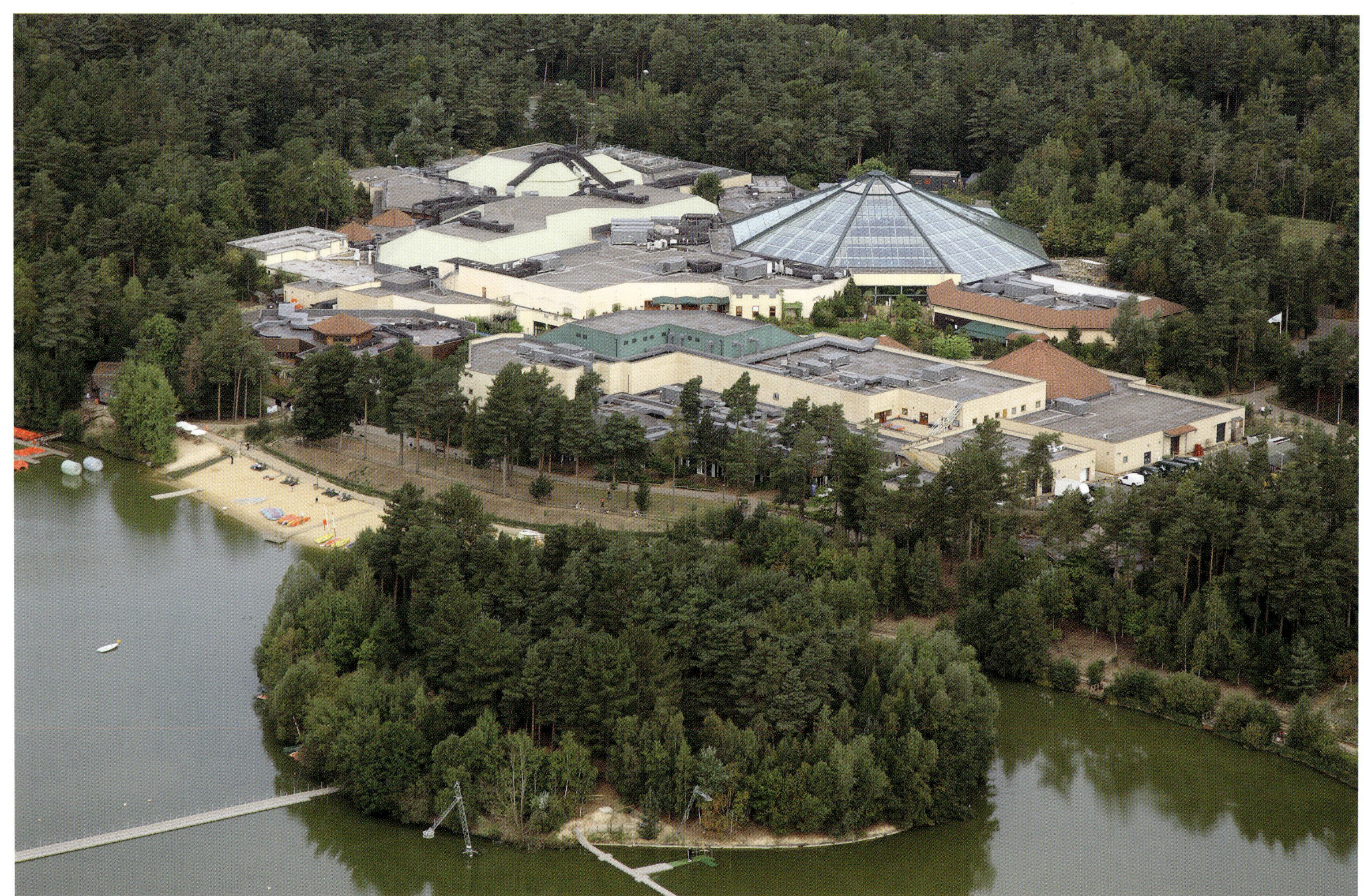

Centre Parcs at Elveden

The idea of the Centre Parcs villages was conceived by a Dutchman in 1987. The 400 acres at Elveden, one of five sites in the UK, provides a holiday destination for those who enjoy outdoor activities. The swimming pools are especially popular. The resort is well situated at Elveden being almost at the county boundary with Suffolk.

Winterton and Horsey

A complete contrast to Centre Parcs, very few people and (hopefully) some seals.

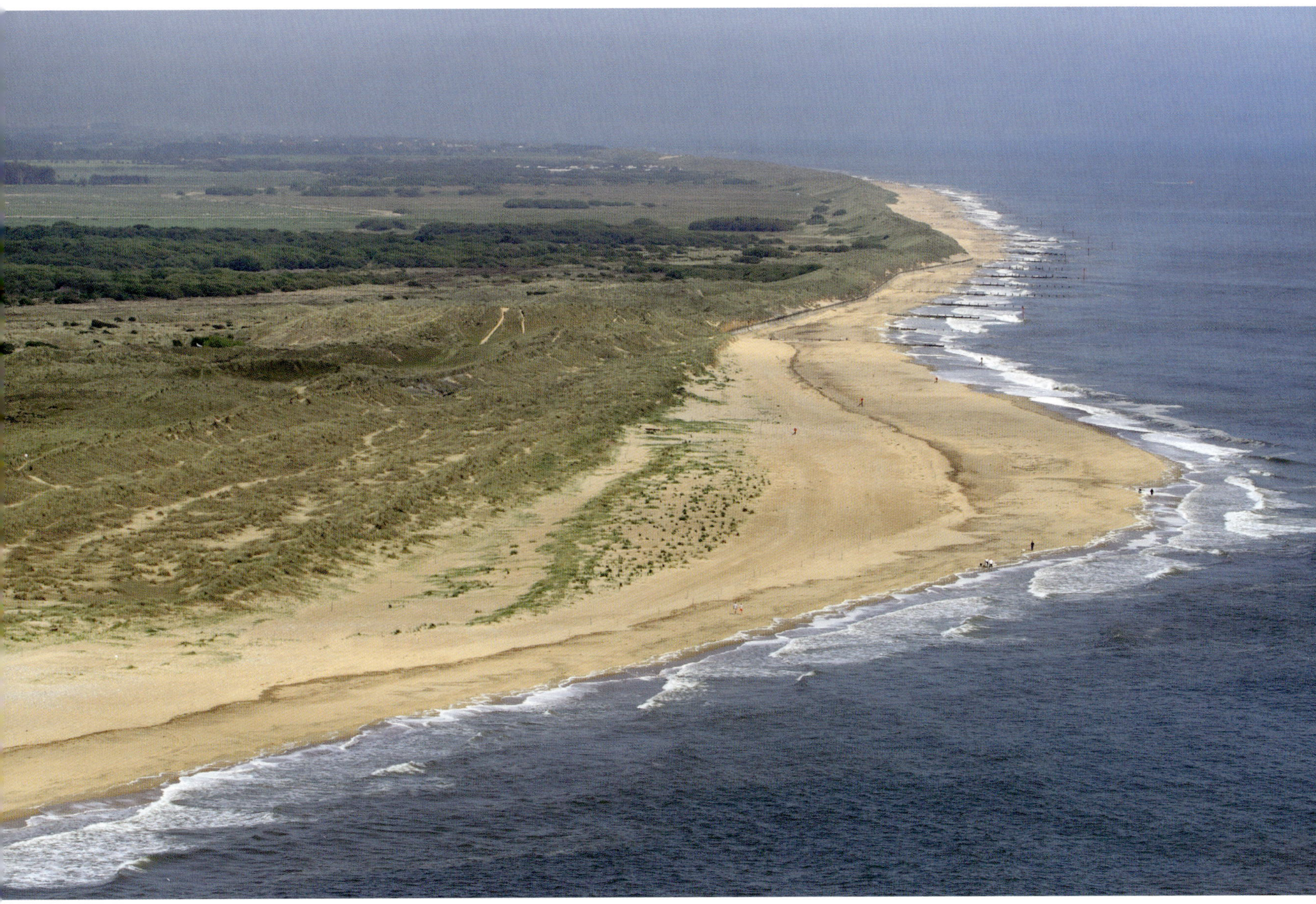

Great Yarmouth's Golden Mile

There's nowhere else quite like it in Norfolk.

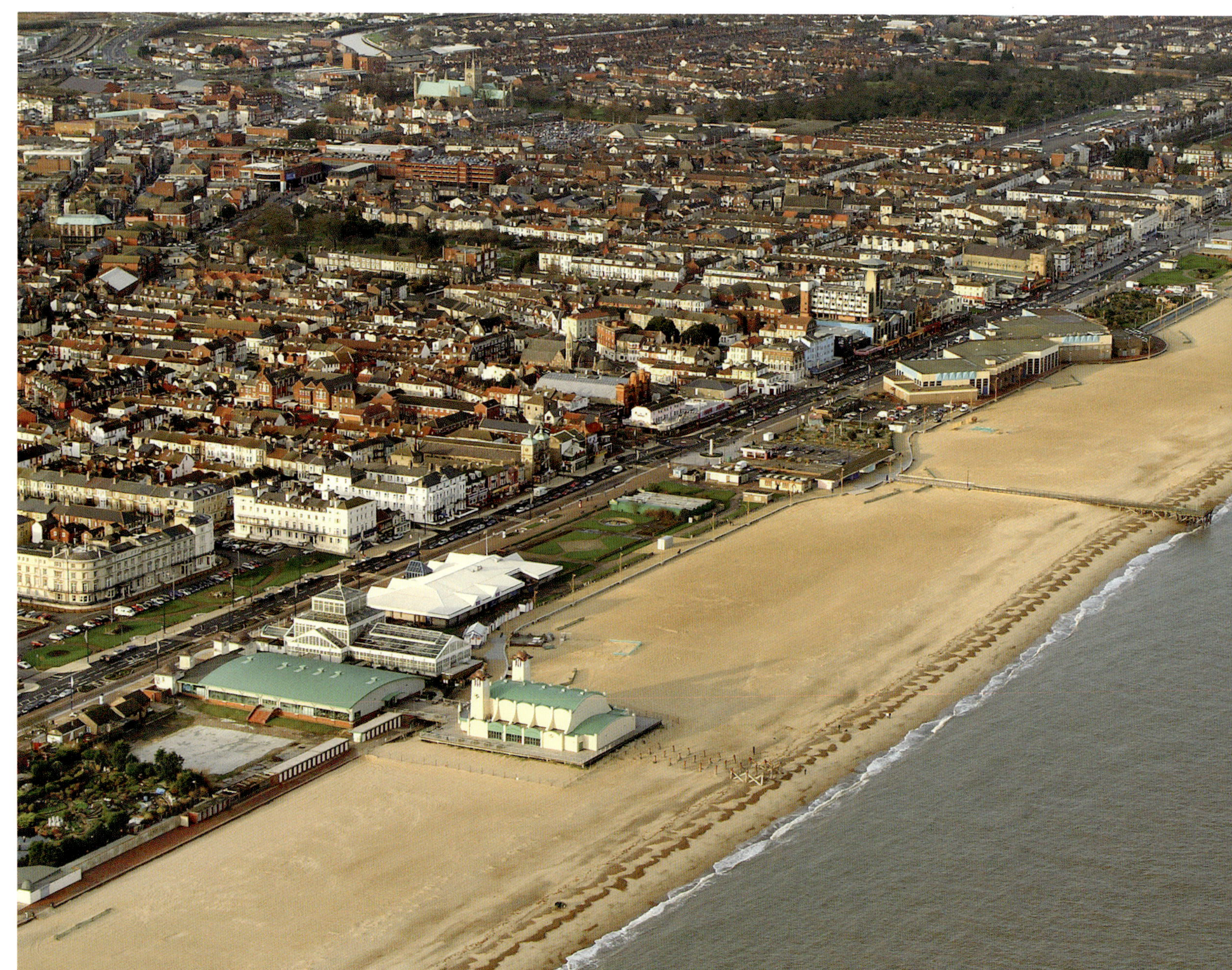

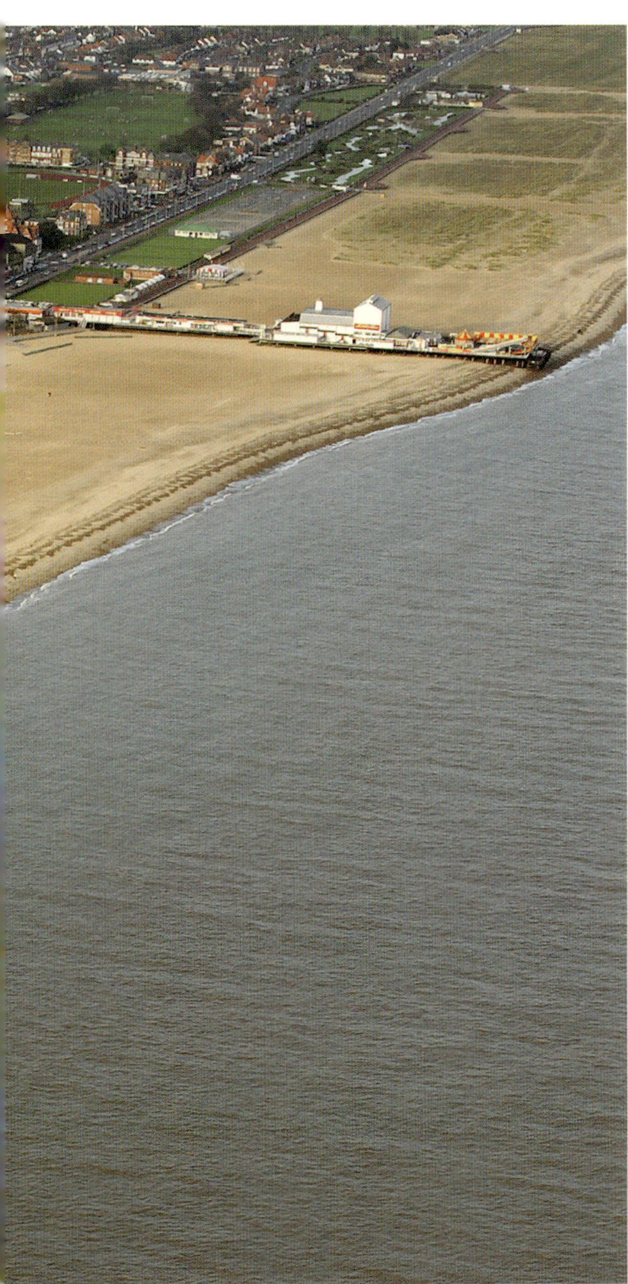

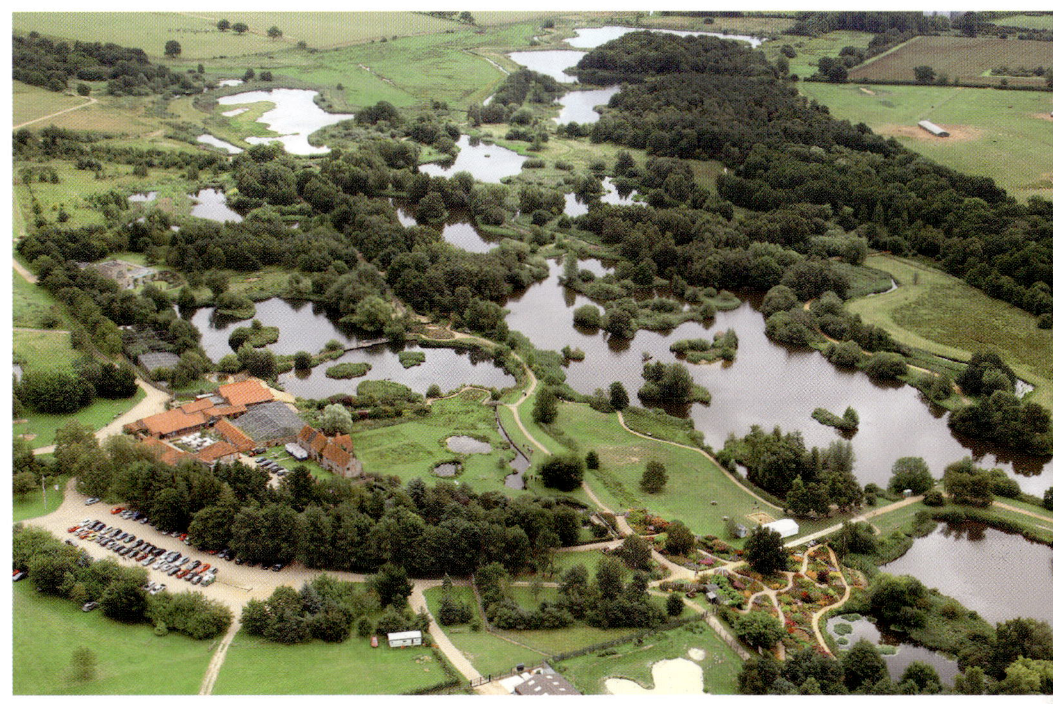

Pensthorpe

There are 700 acres containing wildlife in and near the River Wensum which flows through the site. There's also a red squirrel enclosure and plantings including Piet Oudolf's Millennium Garden with its characteristic flower drifts to which he has returned recently to update.

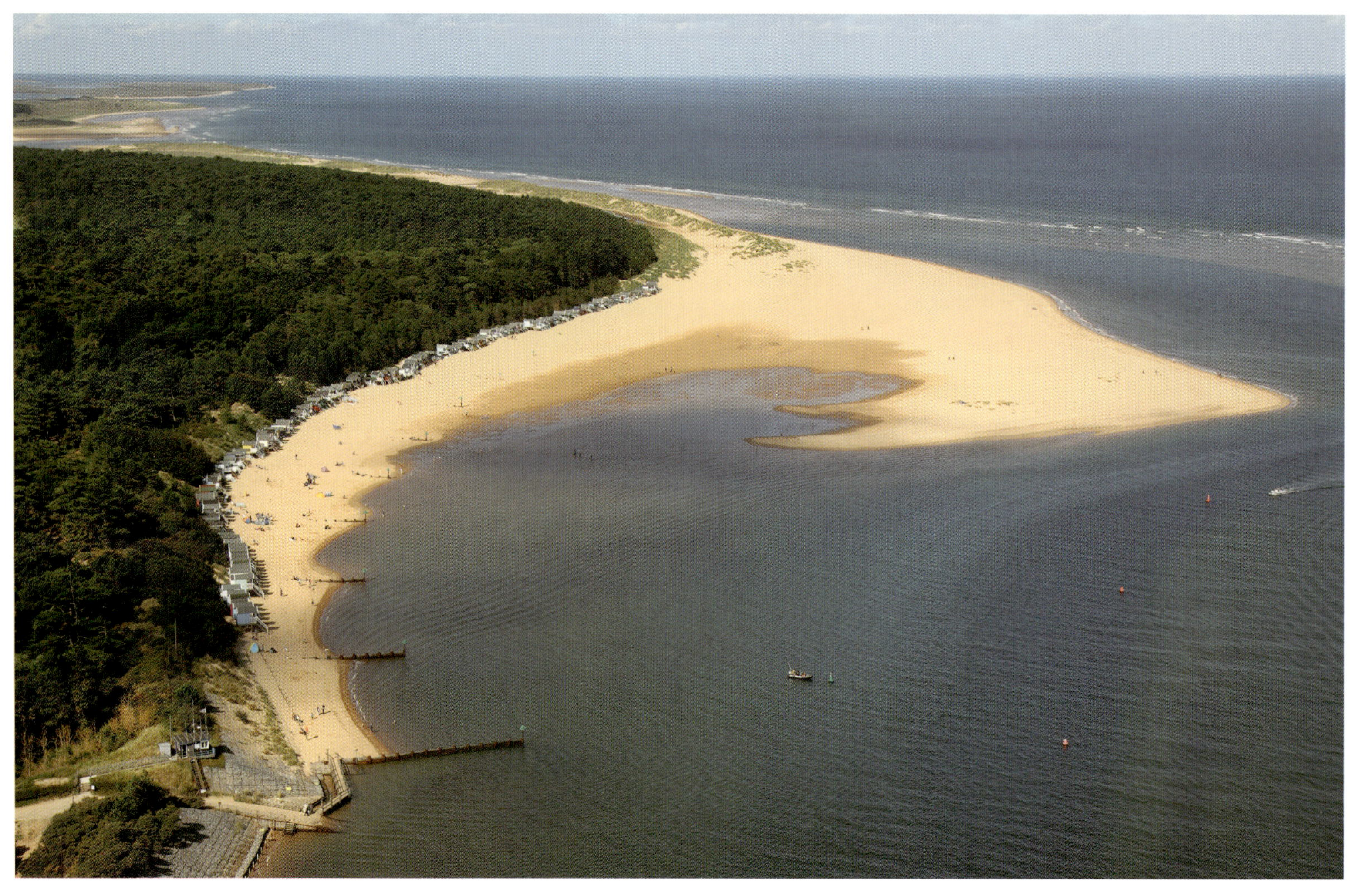

Seaside Paradise at Wells-next-the-Sea

Beach huts, sand and a background of pine trees in Holkham Bay.

Cromer by Rail

During the late nineteenth century the coming of the railways boosted Cromer's appeal as a seaside resort.

The first line into the town was the Great Eastern Railway route from Norwich and the London main line, which reached what later became known as Cromer High Station in 1877. Ten years later this was followed by the Midland and Great Northern Railway's line into Beach Station, which provided a more direct route to the town from the Midlands and North.

A third station, Cromer Links Halt, was opened in 1923, largely for the benefit of golfers. By 1954 the remaining train services were concentrated on Beach Station which remains open to this day.

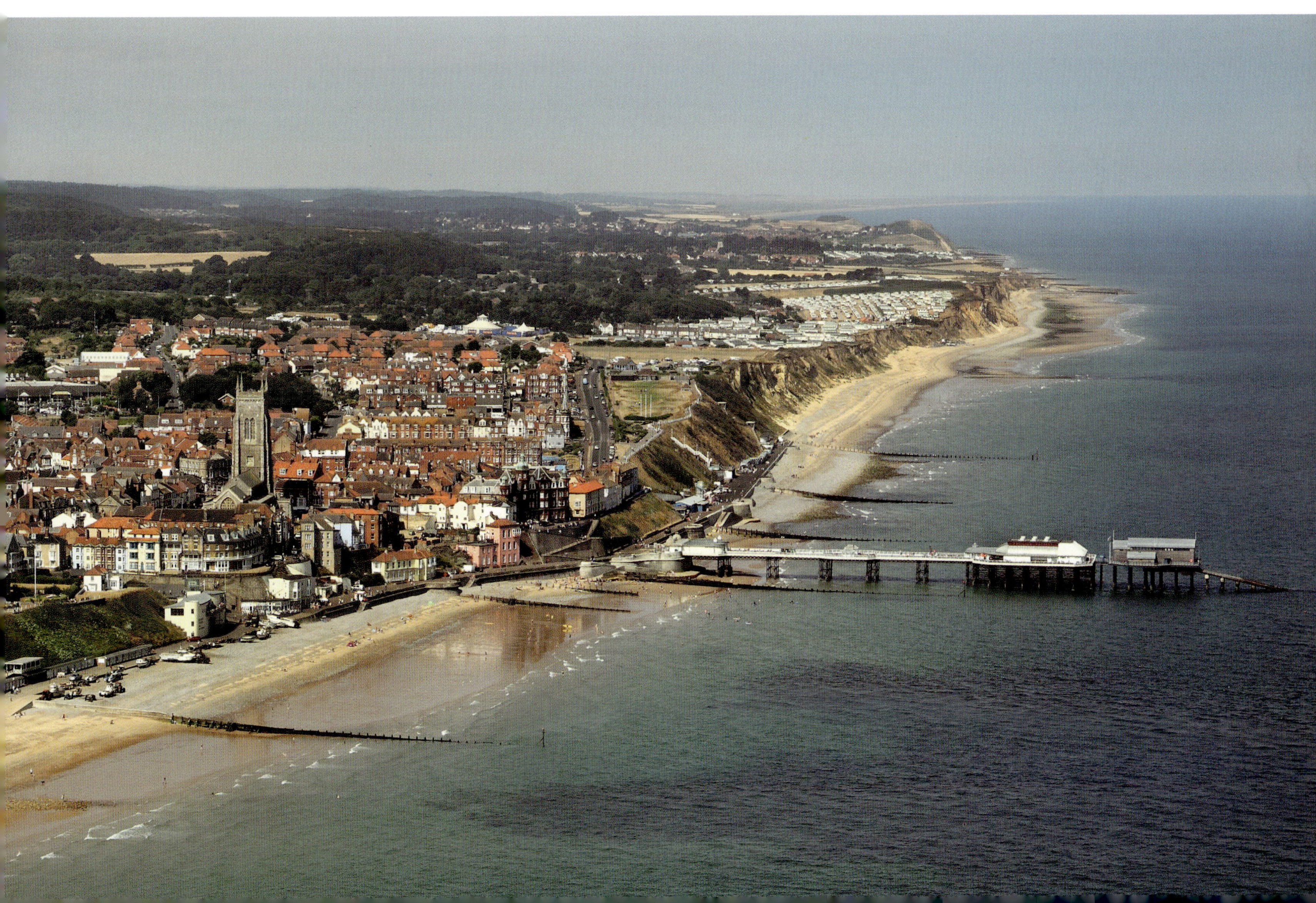

Eaton Park

Eaton Park, covering 80 acres, is one of four major Norwich parks created to provide jobs for the unemployed in the early 1920s. There's a pavilion and a multitude of sports facilities, a bandstand, model yacht pond and miniature railway.

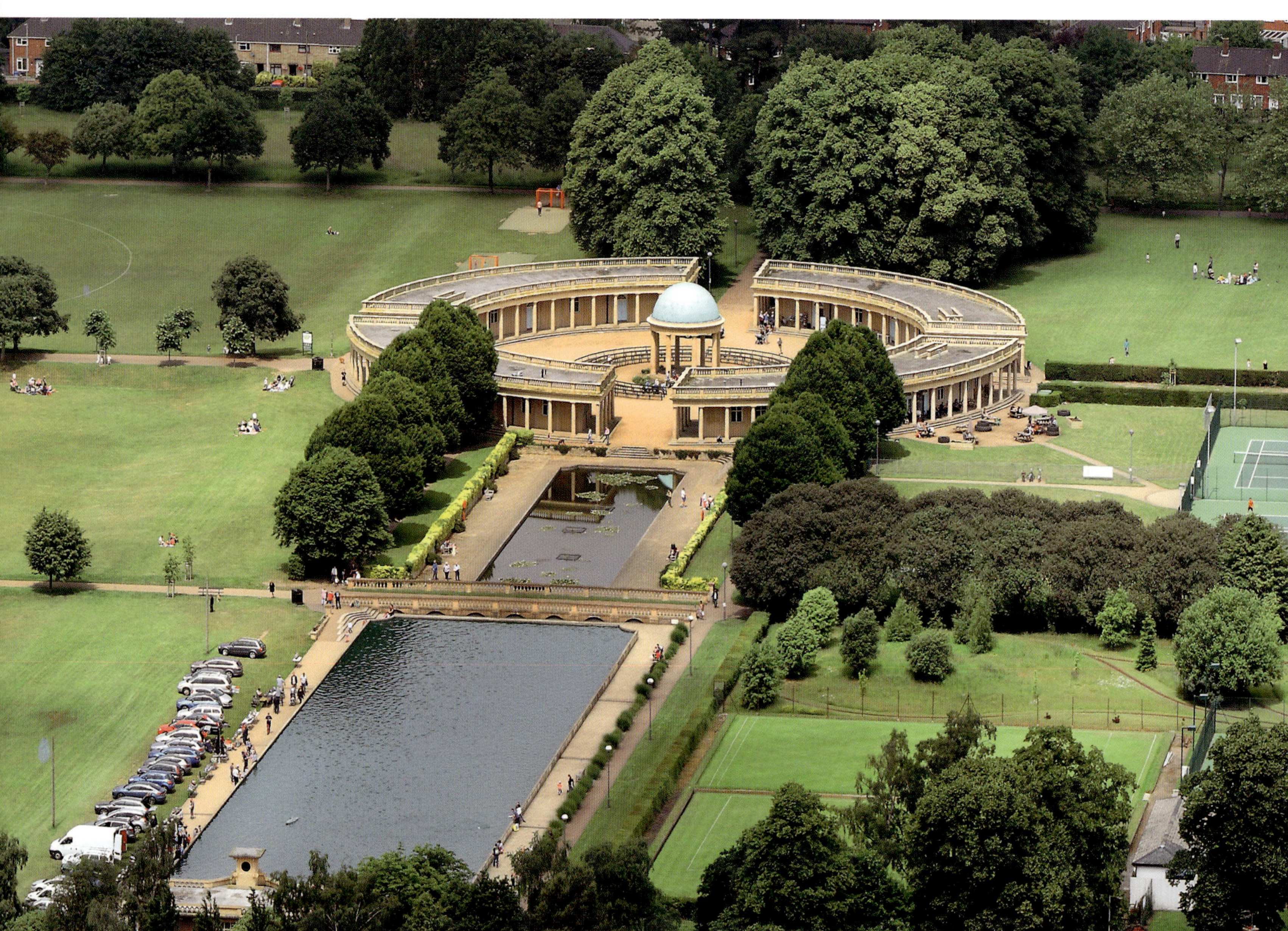

The Sainsbury Centre for the Visual Arts

The long white building in the foreground is the Sainsbury Centre.

From the outside this Norman Foster-designed building resembles an aircraft hangar. The contents were the gift of Lisa and Robert Sainsbury and represent a large part of their art collection. To the right of picture are the ziggurat accommodation units of the University of East Anglia which were built in the mid sixties. They were designed by Denys Lasdun.

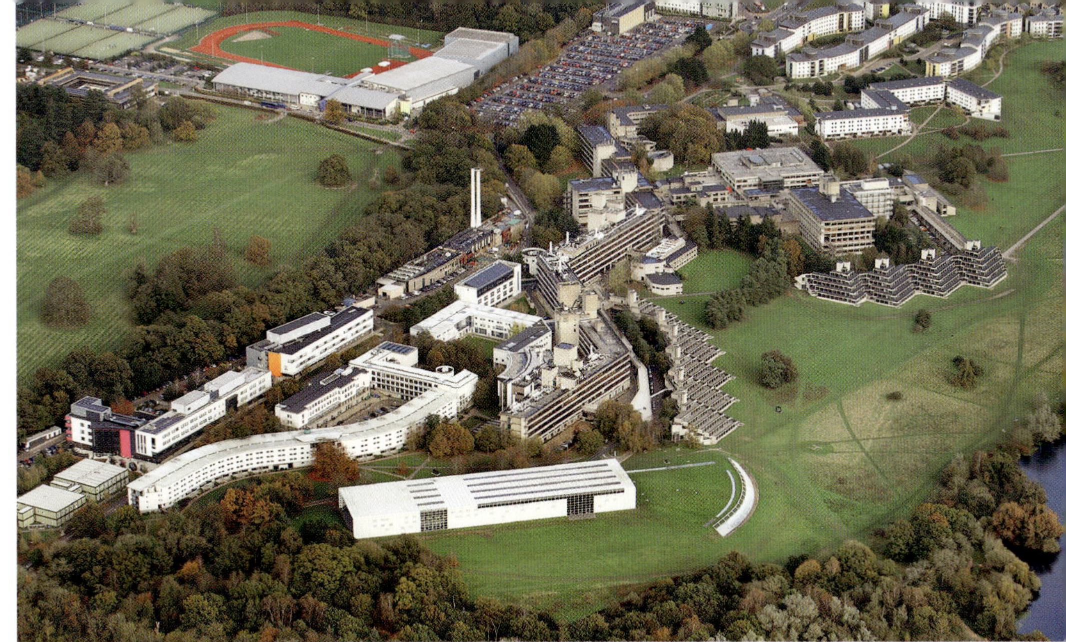

Norwich City Football Ground

The Canaries, Norwich City's football team, is said to be named after the birds brought to Norwich as pets by the Flemish Weavers in the sixteenth and seventeenth centuries. The origin of the team's green shorts? No idea.

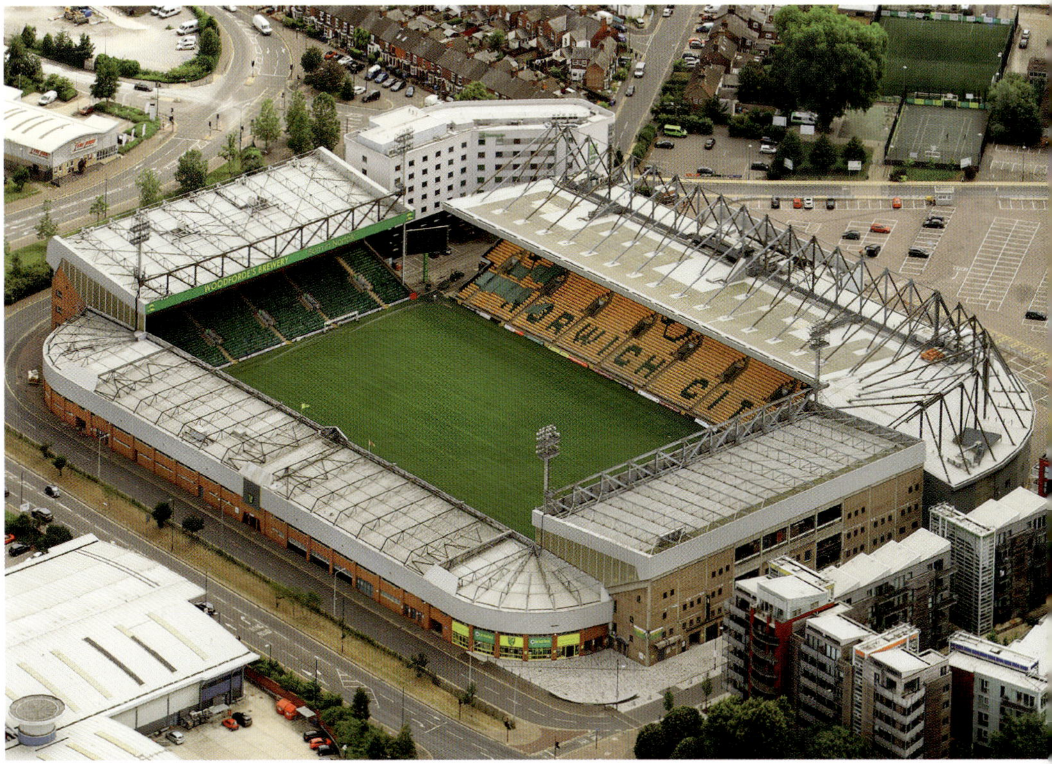

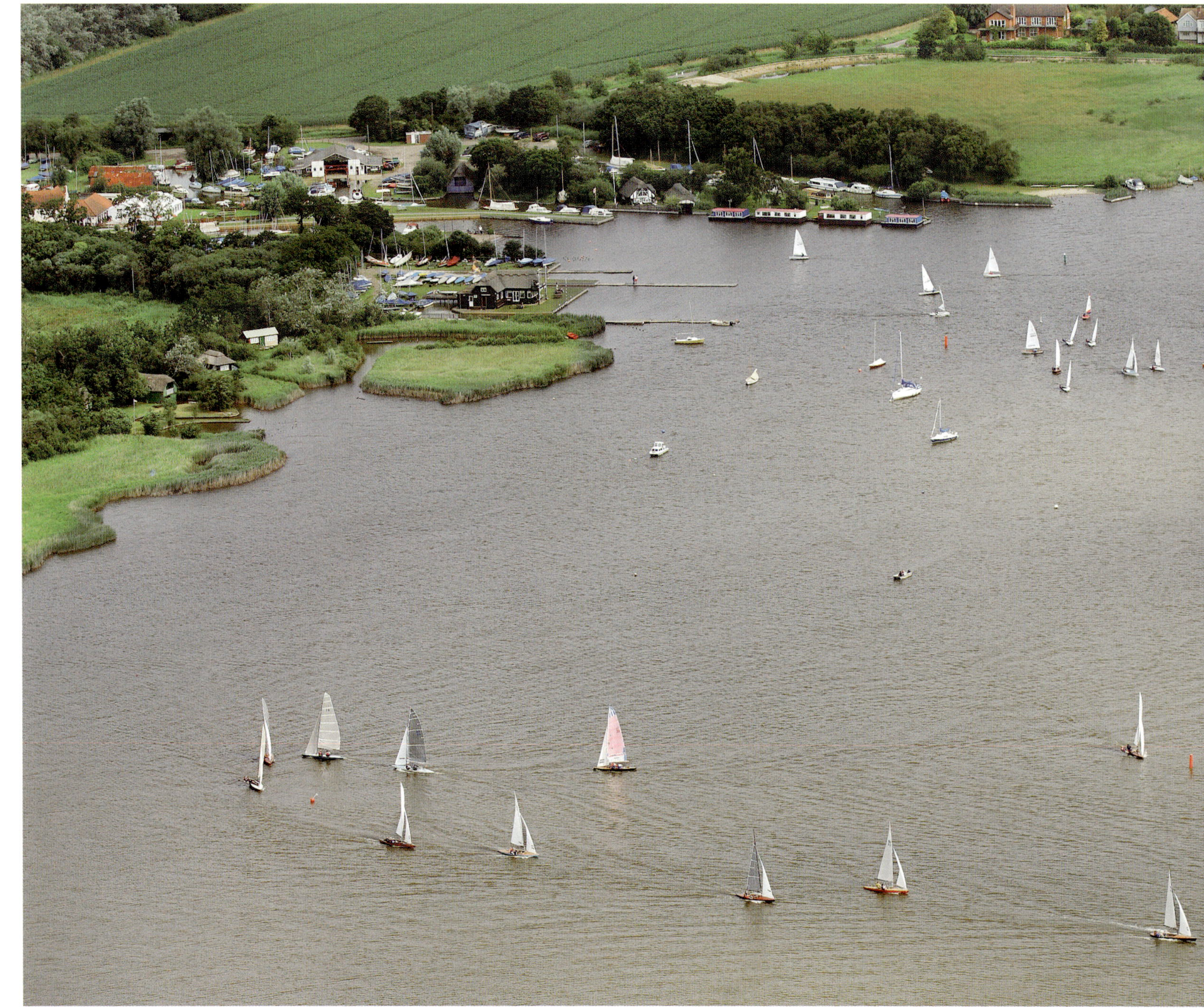

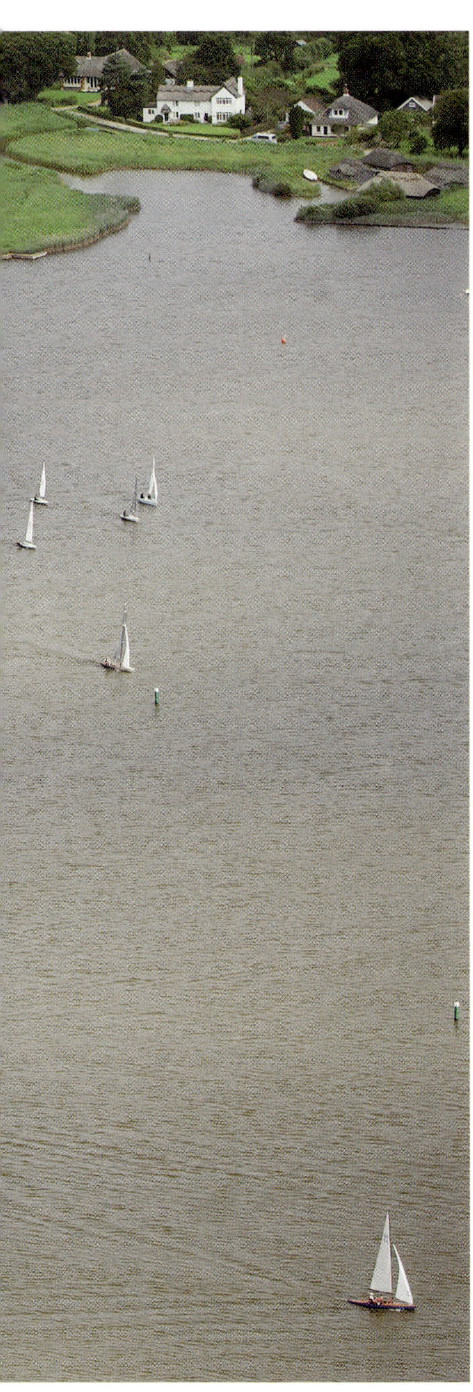

Sailing Dinghies on Hickling Broad

Hickling Broad in the flood plain of the River Thurne is the largest of the Norfolk broads (300 acres approximately).

Norfolk Coast Long Distance Footpath

Starting at Holme next the Sea, the 84 mile coastal path finishes at Hopton on the county boundary with Suffolk. The plan is part of an initiative to have long distance footpaths all over England. This path is now linked to the Peddars Way creating altogether 129 miles.

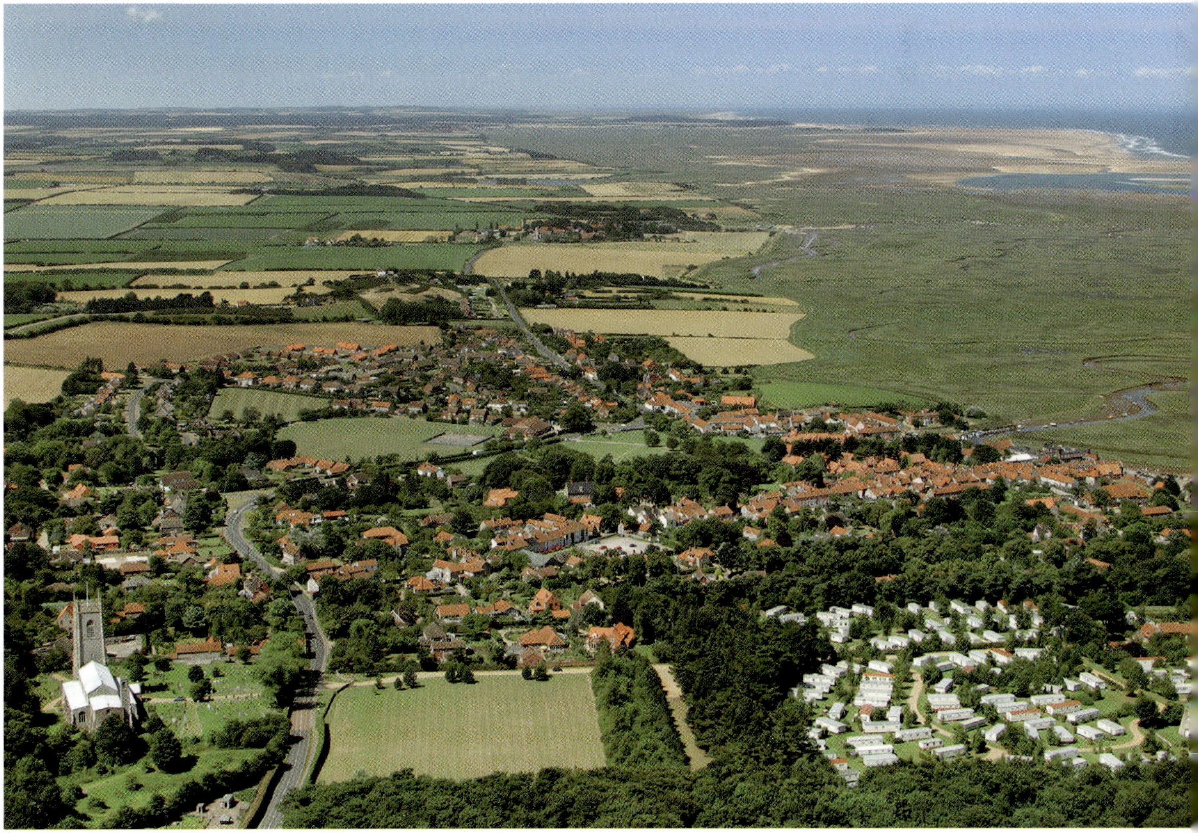

Overhead Blakeney. In places the footpath has to route inland because of the salt marshes.

Banham Zoo

There are around two thousand creatures kept on this 50 acre site. Opened in 1968 the zoo holds numerous events and workshops for all ages to encourage interest in the animal kingdom.

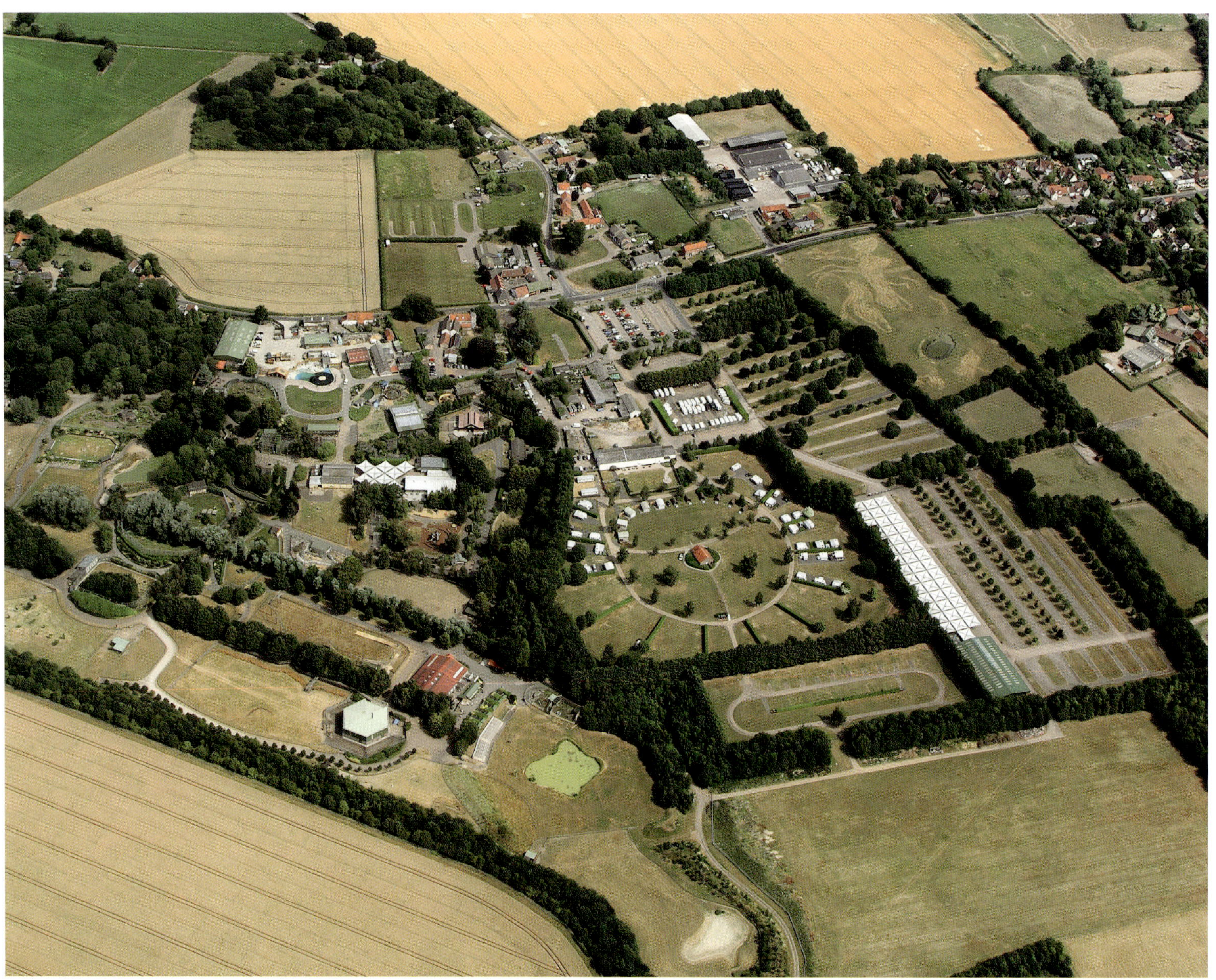

Beeston Maze

Popular since the intrigues of Henry VIII's court, mazes became a regular feature in the grounds of many of the grand country houses. The maze has design similarities with its contemporary, the knot garden, but in vertical form.

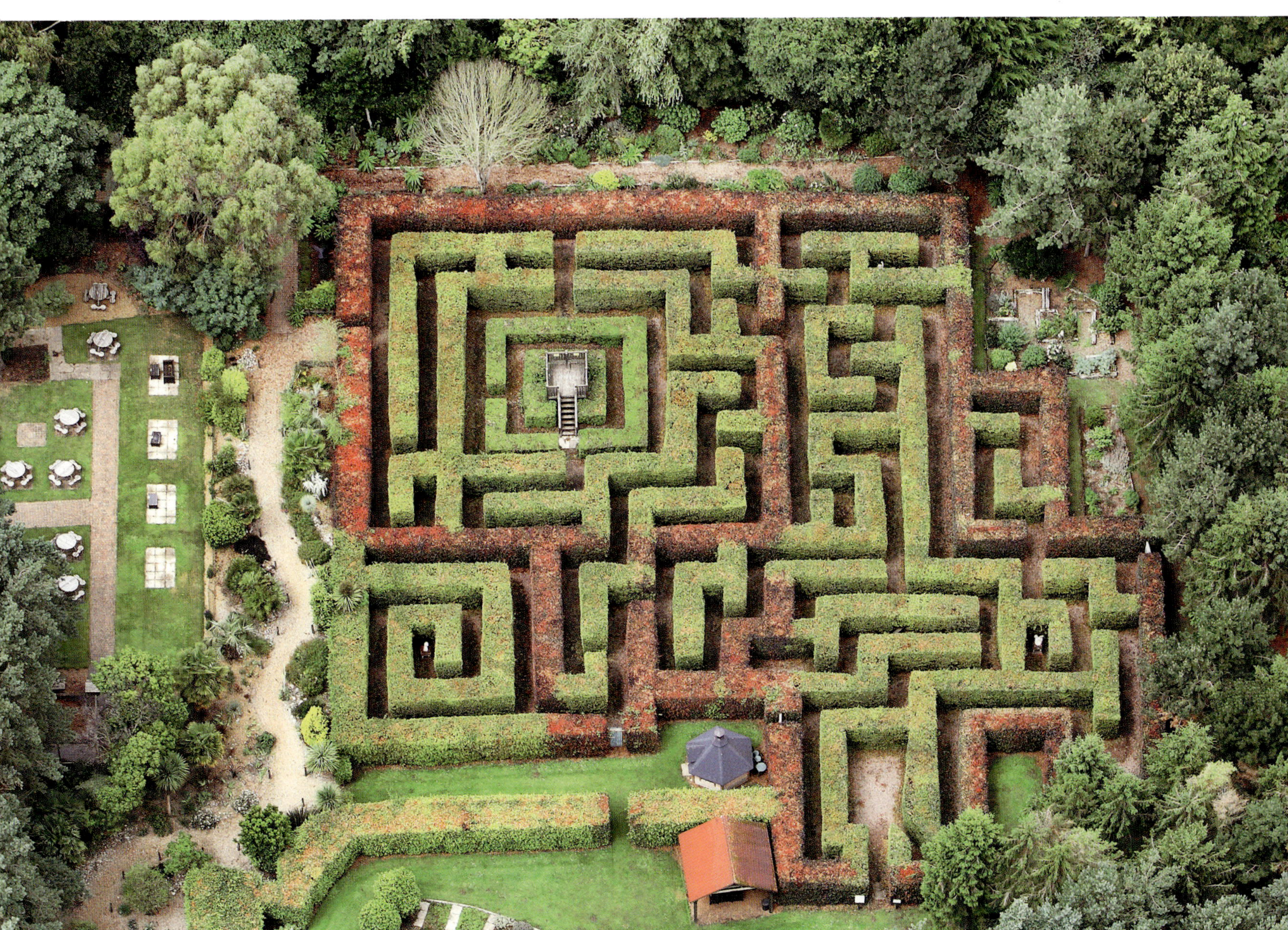

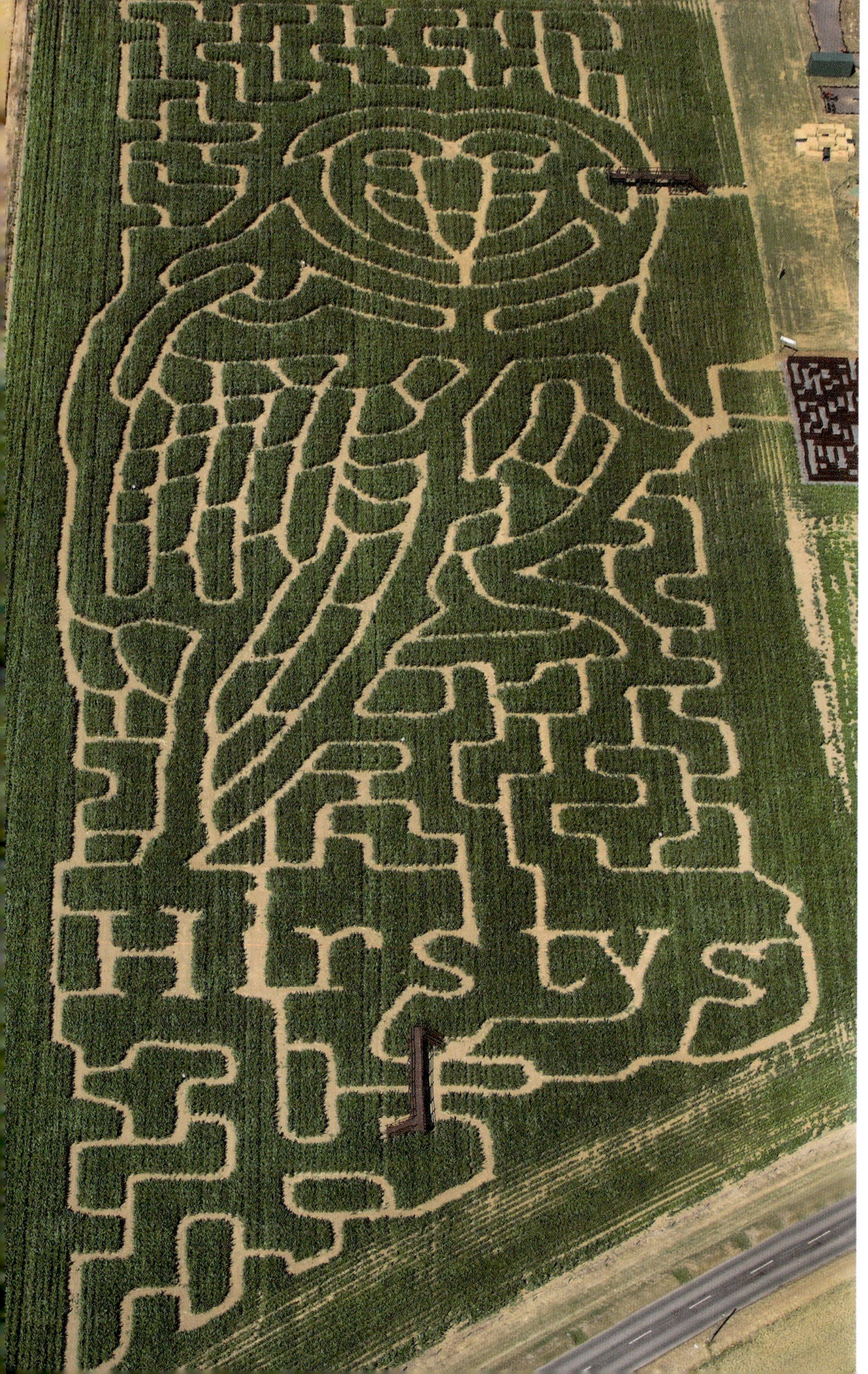

Maize Maze, Hemsby

Maize mazes are a more recent attraction. Their advantage is that maize (corn) grows densely and to an ideal height in one growing season, it doesn't require clipping and doesn't tie up land use for longer than a year. The complicated one illustrated must have been computer generated.

Wroxham: Centre of the Broads

The River Bure separates Wroxham from Hoveton. Roys store is situated in Hoveton, but 'Roys of Wroxham' has an alliterative ring to it and it's a name the company has always used. Its other claim is to be 'the largest village store in the world' and this may well have been true.

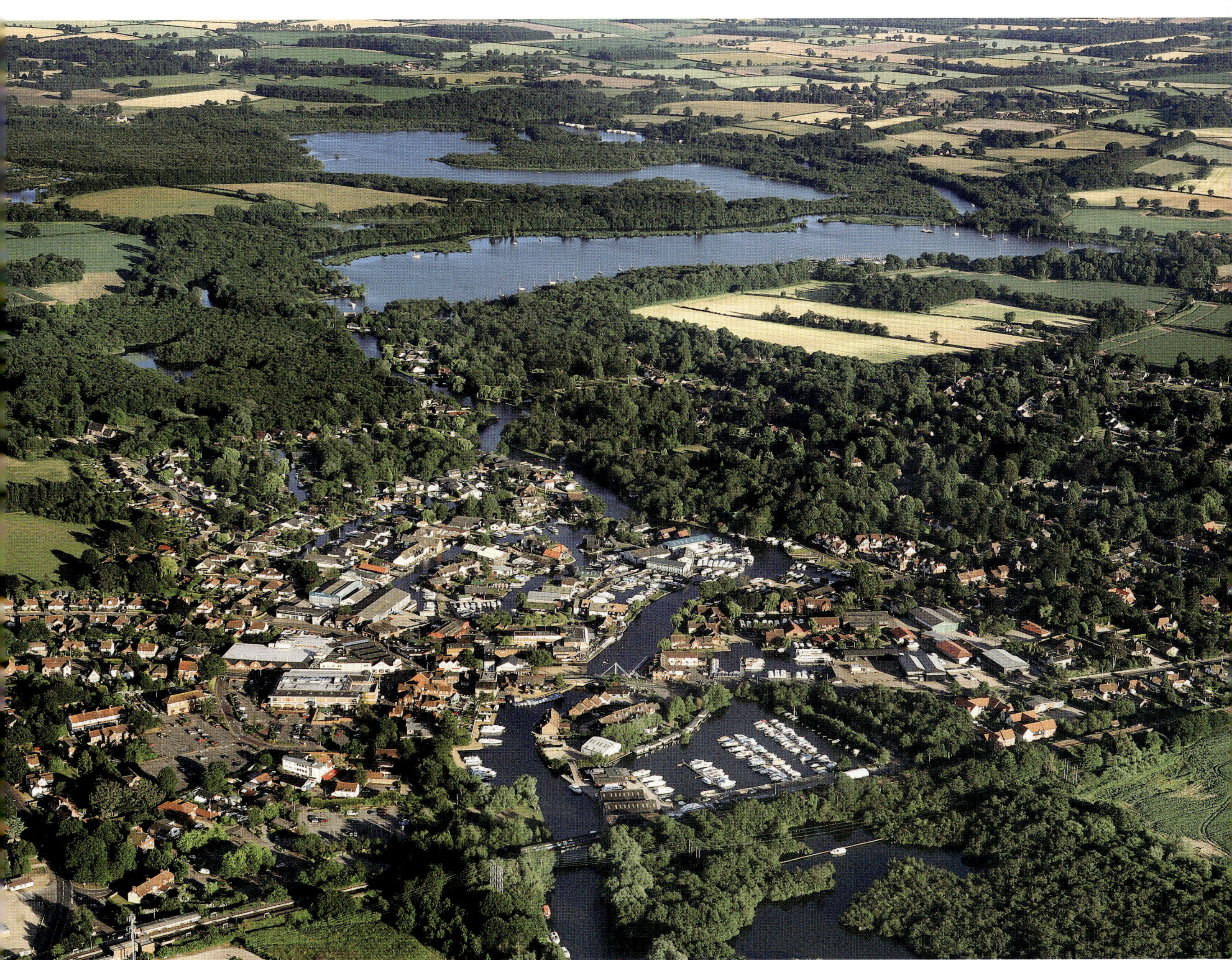

Wroxham village with the River Bure leading to Wroxham Broad and Hoveton Great Broad.

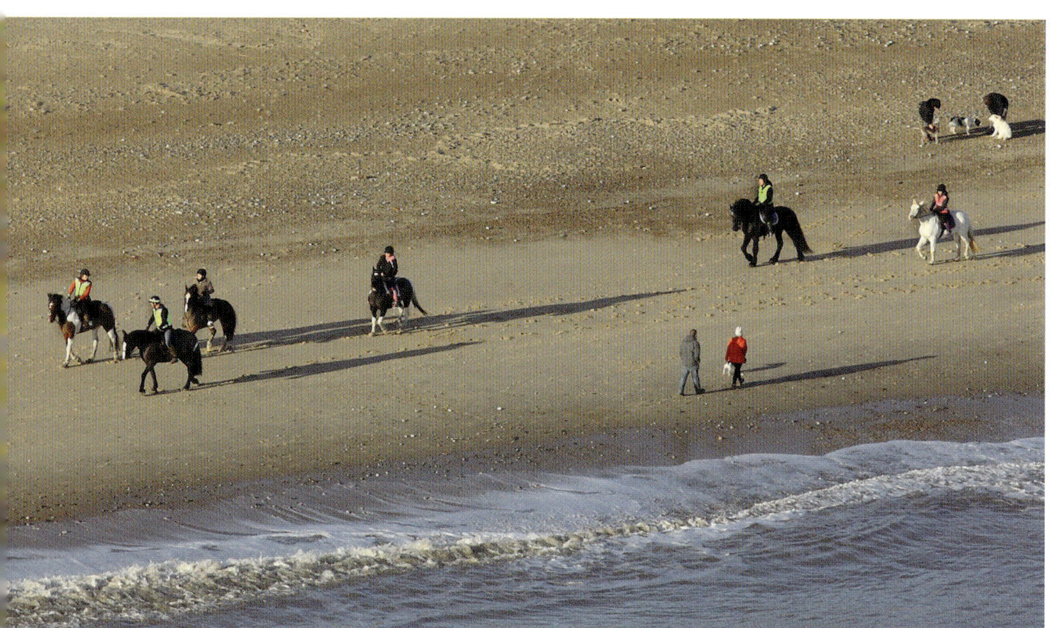

Horses at Hemsby

Acres of space with sea and sand.

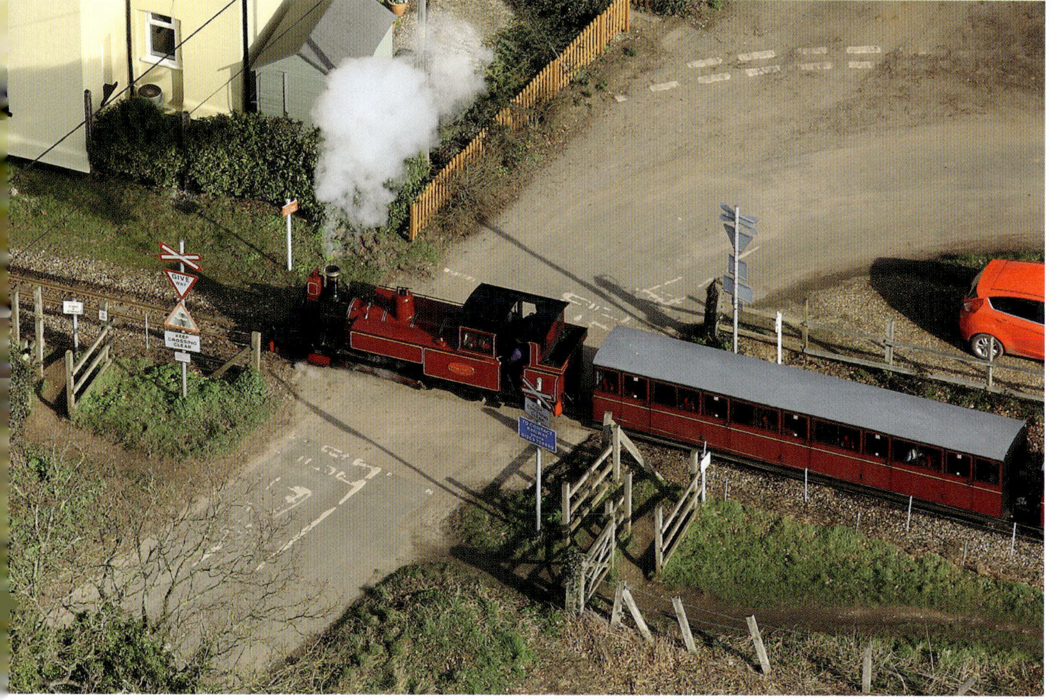

The Bure Valley Railway

The narrow gauge railway runs for 9 miles between Wroxham and Aylsham with halts at Coltishall, Buxton and Brampton. It was built on the track bed of the standard gauge Great Eastern Railway which operated the line from 1880 to 1952. However freight traffic continued until 1982.

The Bure Valley Railway opened in 1990 with a safety fence between the track and the footpath. Walkers, cyclists, dogs and children are welcomed.

Although Norfolk County Council policy was to convert track beds into walks it was Broadland District Council that bought the track bed from Aylsham to Wroxham, and set in motion the events leading to the Bure Valley Railway.

Golf

There are no fewer than five golf courses on the coast's edge: Gorleston, Sheringham, Cromer, Brancaster and Hunstanton. There's only one problem (apart from hitting a ball into the sea) – the coastline is eroding so the courses must be getting smaller.

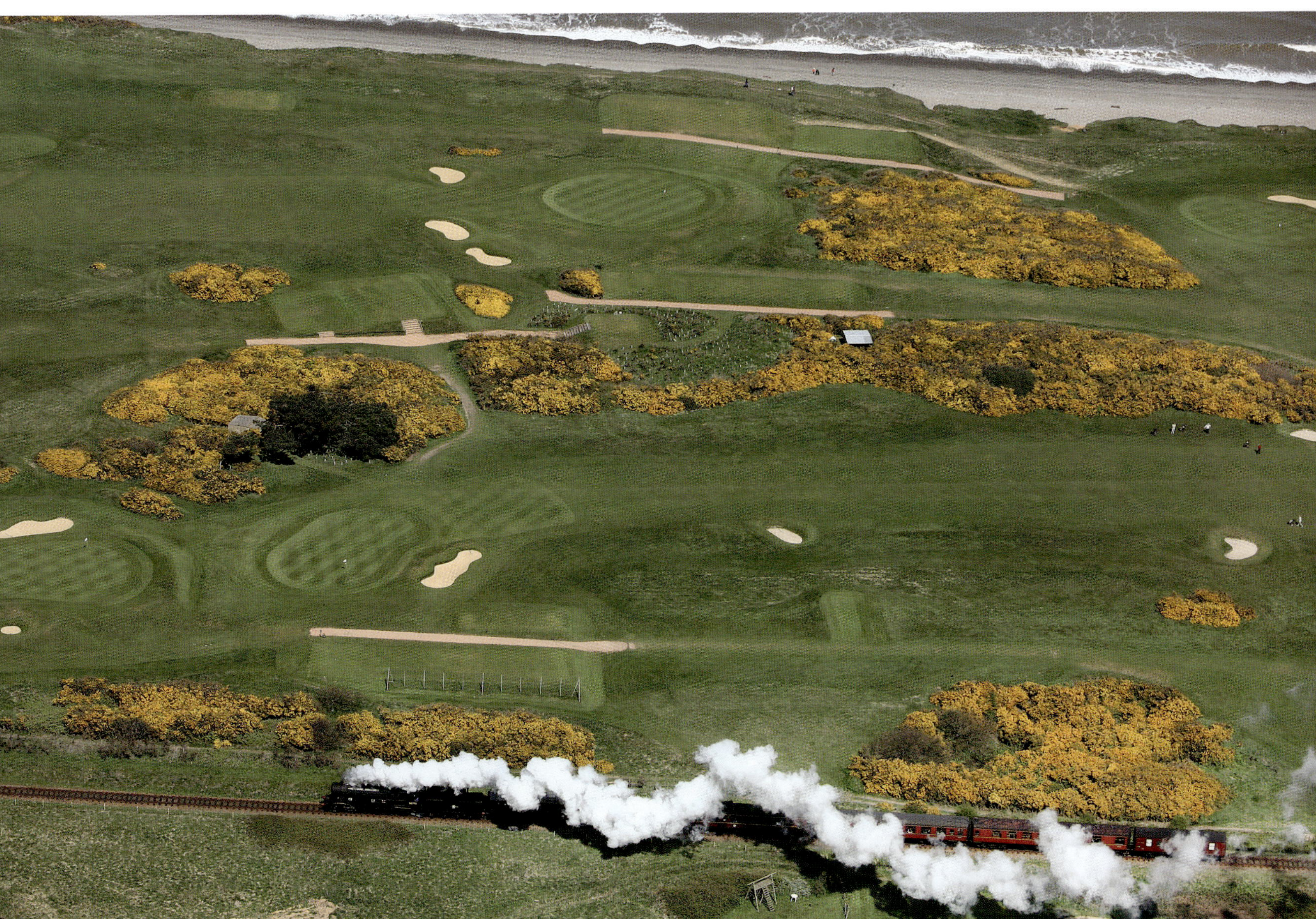

Passing Sheringham Golf Course on the Poppy Line.

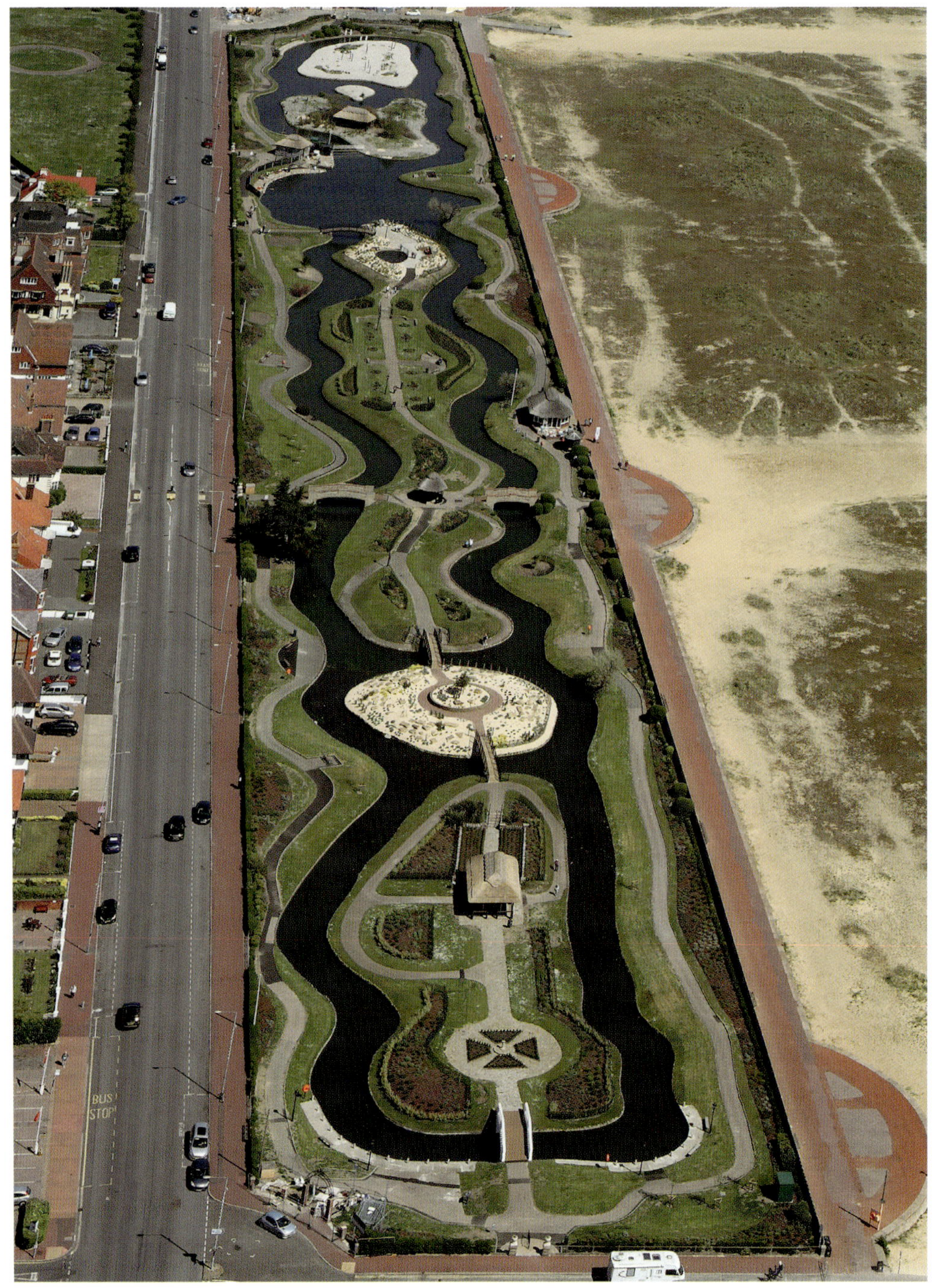

The Waterways, Great Yarmouth

Built in 1928 as an unemployment relief project, the channels were dug by hand and soil for the flower beds was brought in from Caister to replace the sand. Boats chugged round the channels and in the winter the salt water was replaced by fresh to enable ice skating. Unique in the UK, The Waterways became underused when holiday habits changed, but a grant from the Lottery Fund in 2018 enabled its restoration.

Two companies offer hour-long trips from Morston to Blakeney Point to see seals basking on the beach. A local artist sells cards on which the seals are in the boat and the people are basking!

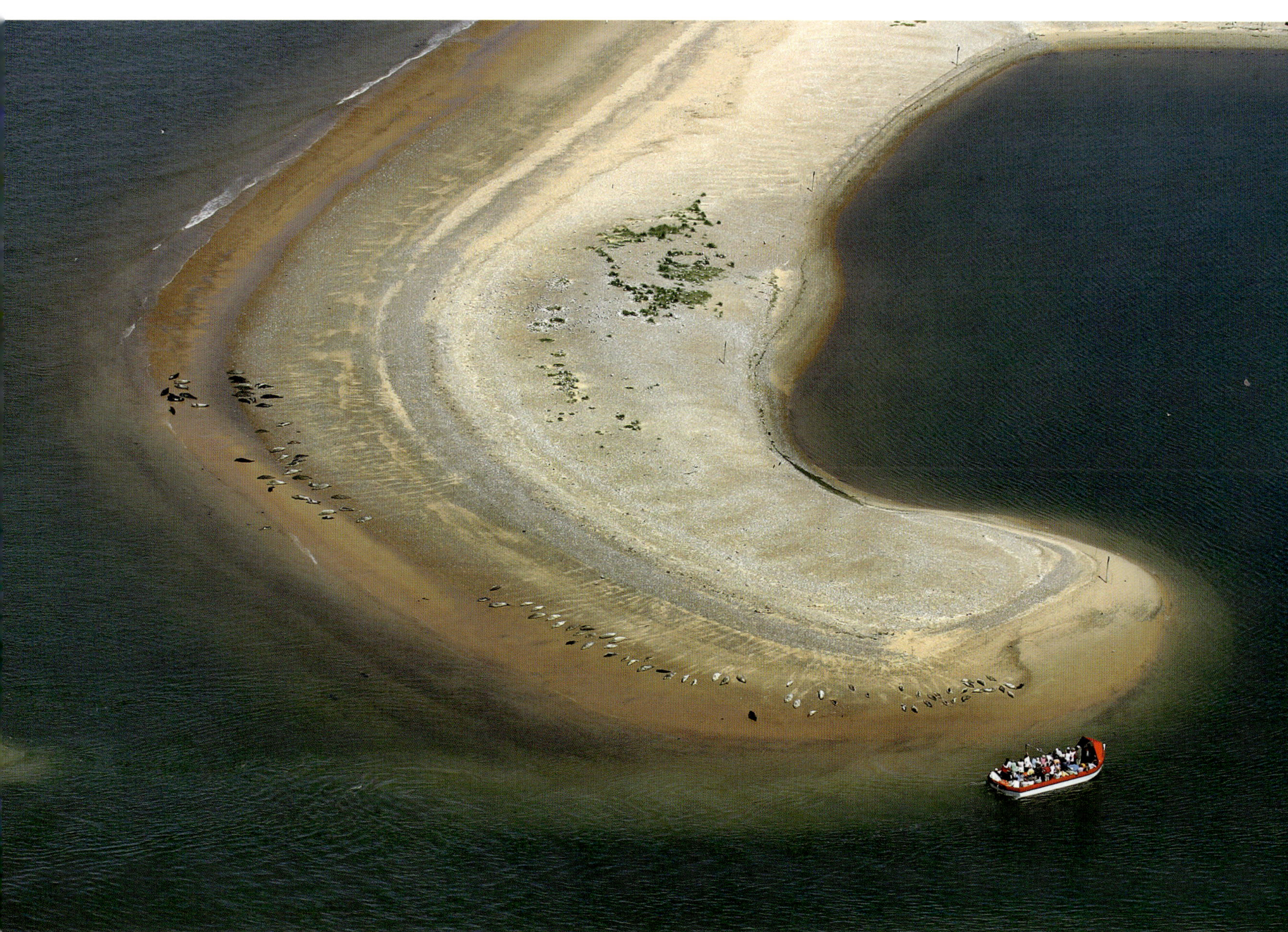

Whitlingham Country Park

Norwich's 'green lung'. Whitlingham's Great and Little Broads were created in the 1980s when gravel was extracted from the site for the new A47. They're not 'proper' broads as they weren't formed by peat digging, but they've become a centre for water-based activities. Together with the rest of the Country Park they're administered by the Whitlingham Charitable Trust.

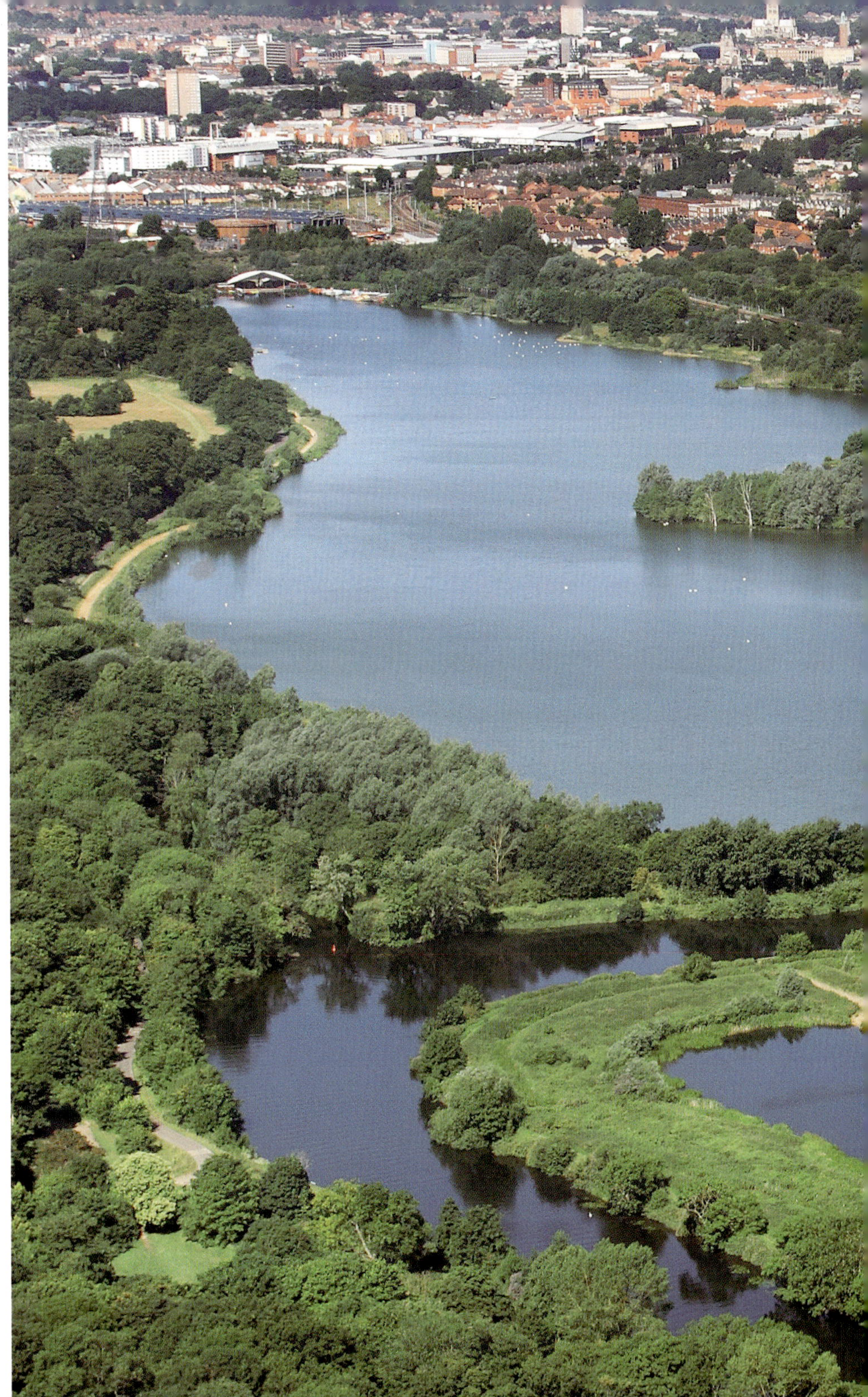

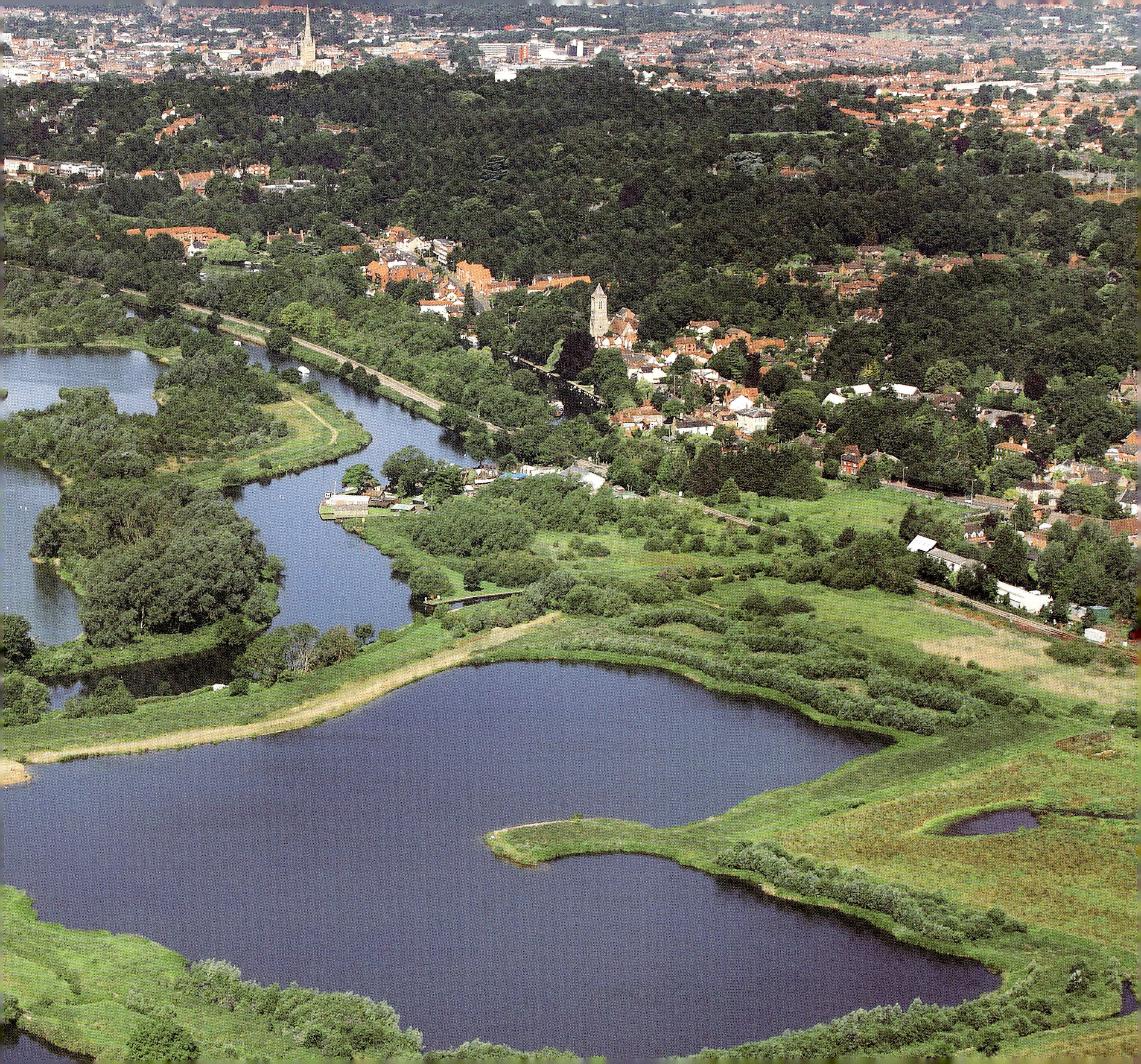

Chapter 4

Murder Most Foul and Other Nasty Happenings

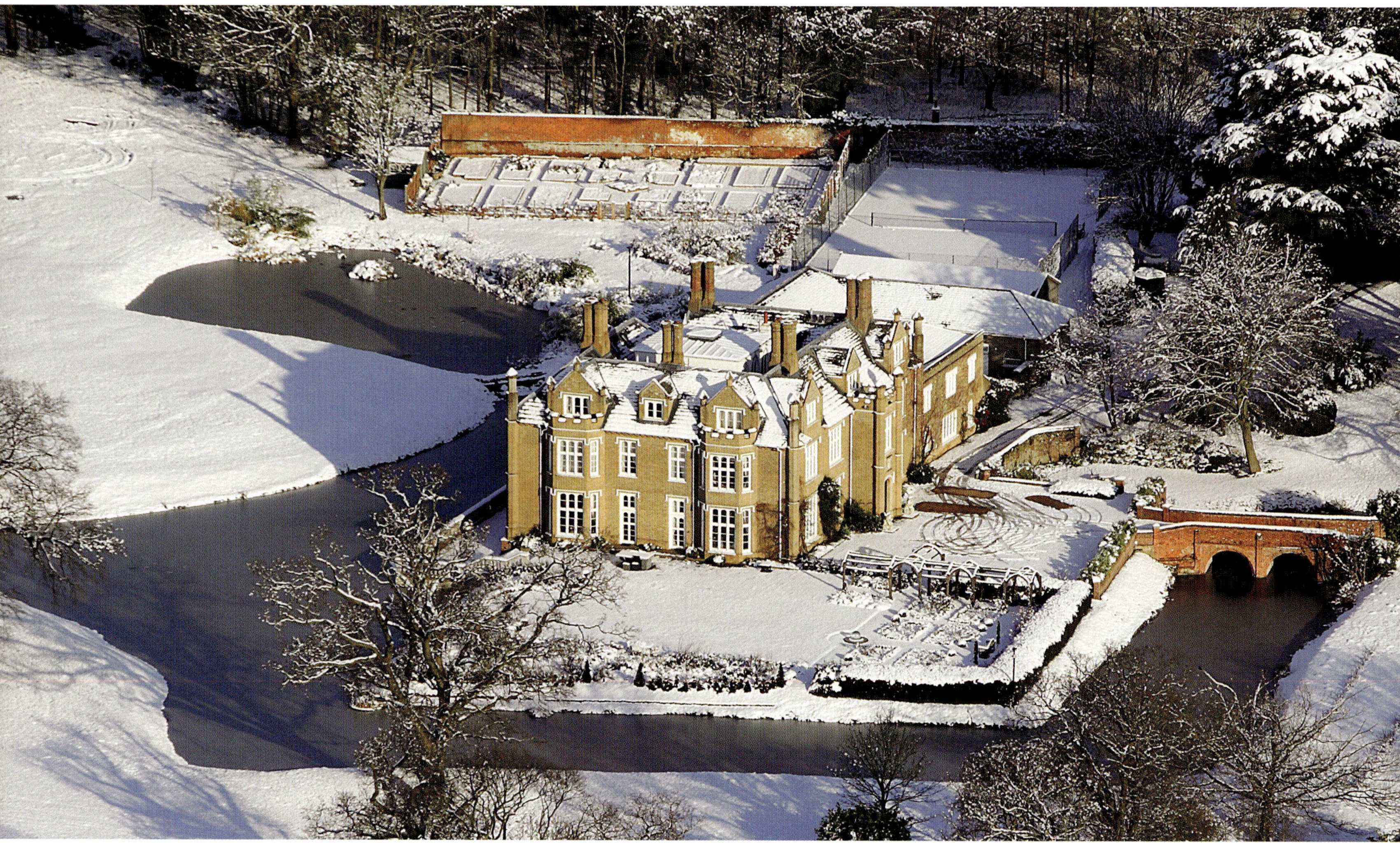

Stanfield Hall.

Murder at Stanfield Hall

In 1848 tenant farmer James Rush of Potash Farm, Stanfield near Wymondham, murdered landowner Isaac Jermy and Jermy's son because of a dispute over money. He was sentenced to death. The public hanging from Norwich Castle caused ghoulish public interest; there were even special excursion trains from London running on the new (1845) railway. Afterwards Potash Farm's name was changed.

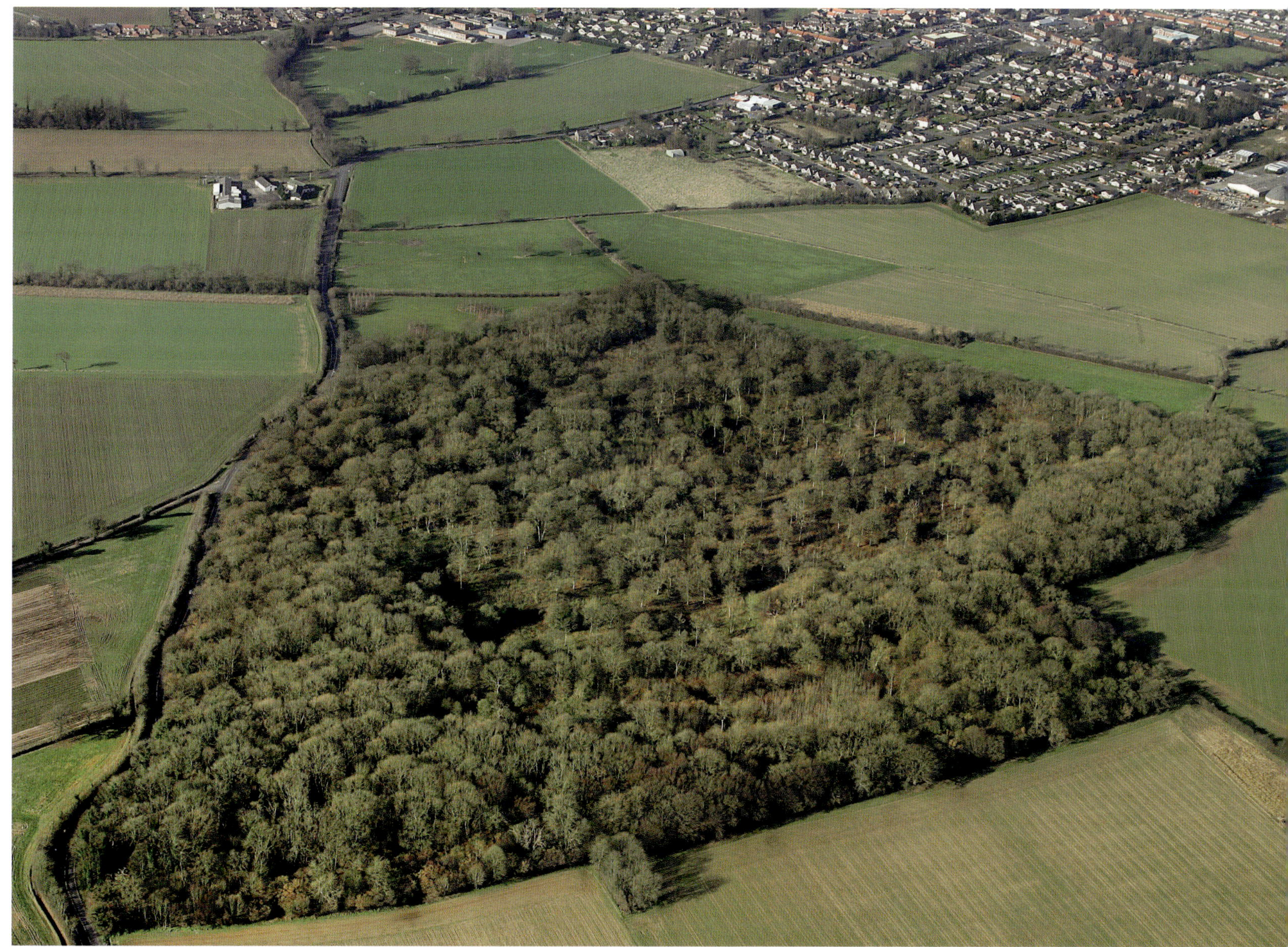

The Babes in the Wood

The story of the young brother and sister murdered by their wicked uncle in Wayland Wood appears often in pantomime… oh yes it does. The children's wicked uncle of Griston Hall near Watton murdered his nephew and niece for their fortunes and abandoned their bodies in Wayland Wood. But forever afterwards nothing went right for him so at least there's a moral. Pantomime ending preferred.

The Brothers Kett

Brothers Robert and William Kett have gained heroic status. As prosperous Wymondham farmers it's difficult to understand why they, Robert as the leader especially, chose to champion the rights of ordinary less fortunate men unless they were guided by altruistic principles. The upset was about the injustices of common land enclosure which, until then, had been accessible to all. Things came to a head in 1549. An army of thousands of ordinary men headed by Robert Kett encamped on Mousehold Heath waiting to march on Norwich demanding change. They failed. Robert Kett, together with nine others, was hanged from the walls of Norwich Castle. William Kett was hanged from the west tower of Wymondham Abbey. An act hardly in the Christian spirit.

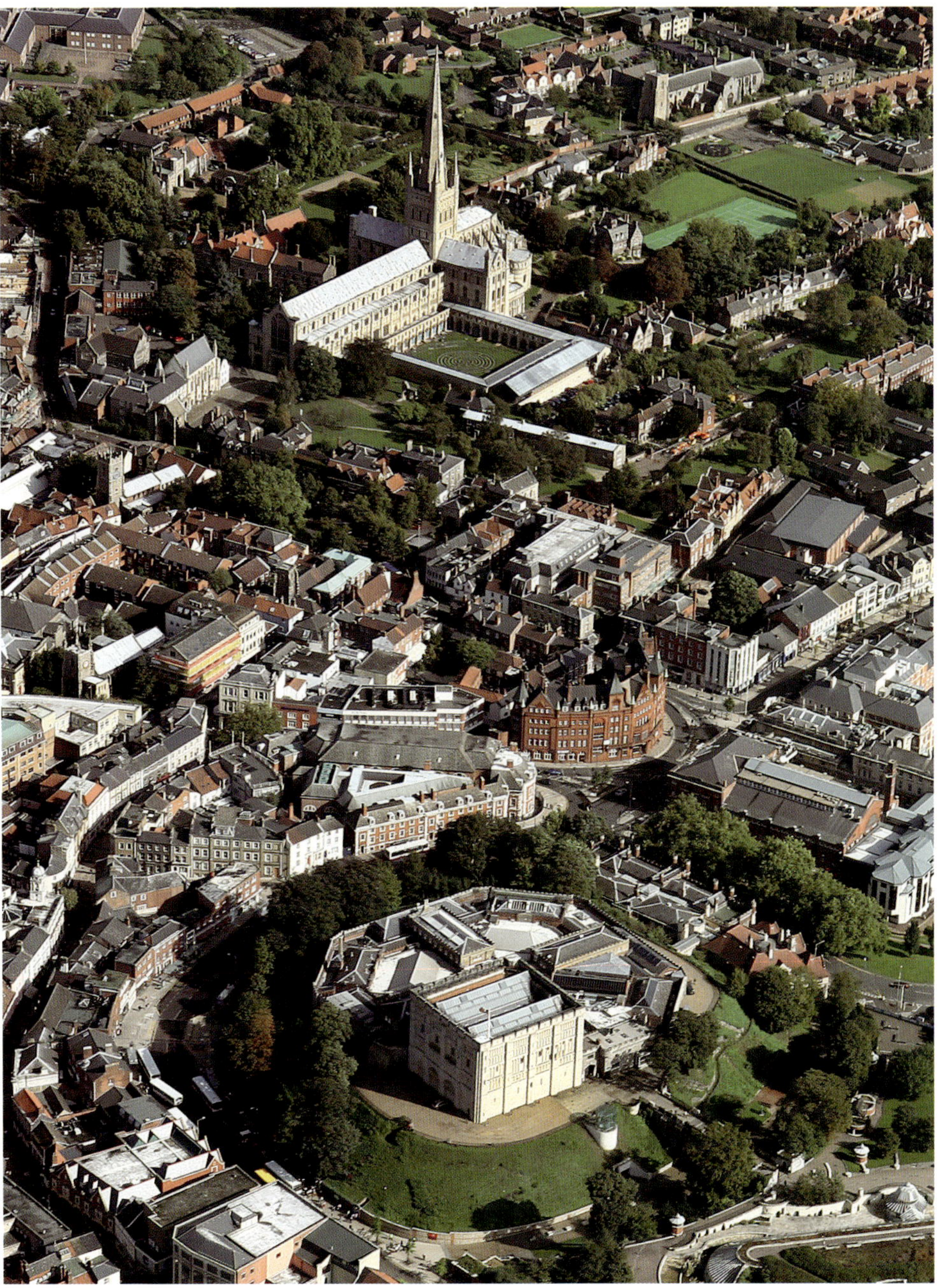

Right: *William Kett was hanged from the west (left) tower of Wymondham Abbey. This was the tower belonging to the townspeople's half of the abbey, the monks occupied the eastern part before the Reformation.*

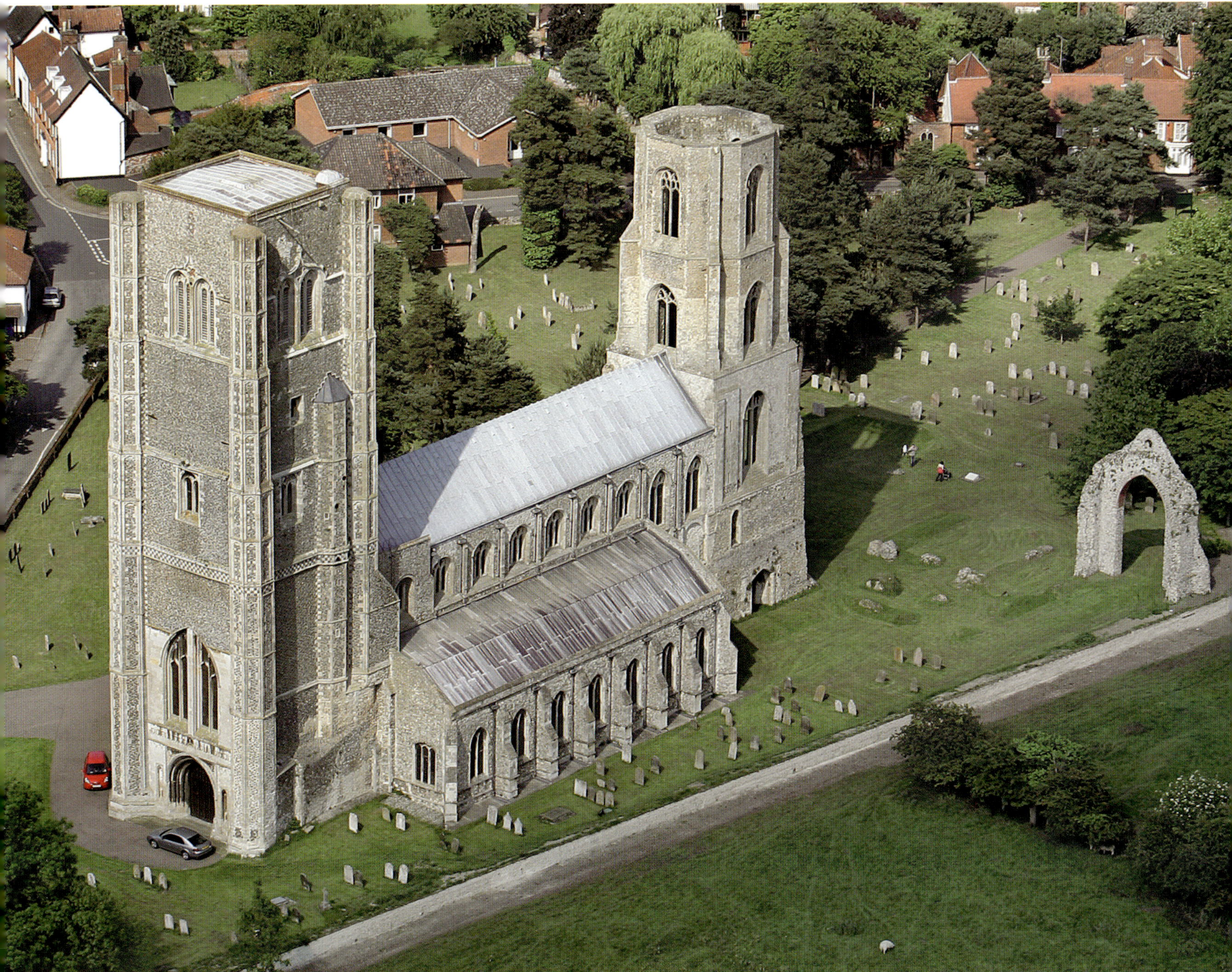

Edith Cavell 1865–1915

Nurse Edith Cavell was murdered by a German firing squad in Brussels. The charge: helping allied soldiers escape. She was the most famous female casualty of WWI and became a national heroine. Her father was Vicar of Swardeston near Norwich and the church's west window is dedicated to her. She's buried in the grounds of Norwich Cathedral. In adjacent Tombland there's both a statue and a pub dedicated to her.

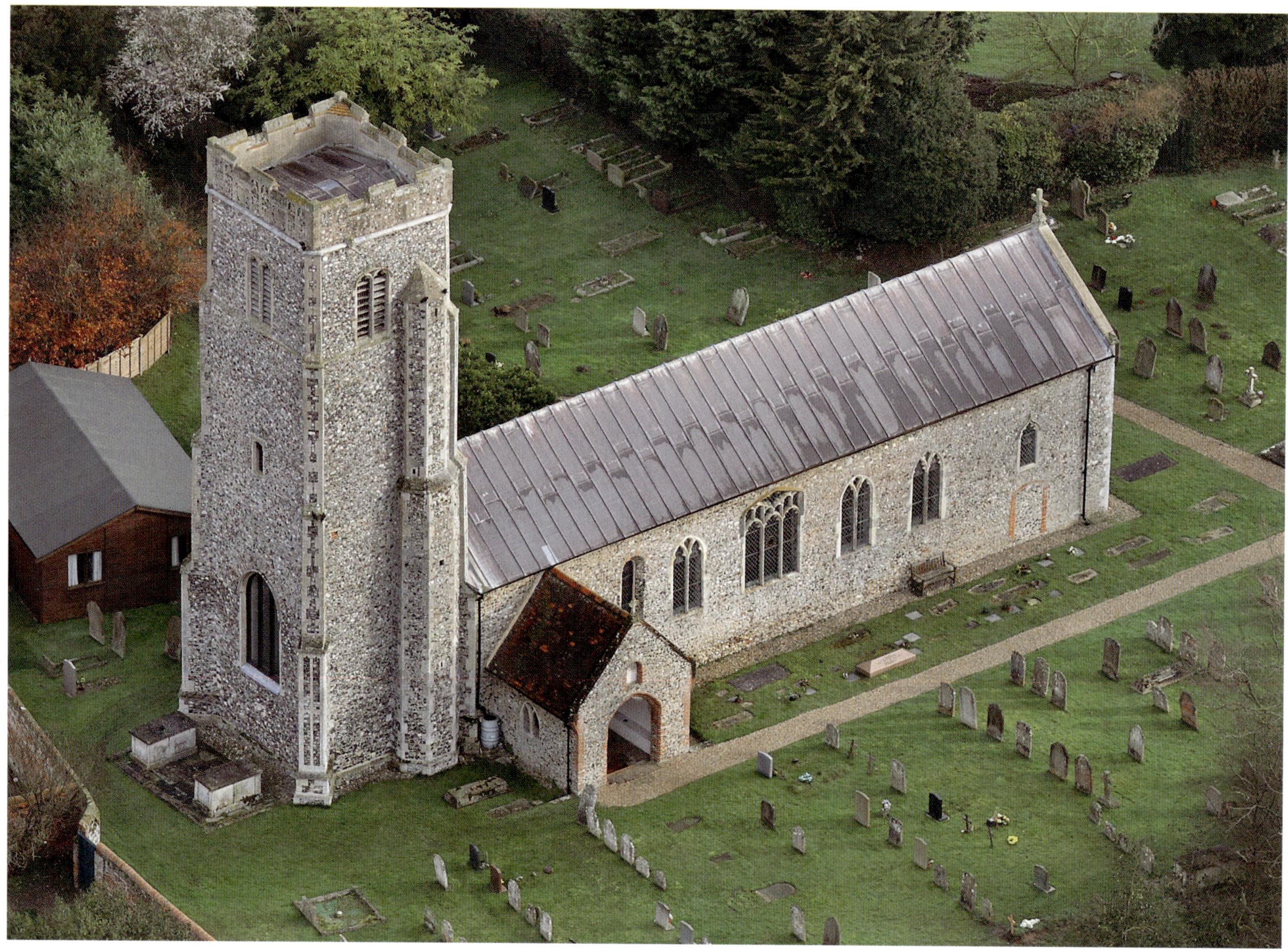

Swardeston Saint Mary the Virgin church.

Boudicca: Queen of the Iceni

After her husband Prasutagas, King of the Iceni tribe, died around AD60, Boudicca and their two daughters assumed control of the wholesale killing and general annoyance of the Romans. Petticoat Government did not suit the Romans at all and in AD 61 they invaded Boudicca's territory setting up forts along Peddars Way and the Pye Road (more or less today's A140). Her kingdom centered on Saham Toney and Ashill where evidence in the form of weapons and jewellery has been discovered. The kingdom lasted only until her death after which Roman rule was restored.

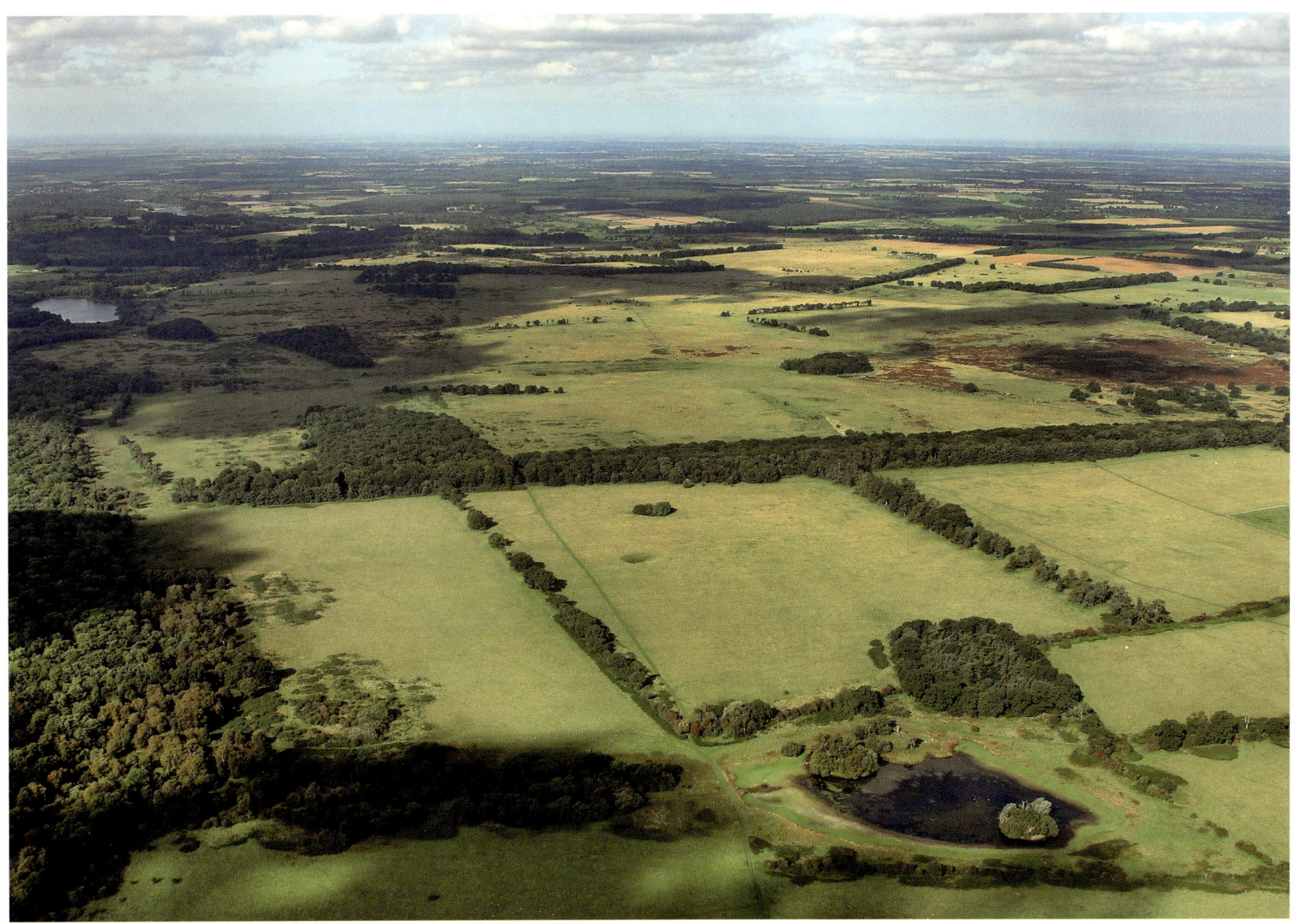

Breckland – Boudicca territory: note the meres – found only in Breckland.

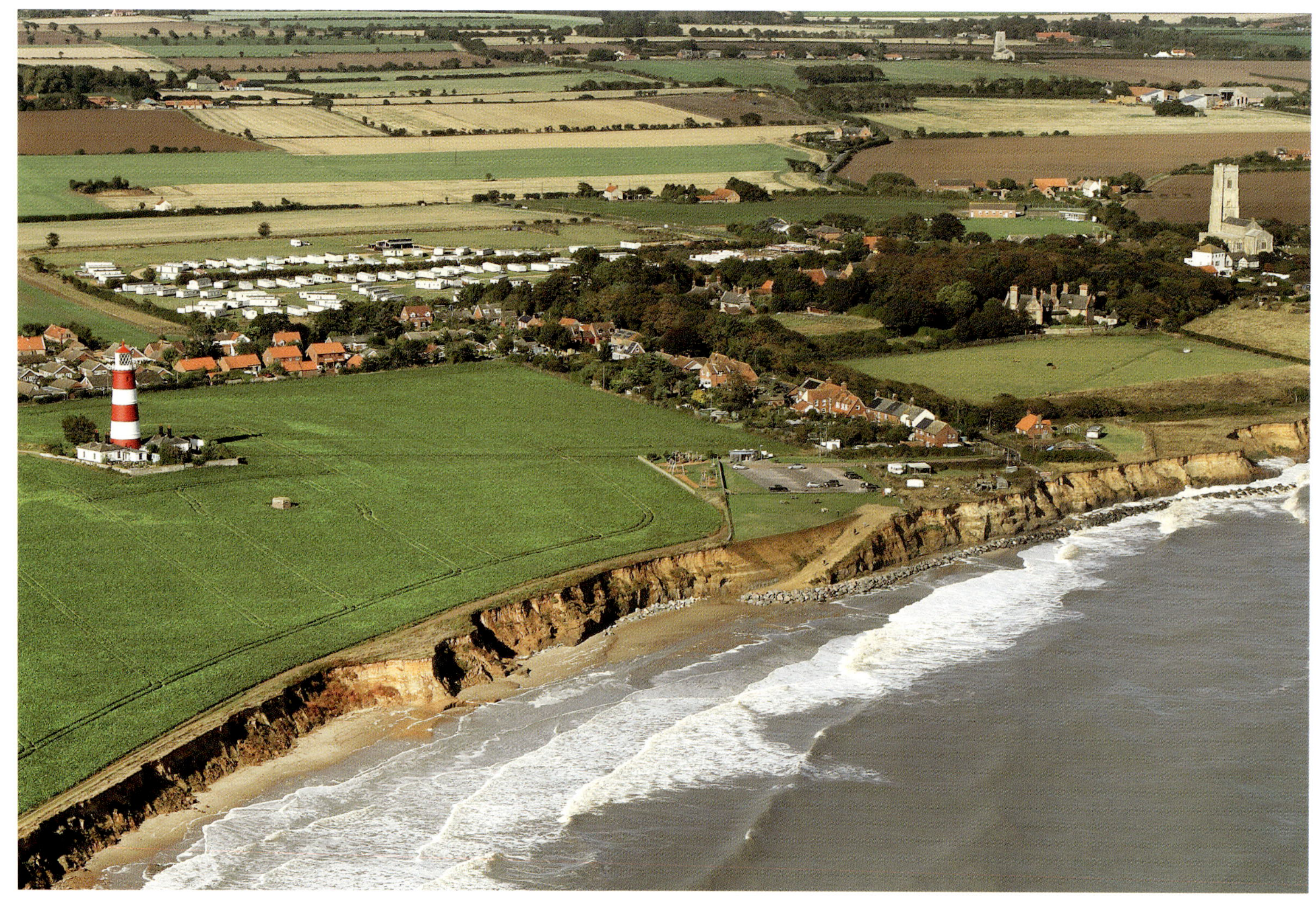

Happisburgh.

HMS *Invincible*

The shallow North Sea has accounted for many shipwrecks and drownings over the centuries that Norfolk has been separated from mainland Europe. Graveyards all along the stretch of coast from Weybourne to Caister contain the bodies of seamen whose ships have foundered. So littered with wrecks were the sandbanks that in 1904 Trinity House sent a team to blow them up.

In 1801 the largest loss of life was suffered by HMS *Invincible* on its way to join Nelson's Baltic Fleet before the Battle of Copenhagen. The ship was overloaded and ran aground on the shoals of Hammonds Knoll before breaking up. Of the 650 men aboard, 400 were drowned and are buried in a mass grave in Happisburgh churchyard. A similar fate had befallen HMS *Peggy* in 1770 when 32 sailors were washed ashore; they too are buried at Happisburgh.

The Siege of Caister Castle

There's not a great deal written about the siege because it wasn't much of a siege and it didn't last very long. But it must have been rather nasty.

The castle had been built for Sir John Fastolf, one of the heroes of the Battle of Agincourt (1415). After the battle he wanted peace and quiet and with the proceeds of the ransom awarded to him for the return of a French knight he'd captured in the battle he built Caister Castle. Eventually (by friendly agreement) it passed to the Pastons but the Duke of Norfolk, Sir John Mowbray, wanted it for himself and moved in. Battle and siege ensued, the Duke won but the Pastons reclaimed the Castle eight years later.

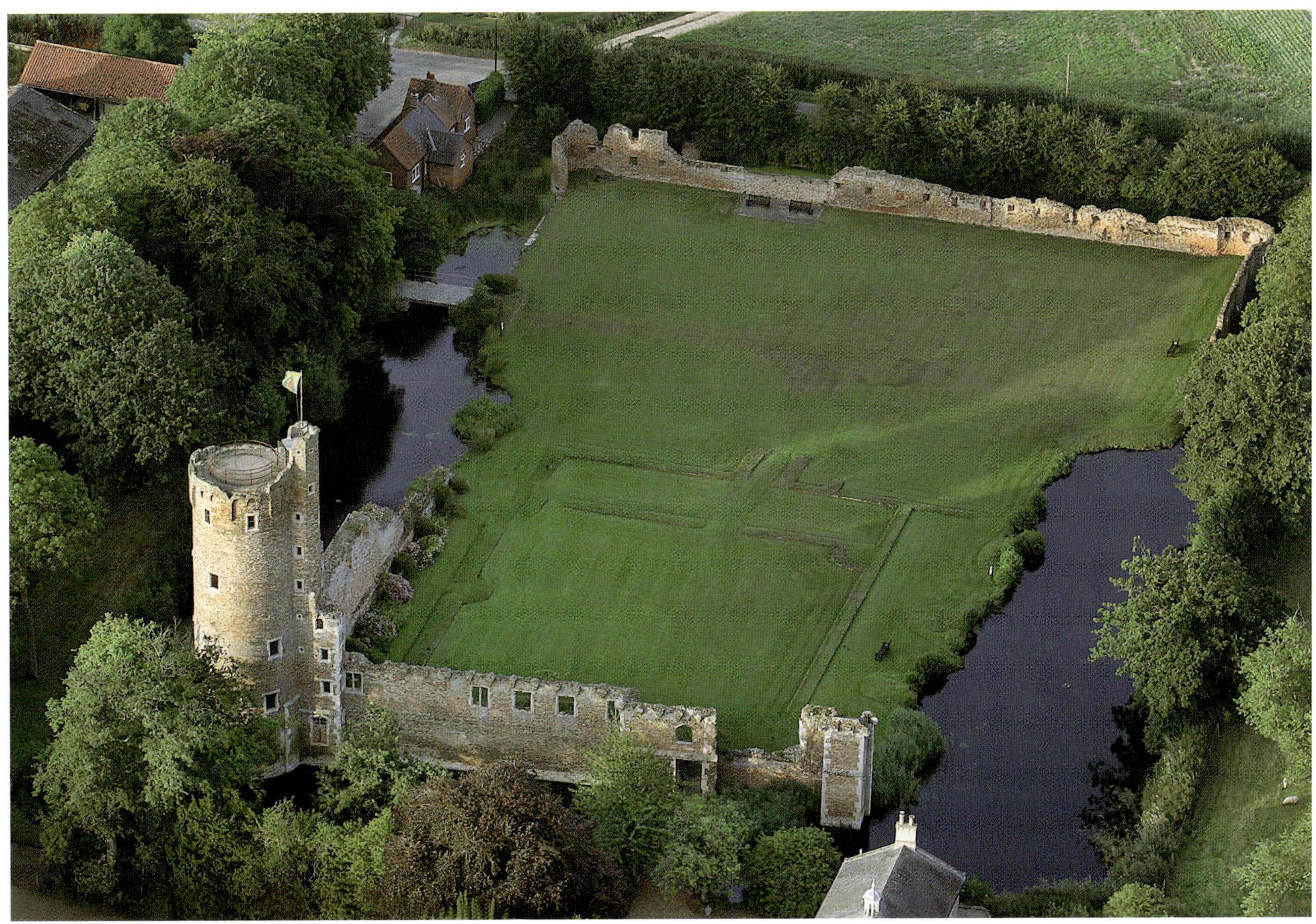

The Thorpe Railway Disaster

On 10 September 1874 the London express heading east and the mail train from Great Yarmouth heading west were both on the single track and crashed head on at Thorpe adjacent to this spot. A contemporary report in the *Illustrated London News* lists the 22 dead which included the crews of both engines and four passengers who later died of their injuries. A guard and 73 passengers were seriously injured. What was then the Three Tuns and is now the Rushcutters pub on the Yarmouth road was used as a mortuary and this building is prominent in the picture above the locomotive.

Human error and the fact that the London train was running late caused the train from Yarmouth to proceed when it should have been held on a loop at Brundall. The local train's driver and fireman are buried side by side in the Rosary Cemetery, their headstones distinguished by a railway engine in relief sculpture.

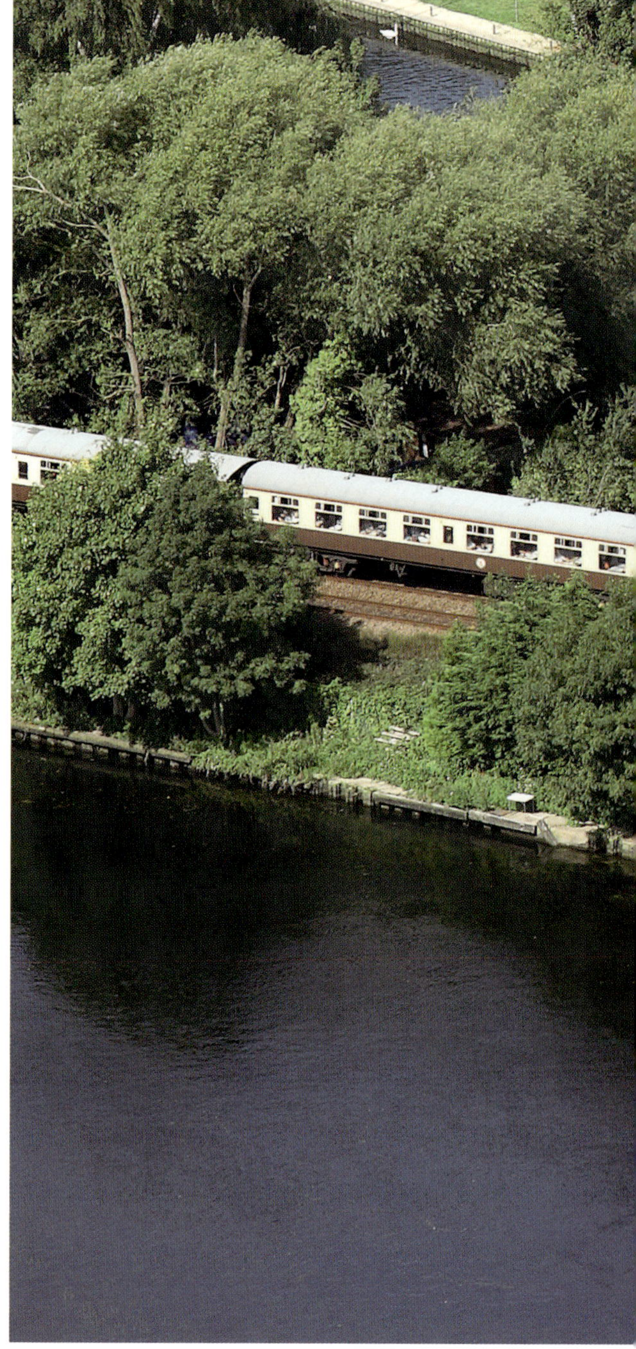

Locomotive No. 60163 "Tornado" crosses the River Yare at Thorpe with an excursion train bound for Great Yarmouth on 28 August 2017.

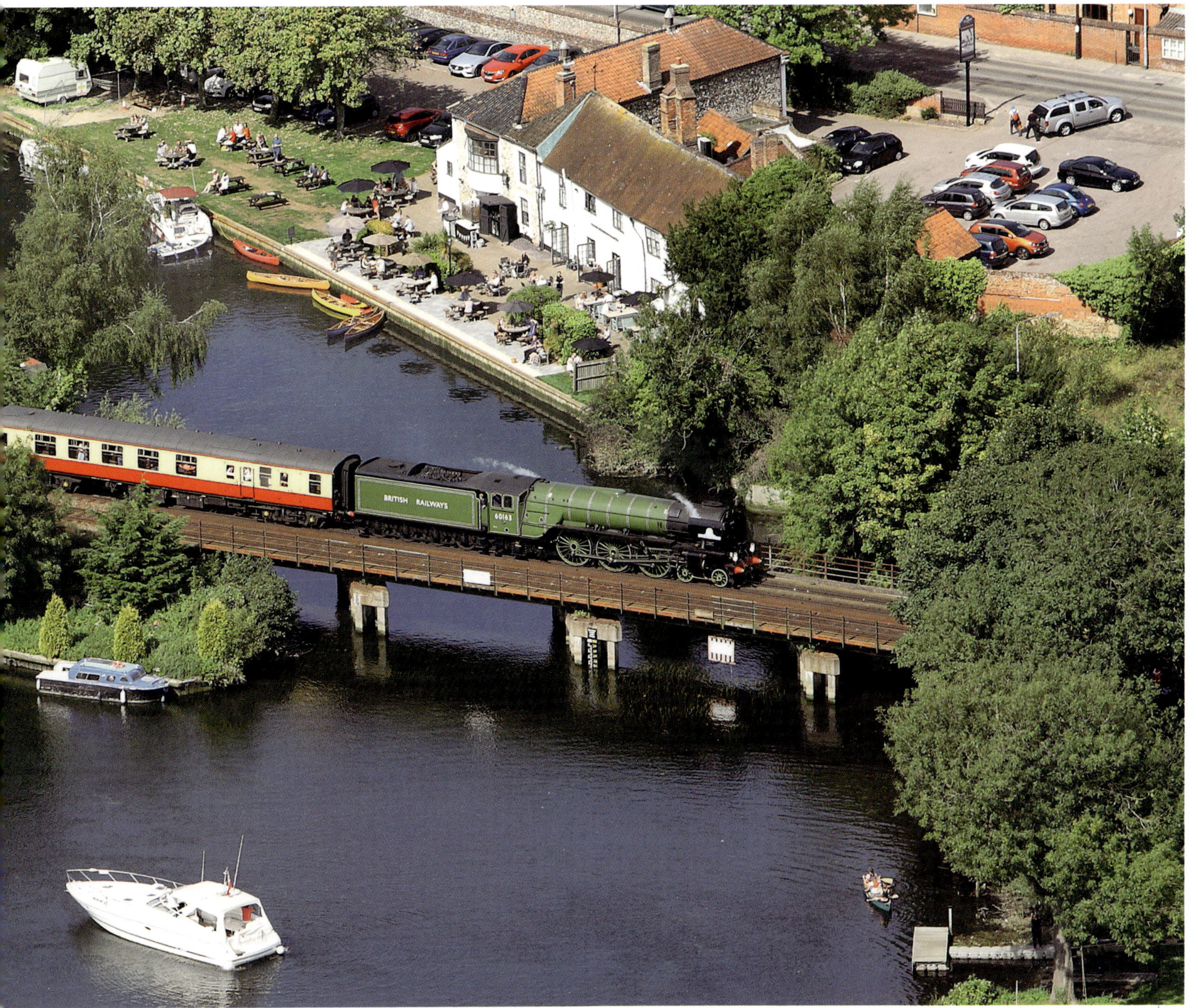

The Reverend Harold Davidson: Vicar of Stiffkey

Stiffkey church is dedicated to St John the Baptist whose head became a trophy for Salome's revenge – much as the Reverend Davidson's did many centuries later. In 1932 Harold Davidson was tried in a court of law on charges of immorality because of his naïve declaration of innocence whilst associating with London prostitutes. Subsequently he was unfrocked at a service in Norwich Cathedral. A broken man, he joined a circus preaching proof of his innocence from an (already occupied) lion's cage. He got it wrong again, and he was mauled to death.

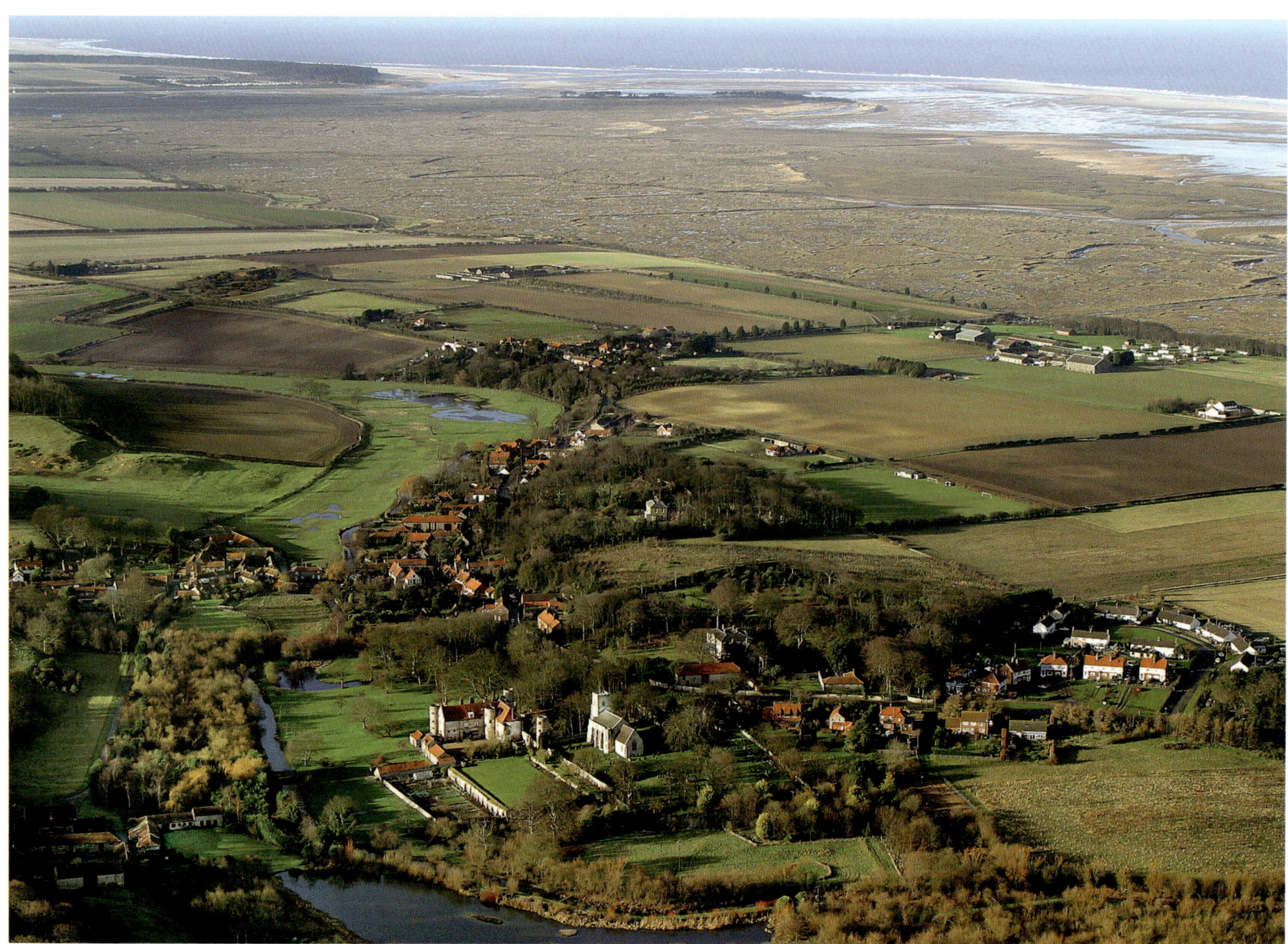

Chapter 5

Metamorphosis: A Change of Character
(How familiar objects are put to alternative uses)

David Copperfield's old nurse Peggoty took David to visit her brother Daniel who lived in an upturned boat on Great Yarmouth beach. The boat had metamorphosed into a house.

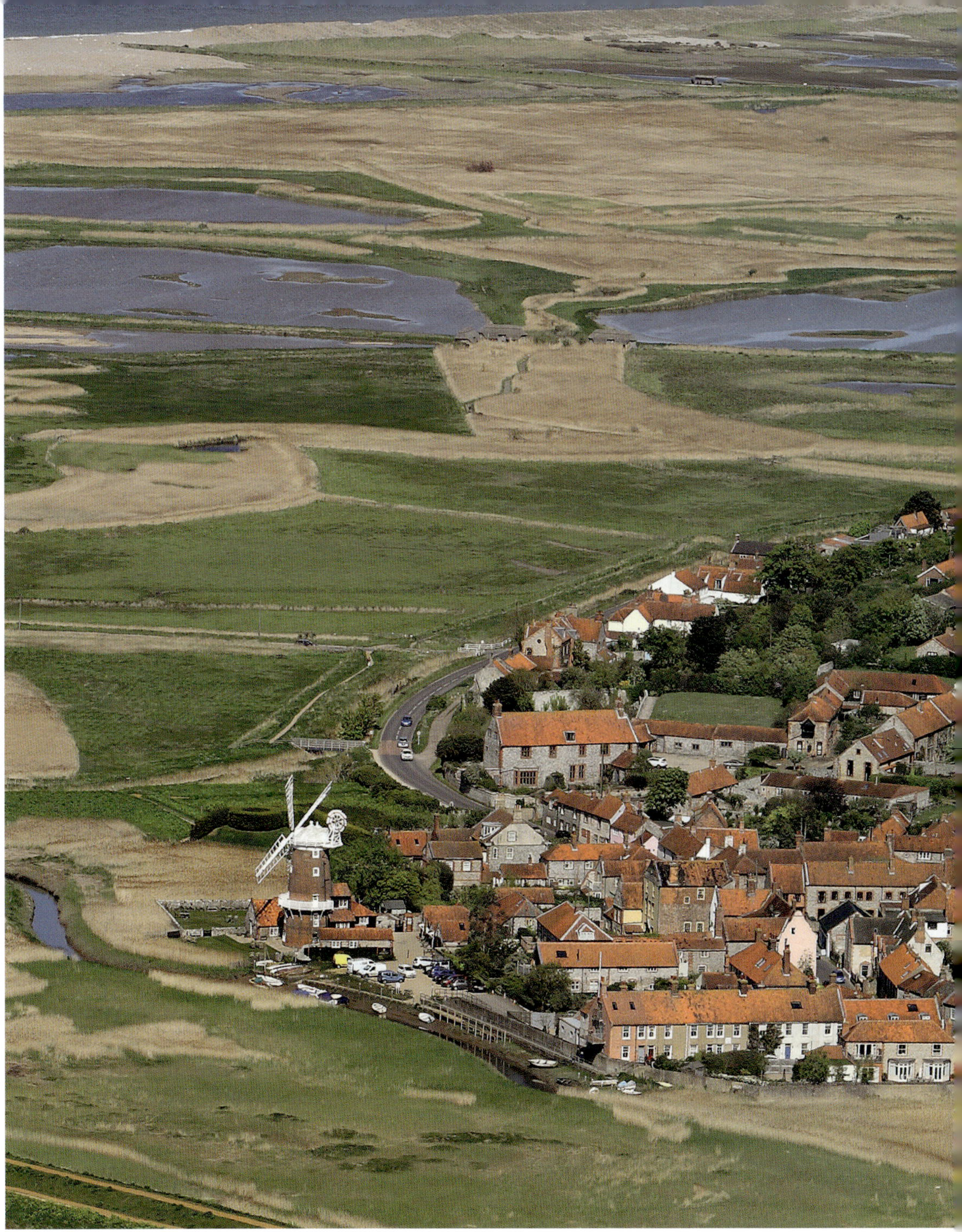

Cley Mill

The windmill with its commanding position on the River Glaven looking out onto the saltmarshes to the coast is possibly the best known mill in Norfolk. Built in 1819 this corn-grinding tower mill has been converted into holiday accommodation. It's very strange but the great cataloguer of the Buildings of England – Nikolaus Pevsner – missed it out!

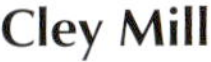

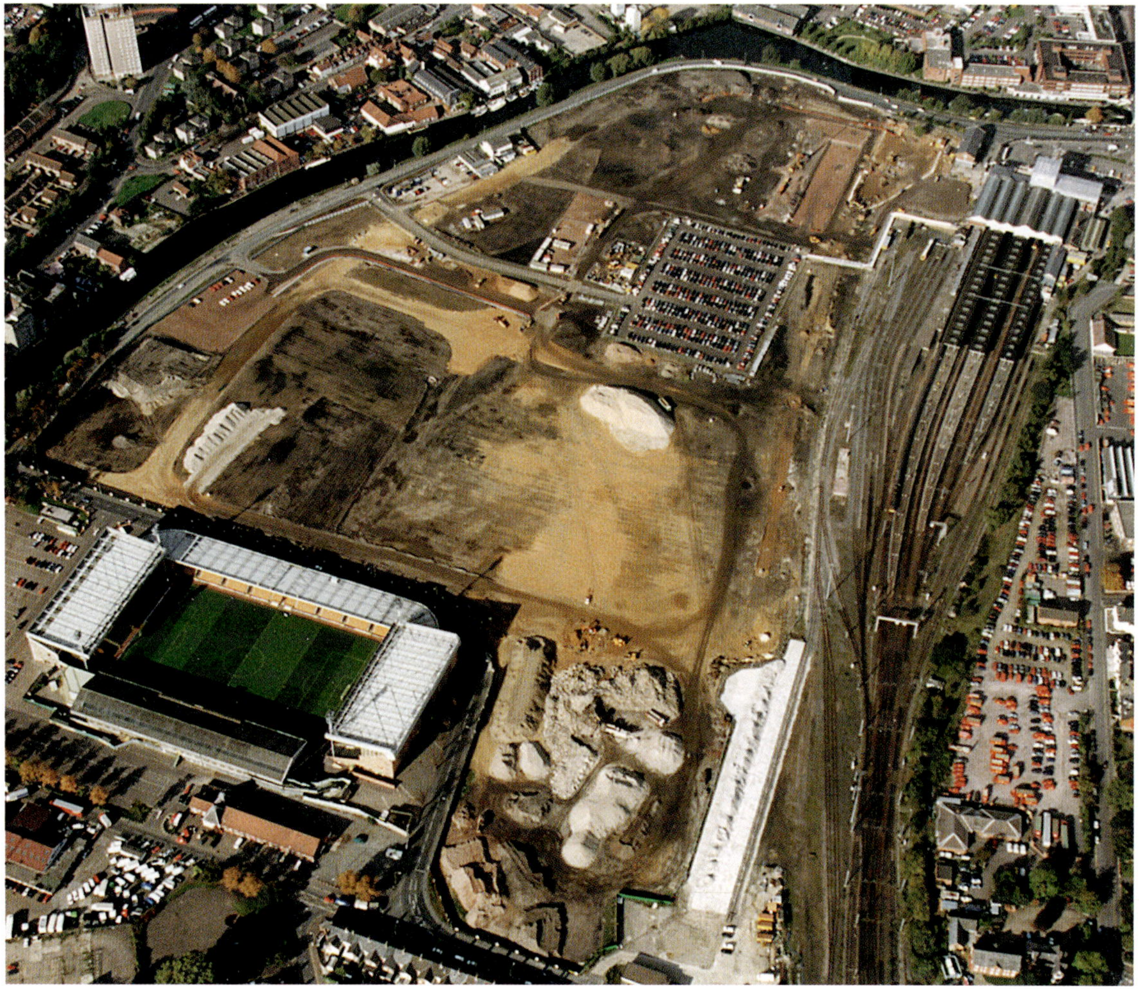

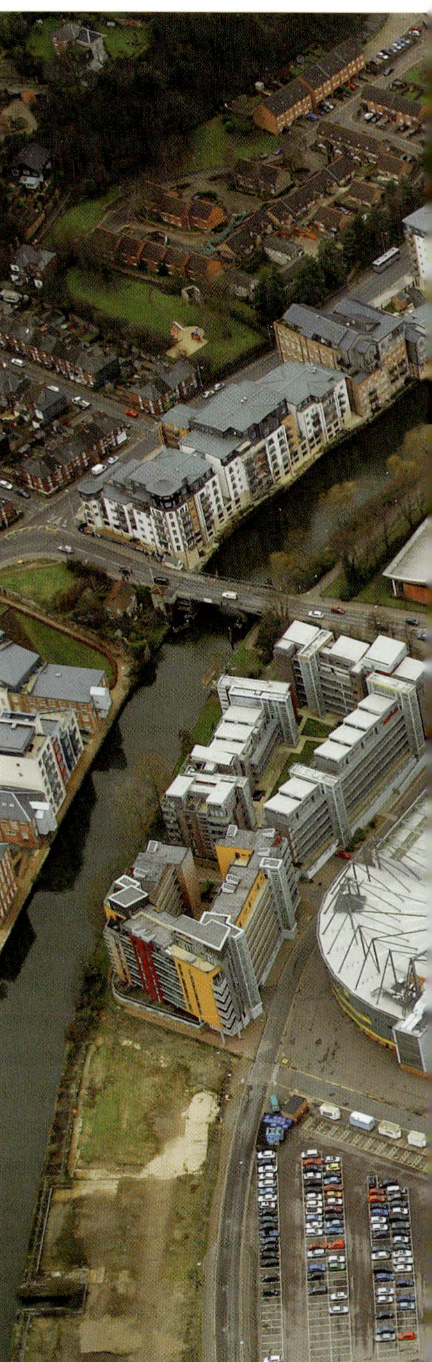

Norwich Riverside in 1993

The contaminated ground whilst under clearance.

Norwich Riverside in 2015

Along the River Wensum in the heart of the city an area has been 'rescued'. Because previously a foundry, railway yard and timber yard stood here the soil was contaminated both with oil, lead and mercury. There was a lengthy operation involving wholesale carting away by river of the affected top soil which has been spread on waste land to leave for decades. The site now houses shops, flats and entertainment venues and is known as 'Riverside'.

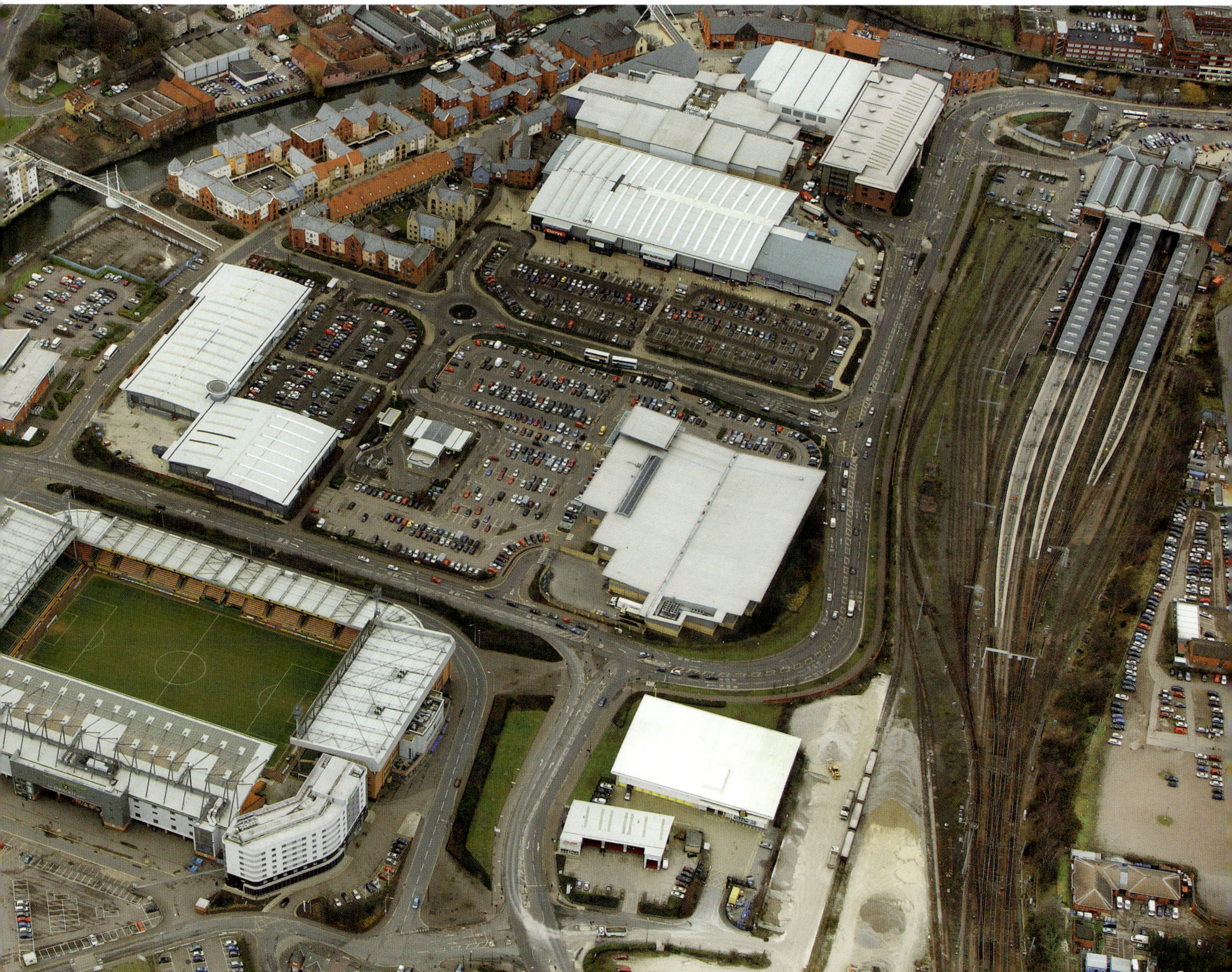

Albatros

Dutch sailing clipper to floating restaurant at Wells-next-the-Sea.

Albatros has spent the last forty years in the ownership of Dutch captain Ton Brouwer. Built in 1899 the sailing clipper was instrumental in carrying Jews and dissidents from Nazi occupied Denmark to neutral Sweden during WW2 with armaments and explosives hidden among the cargo for the Resistance on the return journeys. The last commercial trips for the *Albatros* were into Wells (no easy feat) with cargoes of soya beans between 1990–96. For the last twenty-five years, still under Ton Brouwer's ownership, she's been trading as a popular quayside restaurant with Dutch pancakes a speciality. The restaurant closed in late 2019 and the *Albatros* has since been advertised for sale. In 2020 with new owners, the *Albatros* sailed to Maldon in Essex for specialist restoration at the Marine Heritage Foundation.

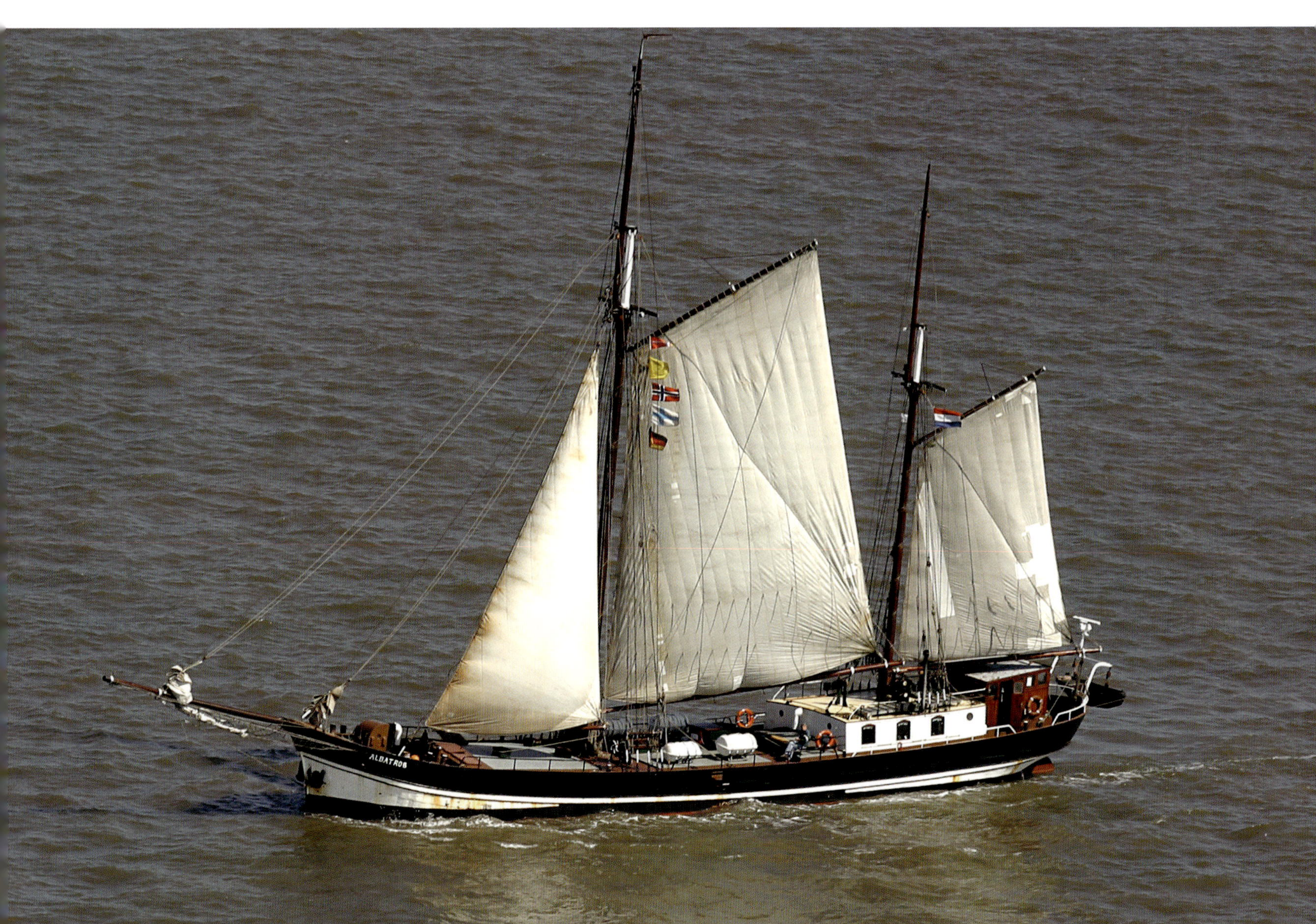

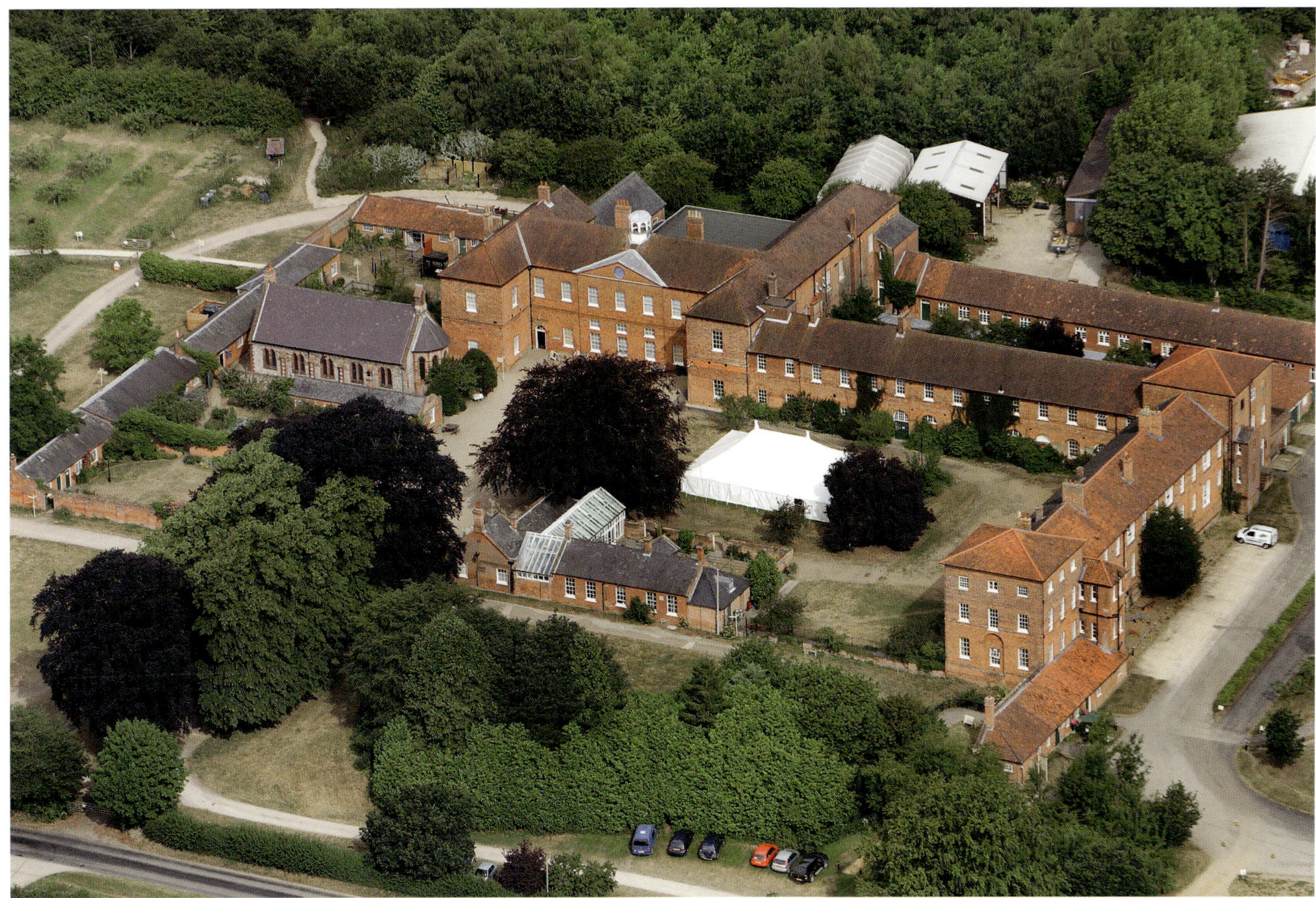

Gressenhall Rural Life Museum

The 'House of Industry' (the workhouse) set up in 1777 gave shelter and employment to the destitute of the parish. Even today the building has the typical grim appearance of the workhouses of the time. Attempts were made to reduce its stigma. Over time children were educated in state schools and in 1919 the Registrar General refused to accept the word 'workhouse' on Birth and Death Certificates. Gressenhall Workhouse was renamed 'Beech House.'

Today the building is a Rural Life Museum and farm with rare breeds of livestock. It's also the headquarters of Norfolk's Archaeological Department and the Norfolk Air Photo collection. A change for the better.

Former Workhouse in South Norfolk

The metamorphosis has been that the building has been changed into luxury houses and flats. It's not lack of money which qualifies anyone to live there – just the opposite!

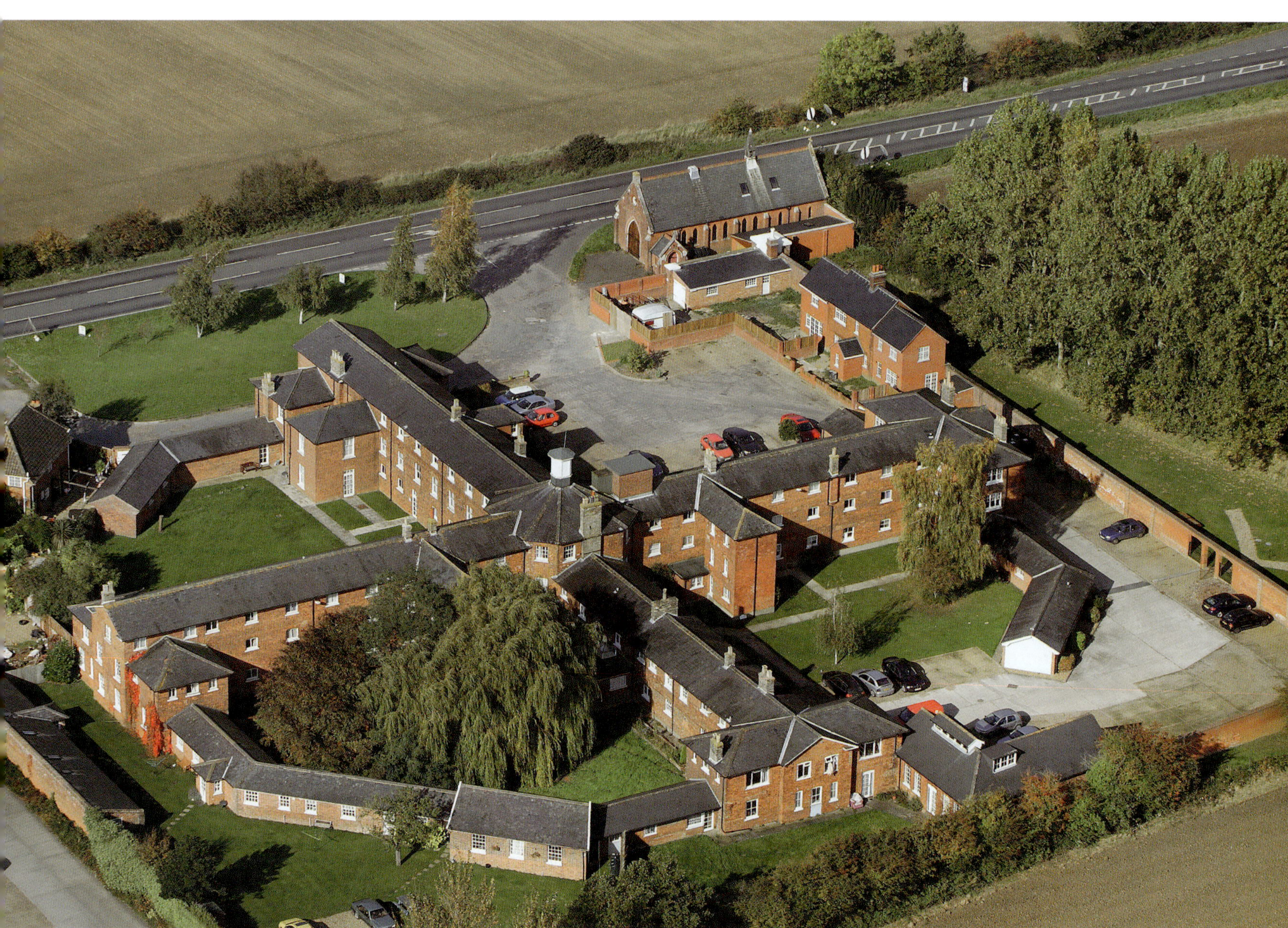

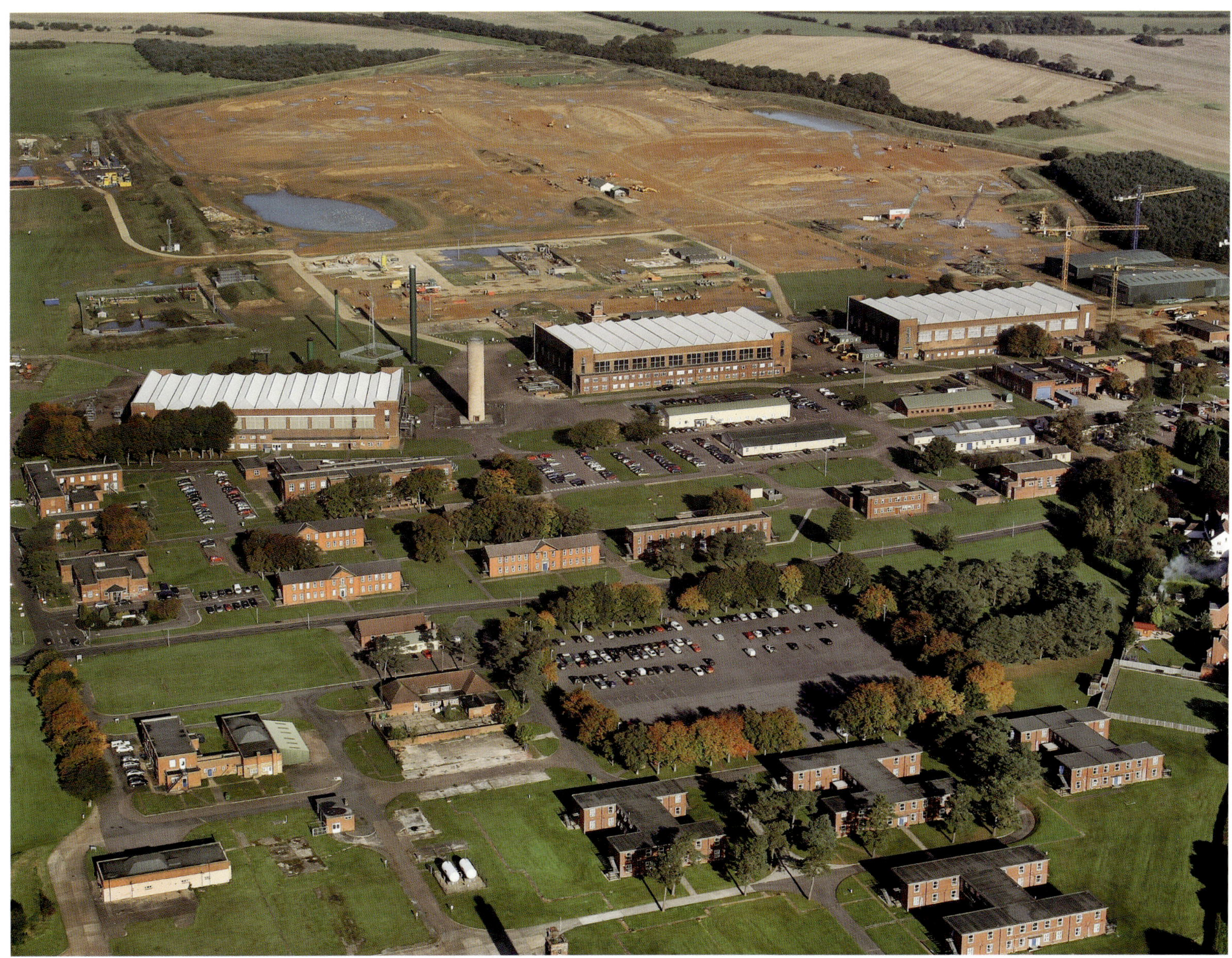

Swords into Ploughshares

RAF Bircham Newton (1918-66) was very much to the fore in coastal defence and shortly before its closure was involved in the development of the Hawker Siddeley 'Kestrel' V/STOL, forerunner of the 'Harrier'. The site was sold to the CITB (Construction Industry Training Board) which in turn sold it on to the West Suffolk College in 2020 – its teaching role remains the same.

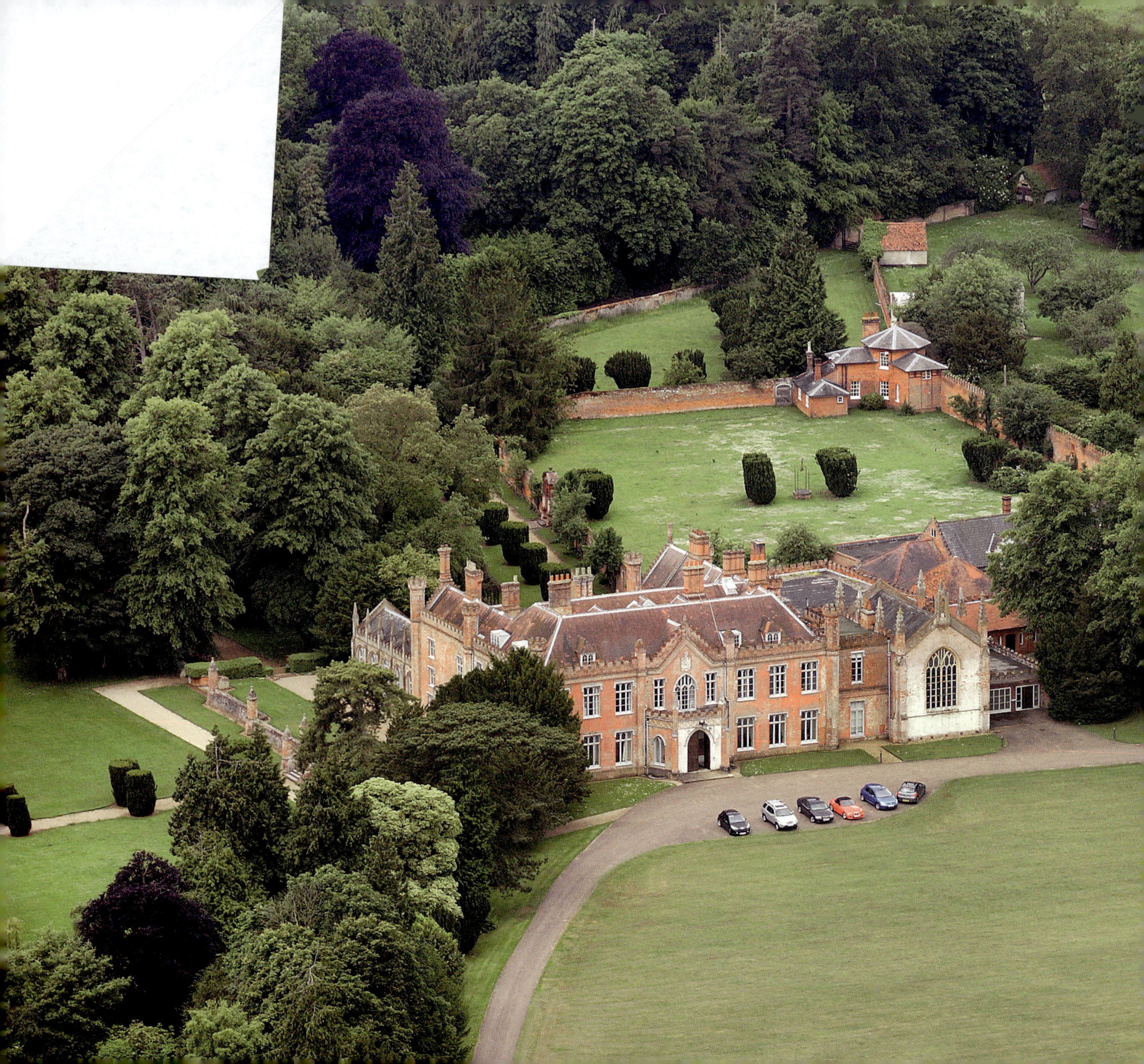

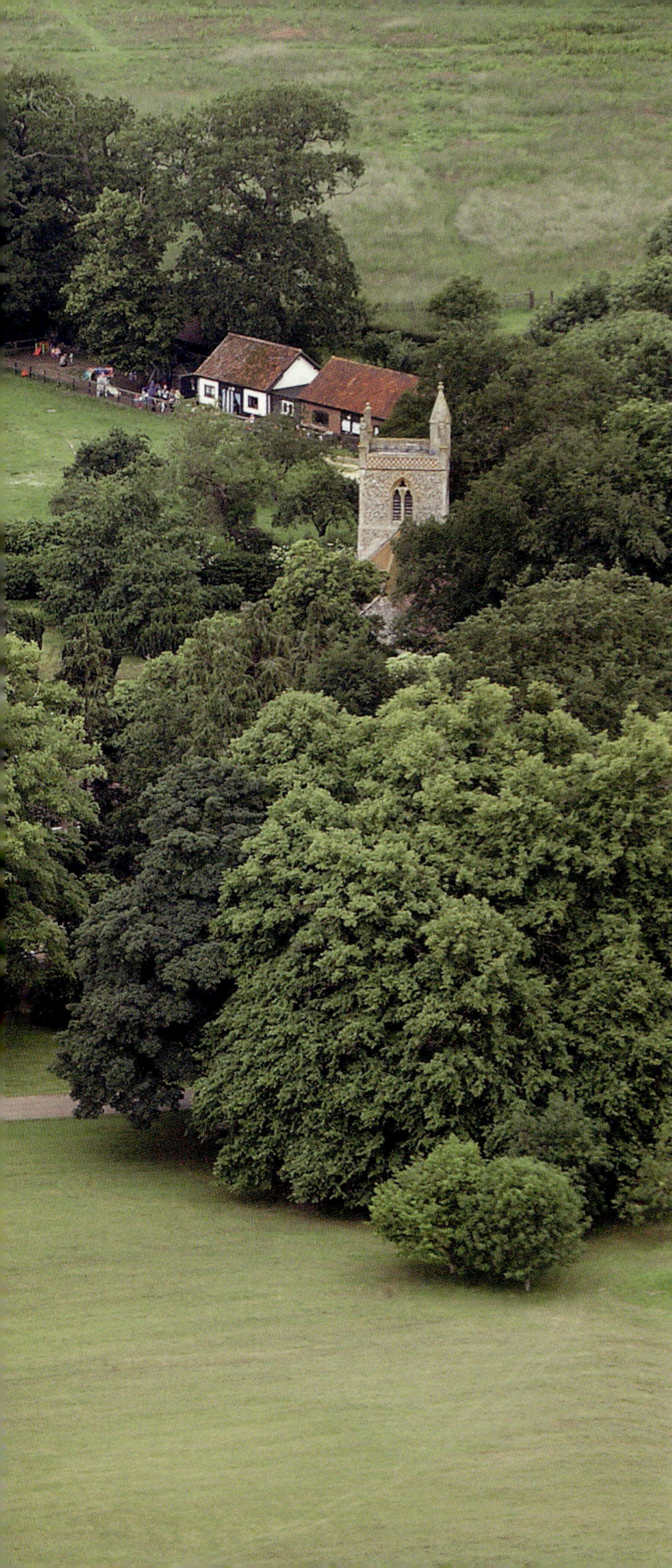

Ketteringham Hall

Much of Ketteringham's history of two centuries involves the ongoing power struggle between the Lord of the Manor Sir John Boileau and the vicar, the Reverend William Wayte Andrew of Wood Hall, Hethersett. The situation is chronicled in Owen Chadwick's book *Victorian Miniature*. And of course it was inevitable that eventually they would share the same churchyard.

It was Sir John who had remodelled the original Tudor hall into the Gothic form it has today. During WW2 the Hall became the HQ of the United States Air Force. Afterwards it had another metamorphosis into Colin Chapman's HQ for Lotus cars. Now it houses offices.

Gunton Hall

The Hall and associated buildings were rescued by architect Kit Martin who created elegant houses in a wonderful setting in rural Norfolk near Aylsham.

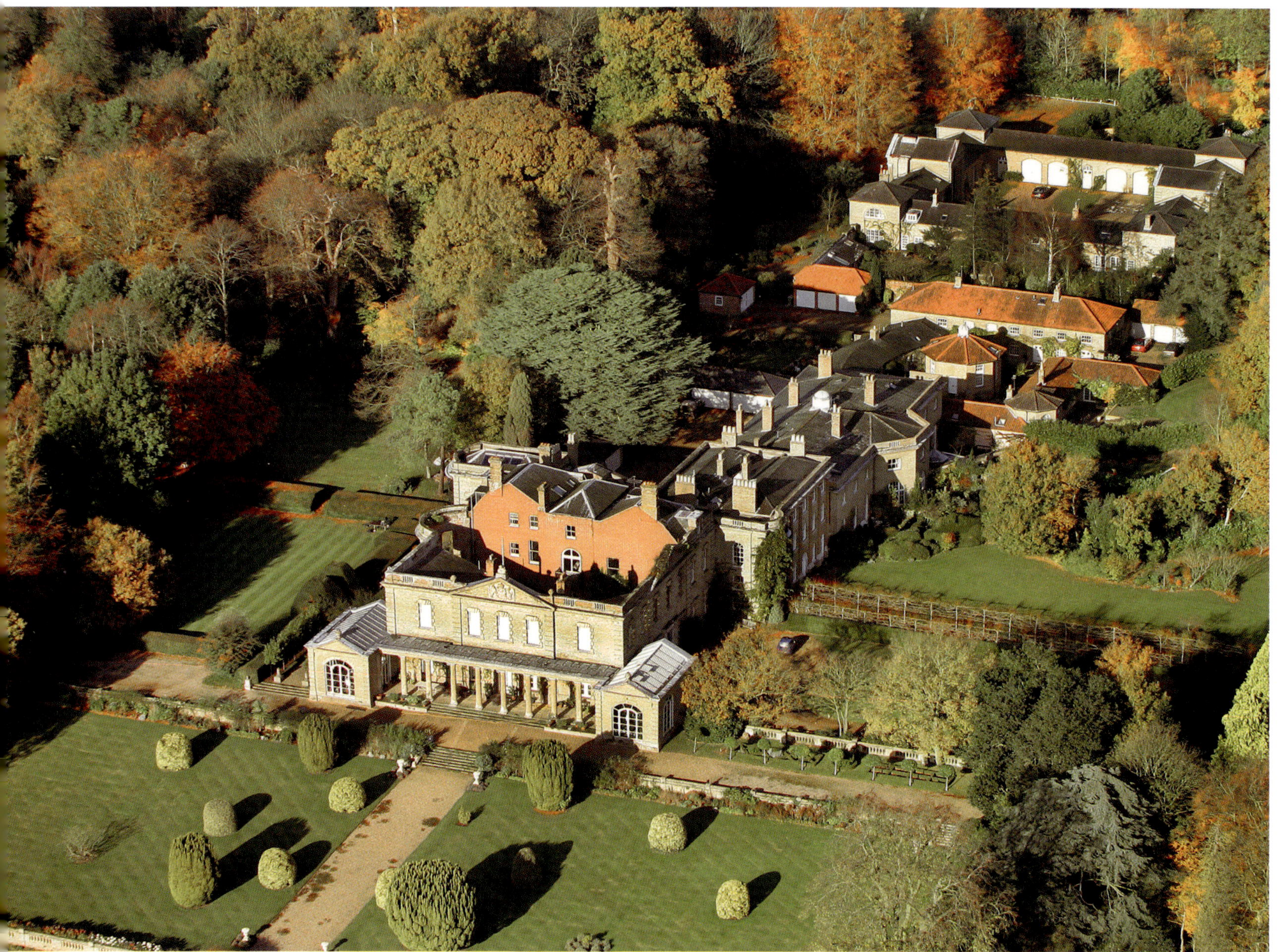

Great Yarmouth Royal Naval Hospital

Great Yarmouth with its safe harbour has long been a place to which disabled ships and injured seamen could return after battle. In Nelson's day sailors were looked after in the earlier hospital near to the parish church.

In 1811 the foundation stone for the new building along the sea front was laid. Bricks were made on the Dunes a few yards away. This hospital first opened for the 600 casualties of the Battle of Waterloo (1815). Over time it nursed victims of various conflicts including those injured in the Indian Mutiny (1858). It closed in 1993 and in 1997 architect Kit Martin (see Gunton Hall) converted it into elegant flats and houses.

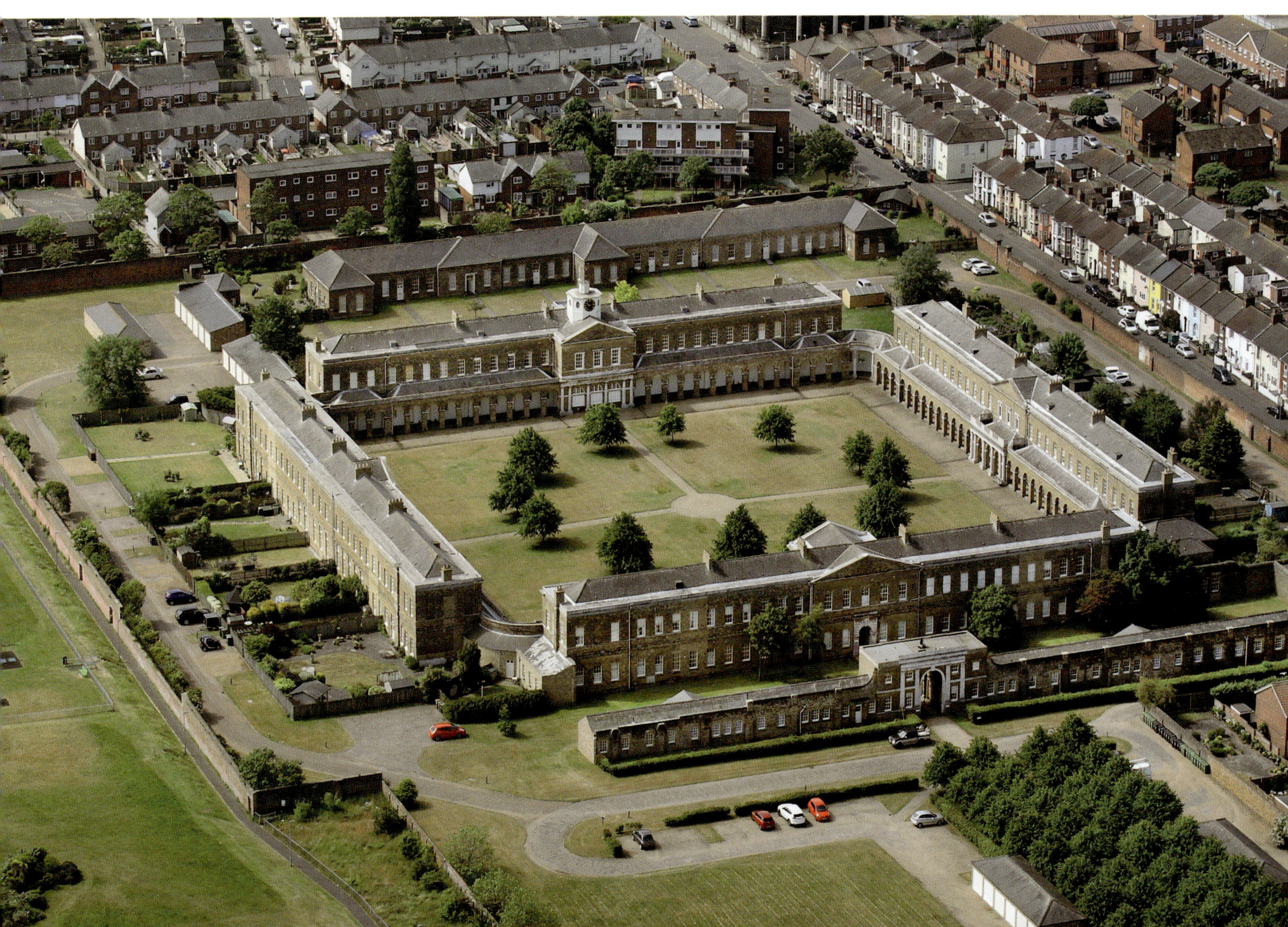

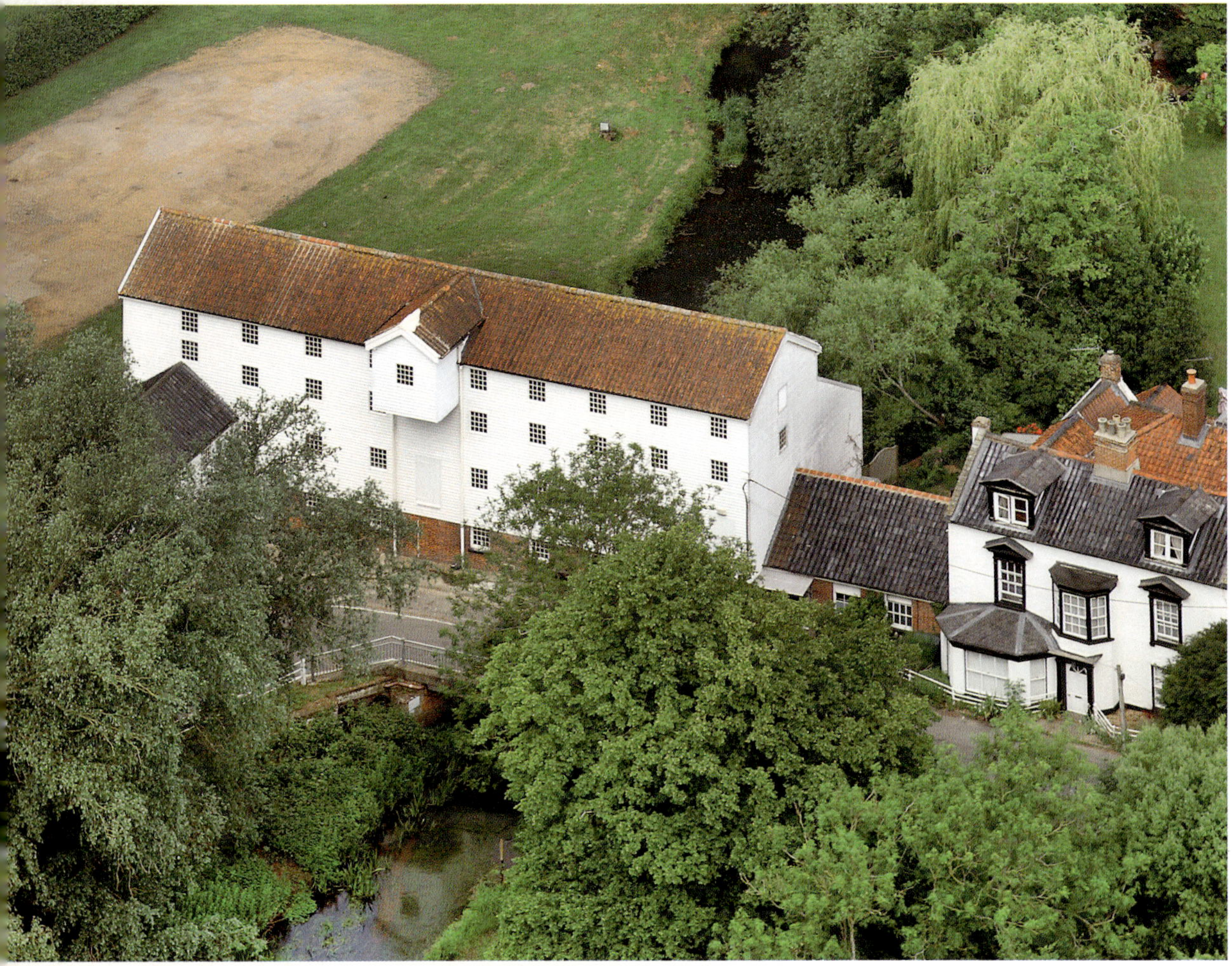

Stoke Holy Cross Watermill

The picturesque water mill is now a restaurant. It was where Jeremiah James Colman first milled mustard seed grown in fields nearby. It is said he made his fortune from the mustard people left on the rims of their plates.

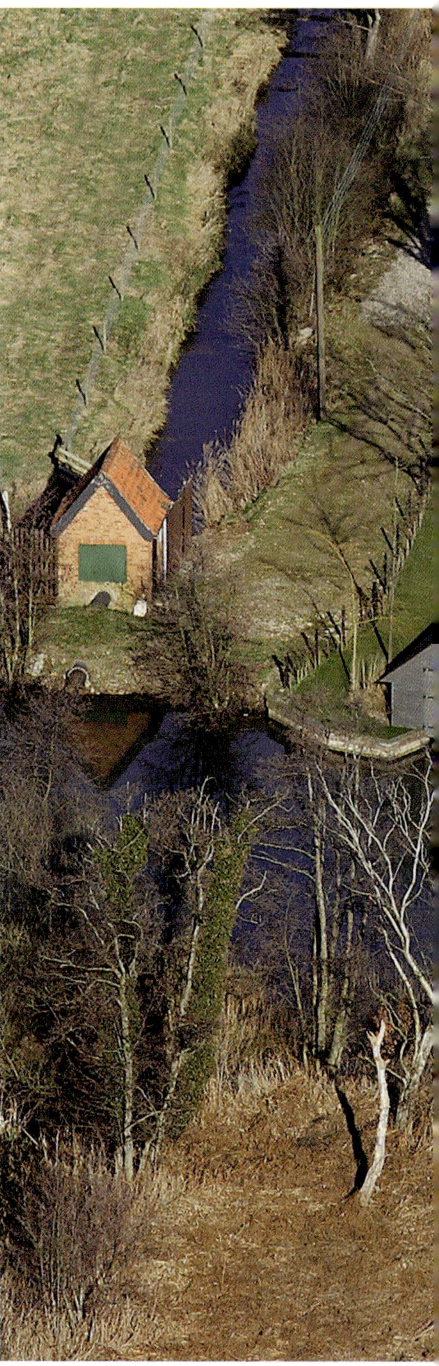

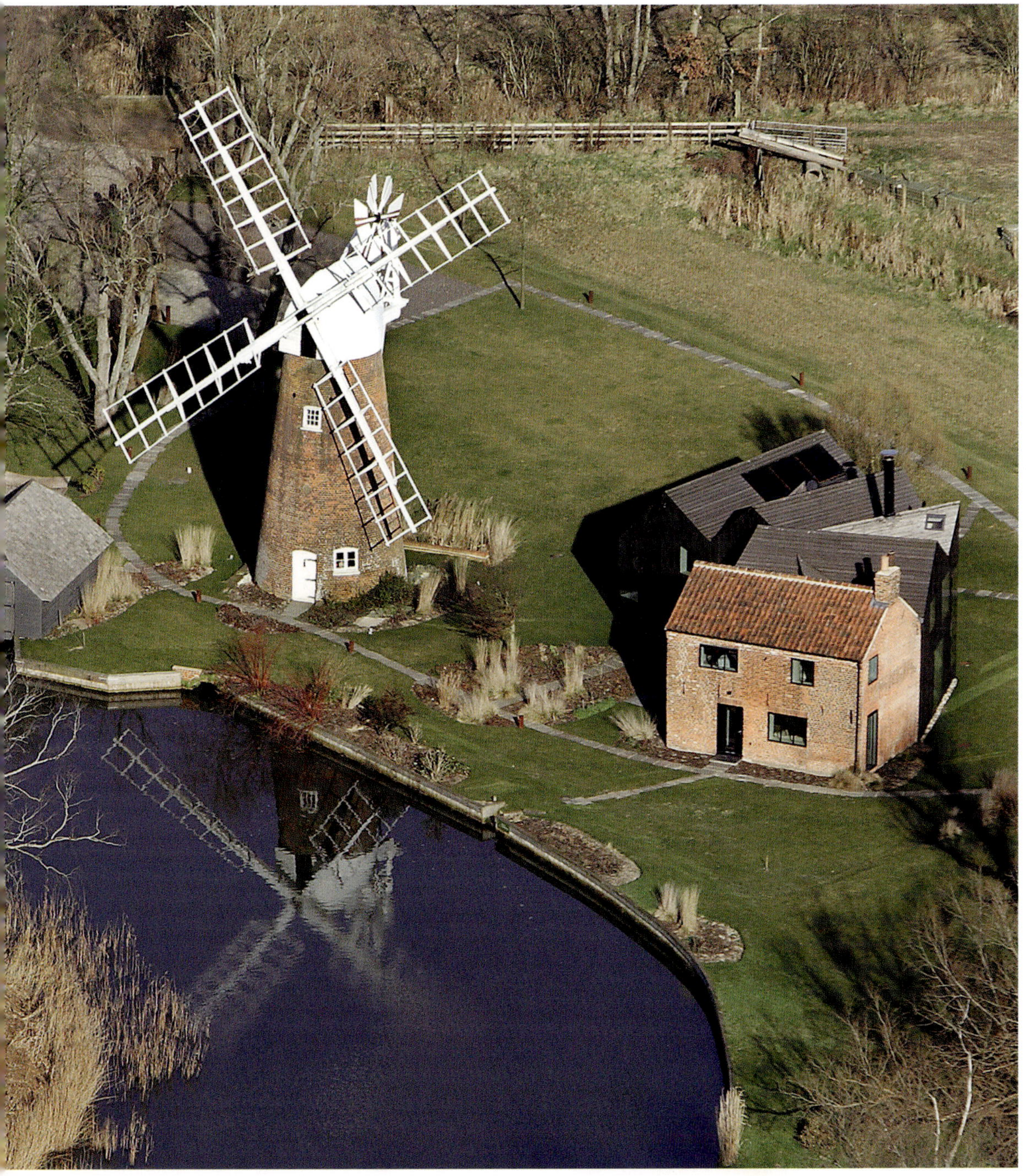

Hunsett Mill

The traditional mill pumped water from the dykes into the River Ant. Eventually a motor driven pump (in the hut next to the cottage) replaced it. Now the marshman's cottage is high tech but the clever thing is that all the eco friendly devices are hidden from the river. The front of the cottage looks as it always has. A ground source heat pump, a well, solar panels and a bore hole are all concealed round the back of the cottage hidden from view.

Dereham Maltings

There was controversy when it was proposed that the building be converted into living accommodation but the conversion fits in very well. To all intents it looks just like a maltings. What is missing is the lovely aroma which came from the barley as it was being malted for beer.

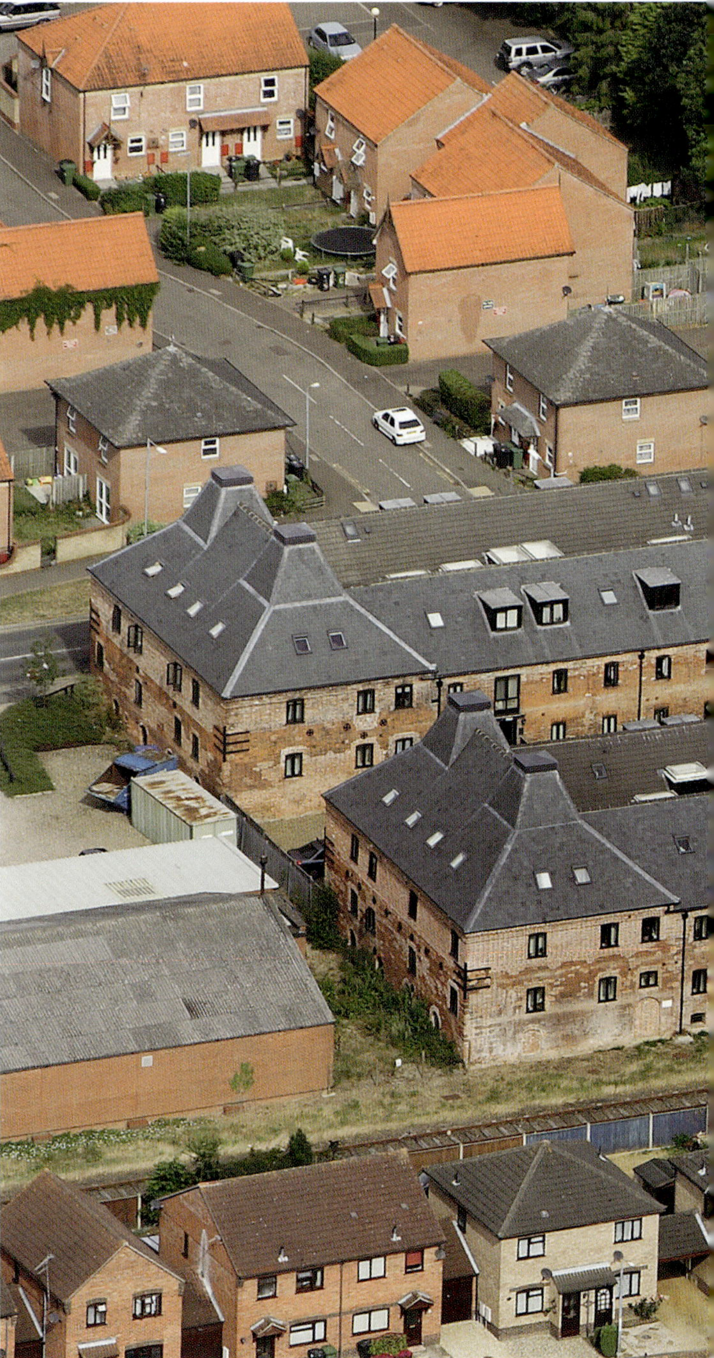

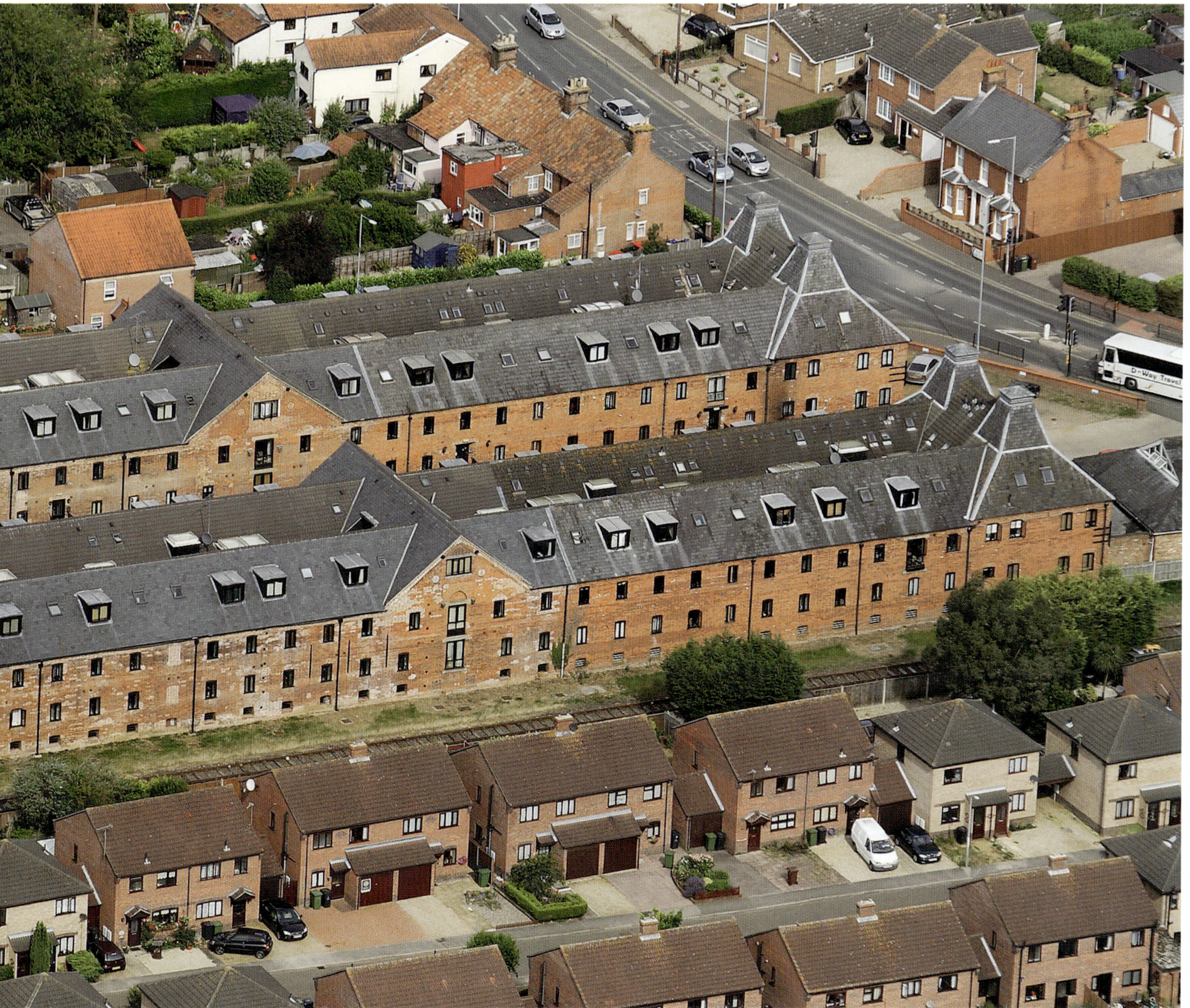

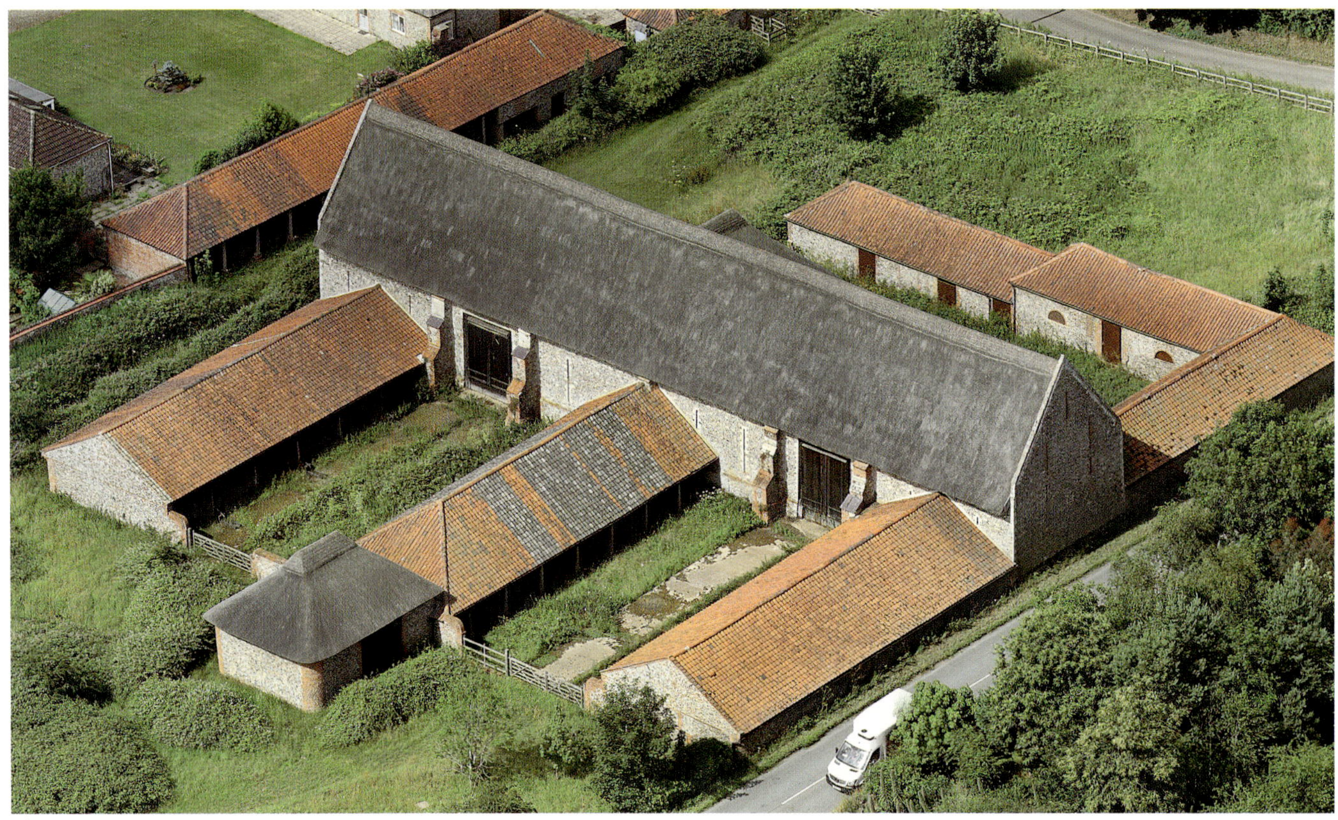

Paston Great Barn

The longest barn in Norfolk (162 feet – 49m) has been designated a Site of Special Scientific Interest. The rare barbastelle bat has set up home here which limits the barn's use for other purposes. It's thought the stone to build the barn originally came from the ruins of nearby Bromholm Priory (recycling is nothing new).

Paston is best known for the Paston Letters – written mainly between a husband (away fighting) and a wife (looking after things at home) in the fifteenth century.

The *Lydia Eva*

Herring fishing was vital to Great Yarmouth (there are herrings – the silver darlings – on its coat of arms). Even the distinctive smoky smell remains. The *Lydia Eva* was built at Great Yarmouth and is the last steam drifter of the herring fishing fleet.

Lydia Eva YH89, the last surviving steam drifter of the herring fishing fleet.

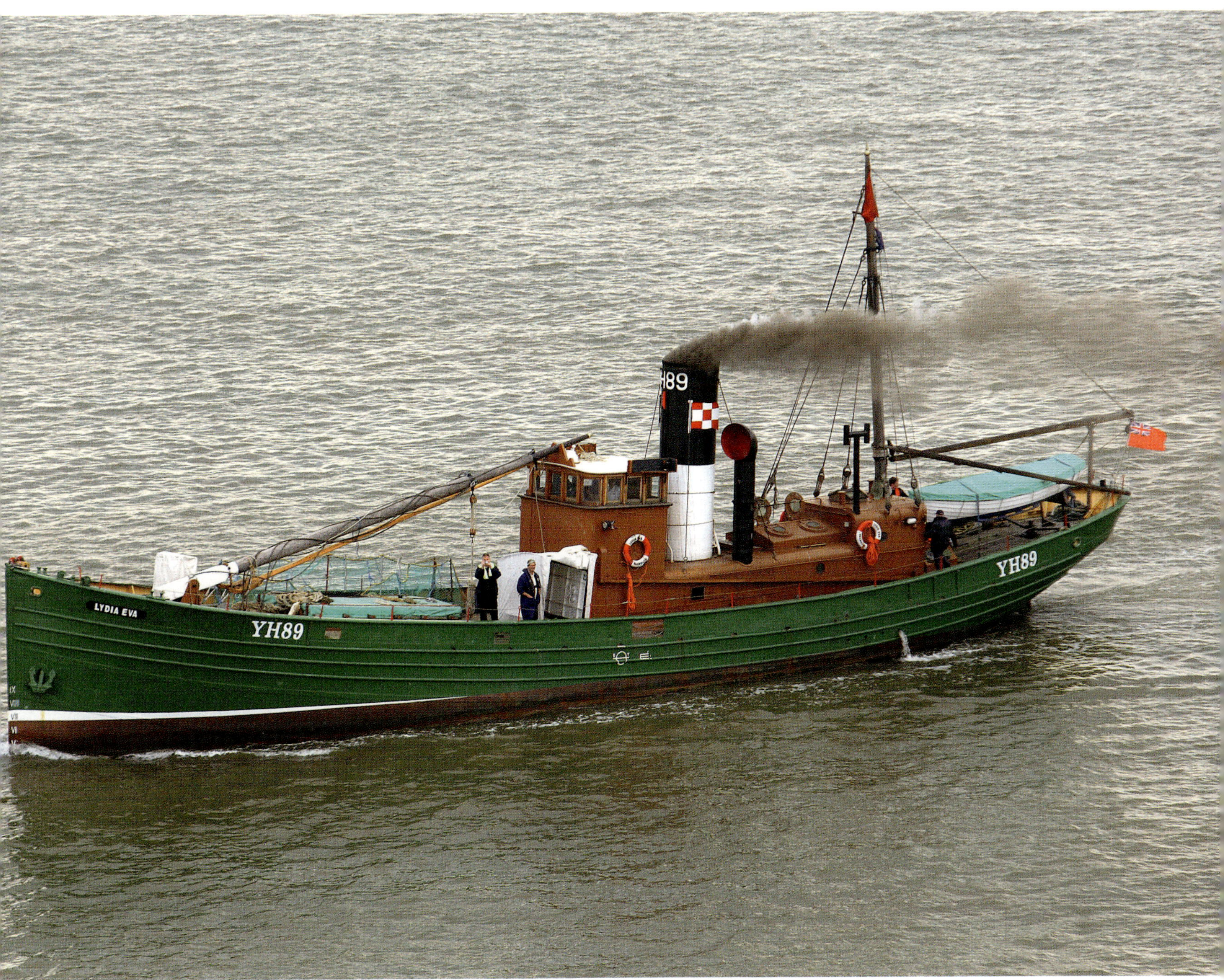

YH89
LYDIA EVA
YH89
YH89

Chapter 6

War

Norfolk is such a quiet and out of the way place, nothing ever happens here. WRONG!

For example in 1933 the Jewish physicist Albert Einstein, against whom German politicians were already campaigning, made a brief and secret stay in a hut on Roughton Common. His purpose was to consult with his friend Commander Oliver Locker-Lampson MP who lived near Cromer. Cdr Locker-Lampson had introduced a Parliamentary Bill to extend British citizenship to Jewish refugees. The Bill failed but he managed to get many Jews out of Germany before the outbreak of war. Einstein was by then exiled in America. His brief stay in England caused security problems which were top secret until the war was over.

Caister.

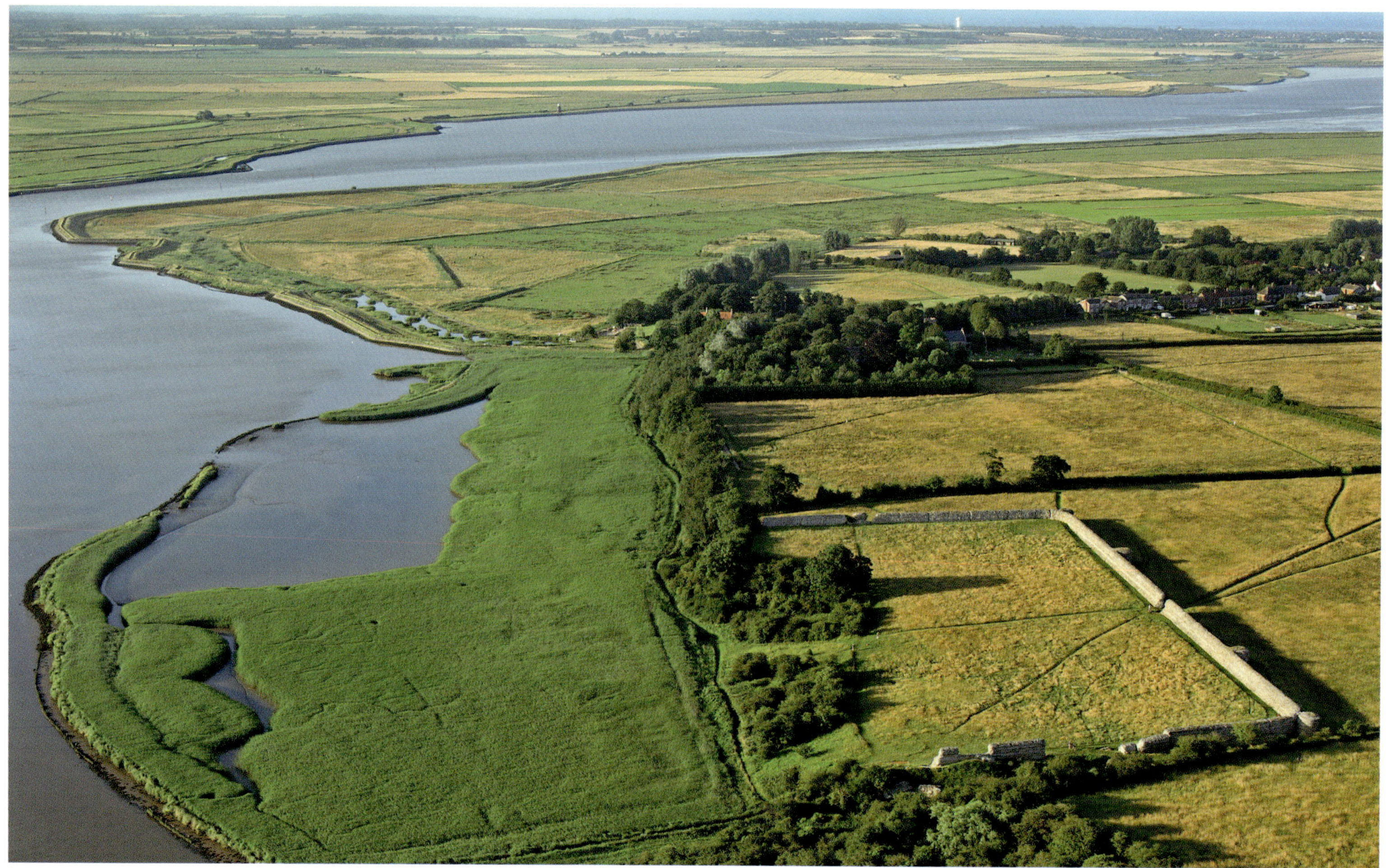

Threat of Invasion

Roman occupation was under threat from tribal invaders – Boudicca wasn't the only menace. To guard Norwich the Romans built two watch stations, one on either side of what is now Breydon Water. From the substantial remains of Burgh Castle to the south of the estuary and the remaining footings at Caister town opposite, the access to the hinterland of the Rivers Yare and Waveney could be defended.

Burgh Castle.

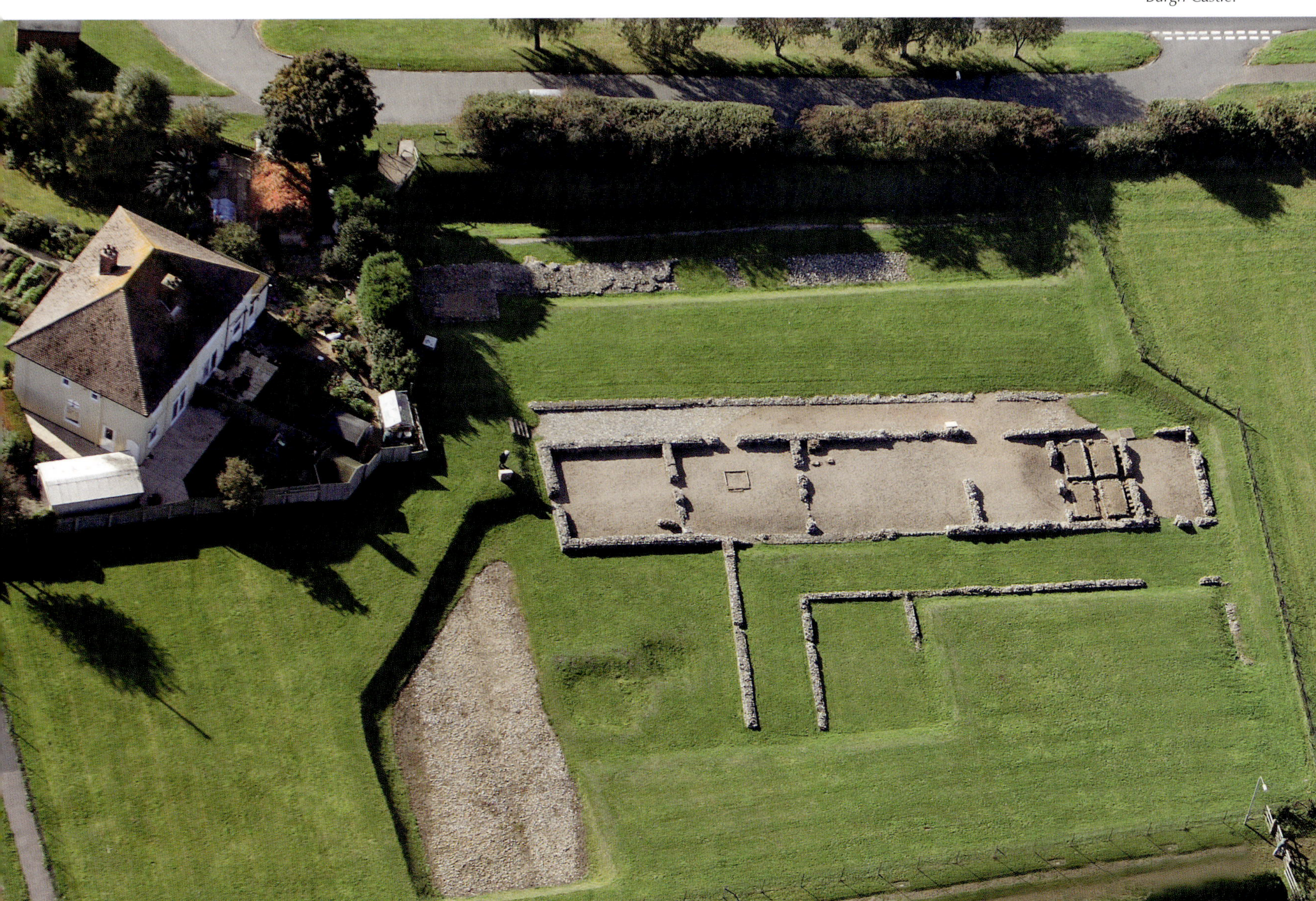

Motte and Bailey Defences, Castle Acre

The massive motte and bailey defence was begun by the deWarrene family who 'came over' from France with William the Conqueror (sounds like a day trip). The family had been awarded land for their loyalty. The castle has been described as 'a monument to Norman ambition'. It stands on a man-made mound (*motte*) as does Castle Rising. The *bailey* is the outer wall of the castle. With its deep moat and massive rectangular keep it's a giant fortress.

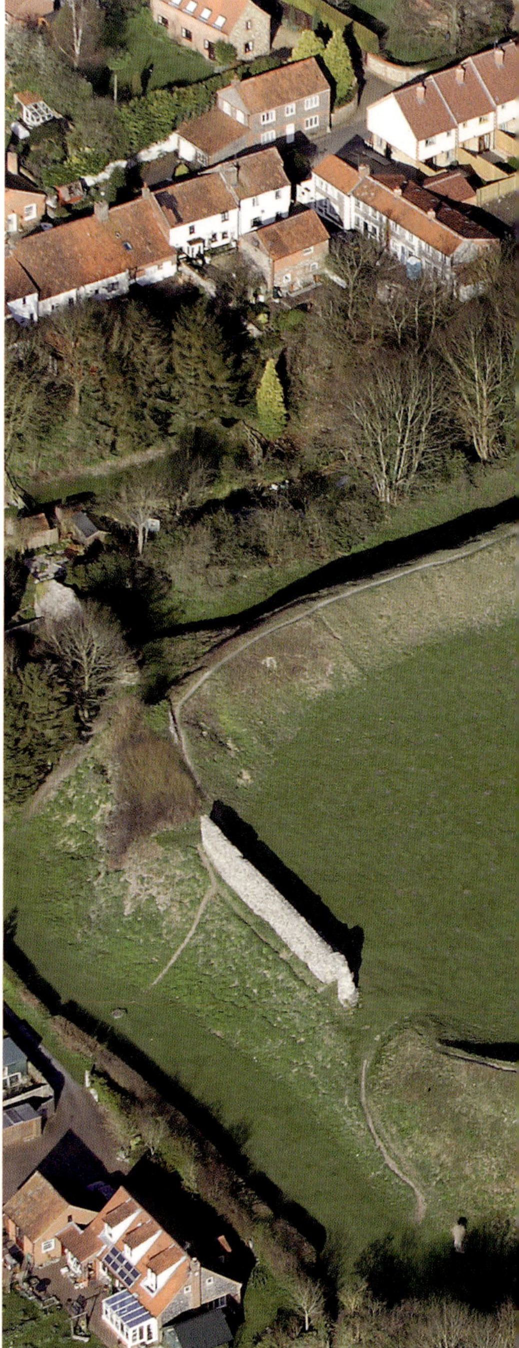

Castle Acre.

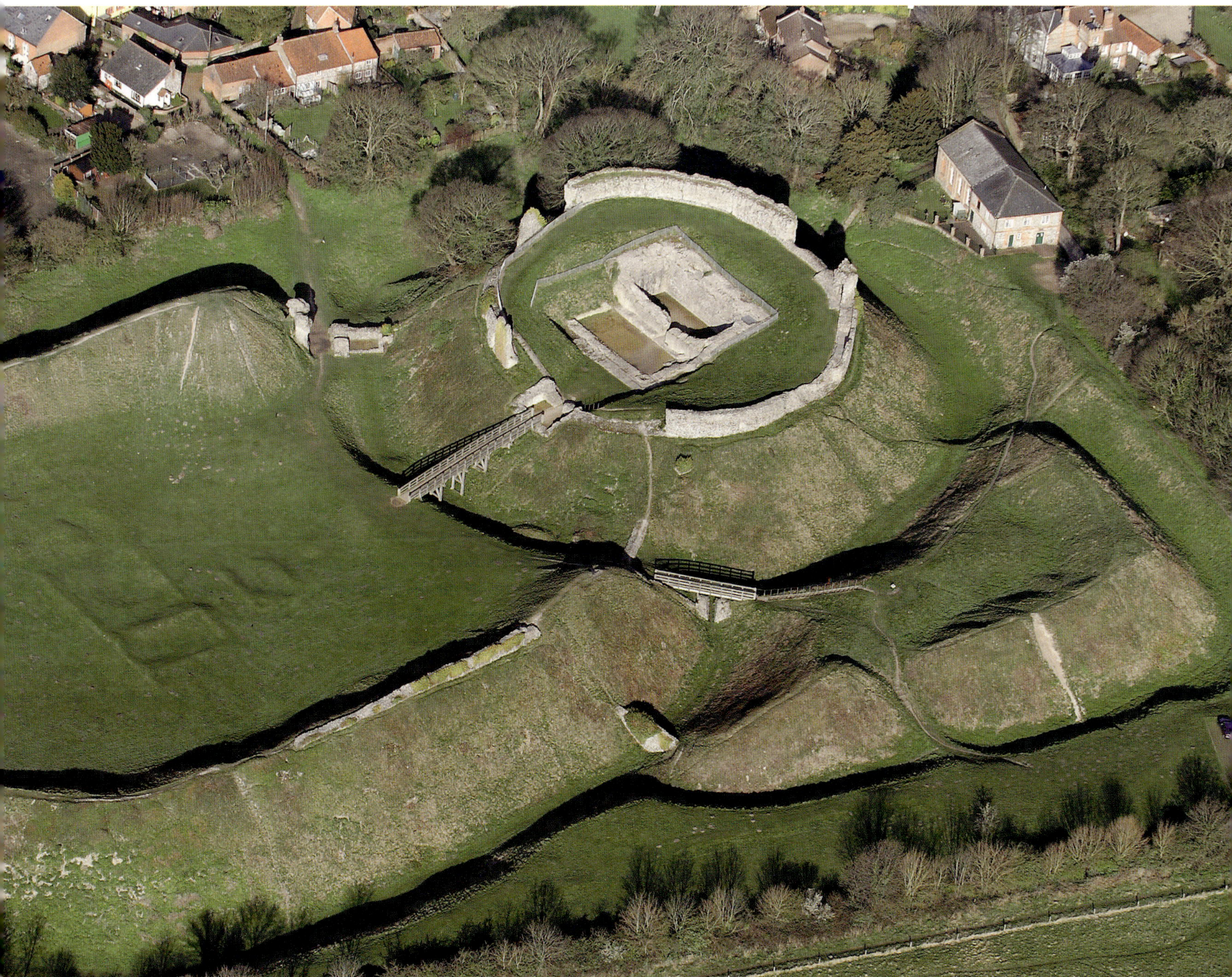

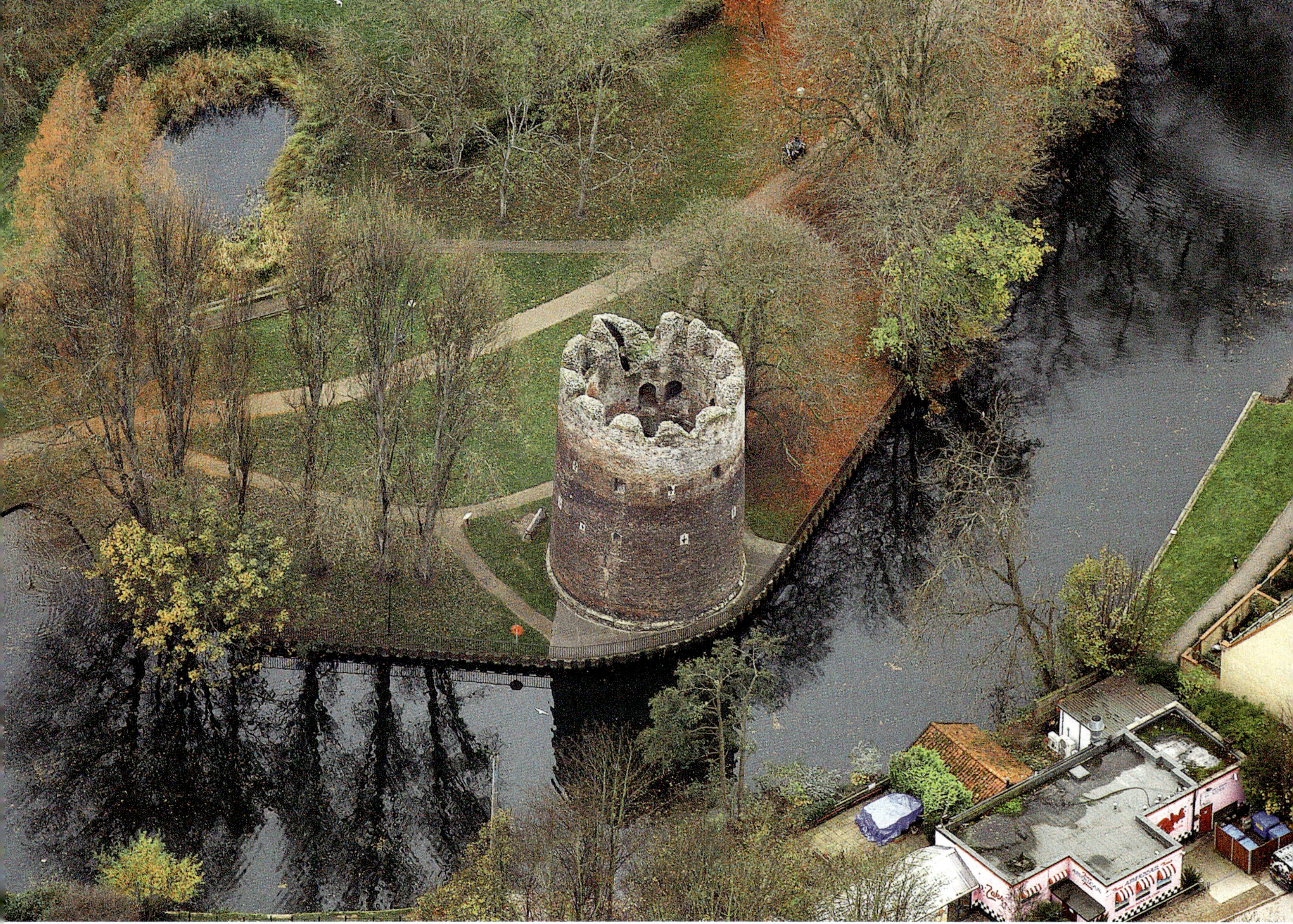

Cow Tower

Standing at a strategic bend in the River Wensum, Cow Tower has guarded Norwich for centuries. It was earlier known as the 'Dungeon Tower' but was remodelled in the fourteenth century as the Cow Tower with mod cons such as hearths and latrines and was large enough to hold a garrison of 14 gunners. It had to be modified to accommodate recently-developed cannon as well as providing arrow loops for crossbows. It suffered damage during Kett's Rebellion and there are traces still of burning at the top of the tower. The surrounding meadows of grazing cattle were called 'Cowholme' hence Cow Tower.

Castle Acre Church

When the church of St James the Great was built in the thirteenth century, Christians from all over Europe were fighting Holy Wars against Muslims. It was almost a badge of honour to be a Crusader. There's a doorway in this chancel tall enough to accommodate a knight on horseback should he wish to ride his horse into church for a blessing before setting off to the Crusades.

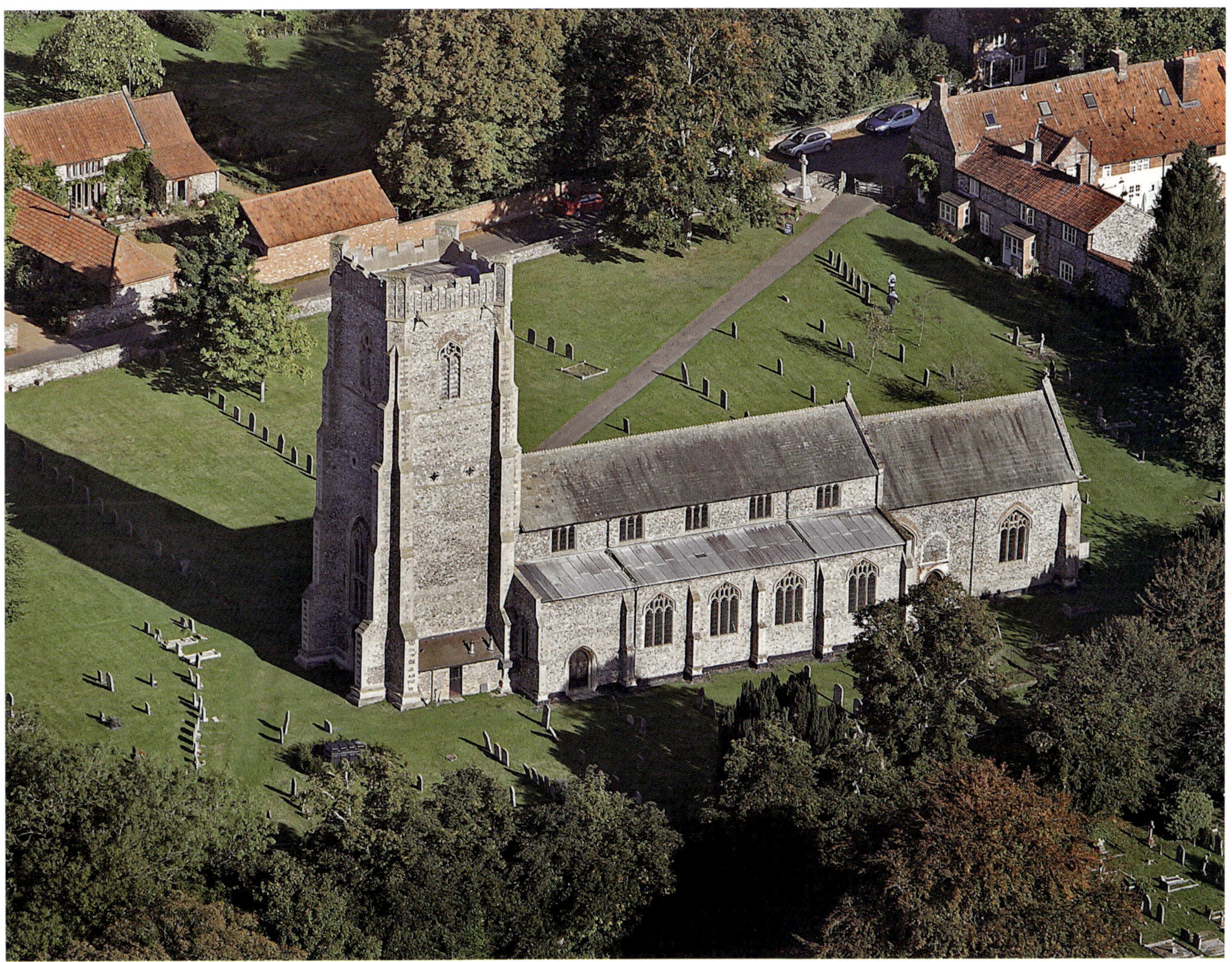

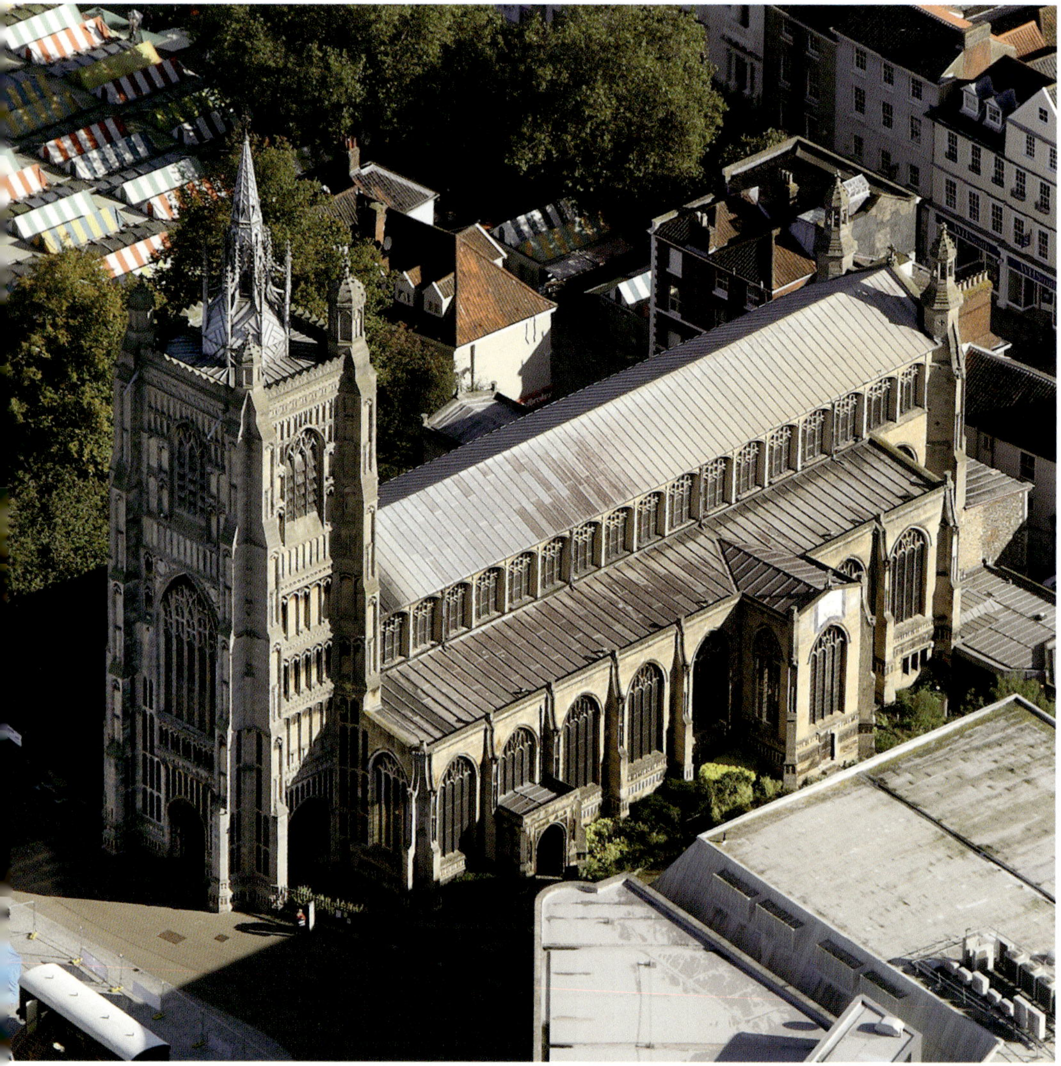

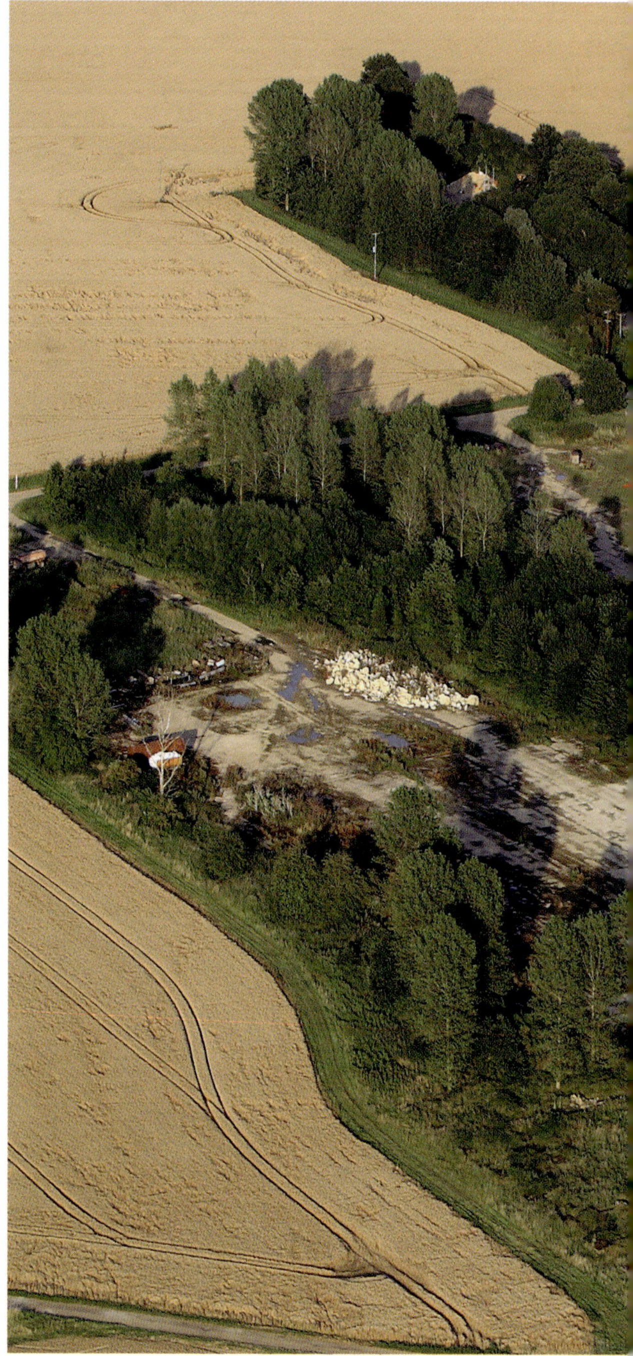

Norwich's St Peter Mancroft church close by appeared to have suffered no damage from the Great Blowe.

The Great Blowe

This extraordinary event occurred in Norwich in 1648. During the English Civil War the majority of Norfolk people were on the side of Oliver Cromwell and the Parliamentarians. But there was a Royalist Committee House in Bethel Street. A skirmish resulted in ignition and explosion from the gunpowder stored with the firearms. The big bang was referred to as The Great Blowe. After the explosion the hostilities were reduced.

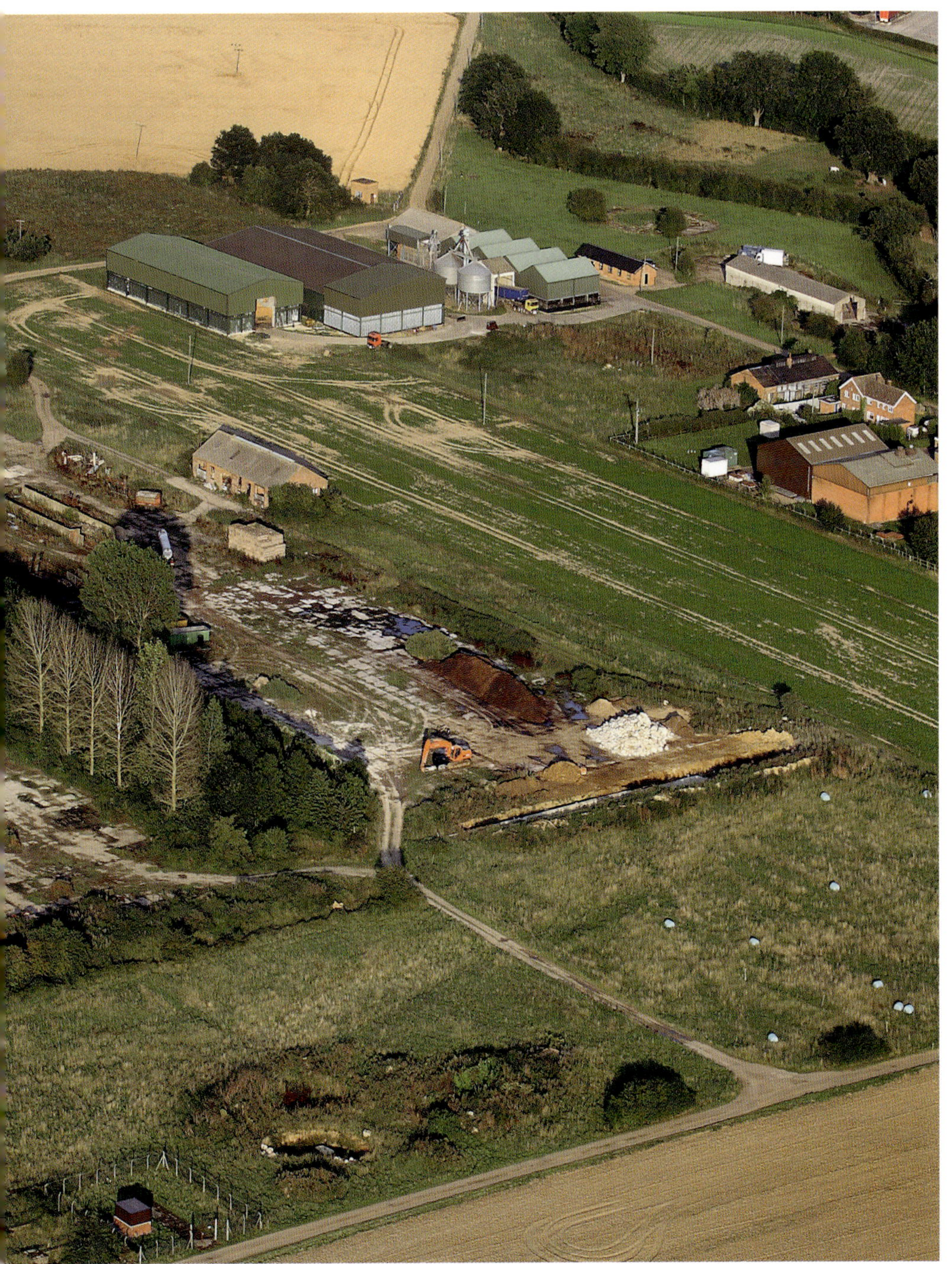

Pulham Pigs

One of the first RNAS airship stations was at Pulham in South Norfolk, renamed RAF Pulham. One of the first landings was here in 1919 when the RN 34 moored en route prior to an Atlantic crossing. In WW1 the airship's role was North Sea surveillance. In the nearby village of Pulham St Mary in the Pennoyer Centre there's a permanent exhibition about the Air Station's role.

And the pigs? A local seeing an airship aloft observed 'That look loike a gret ole pig'.

It's surprising that such an important development in aviation is not publicised more, apart from the Pennoyer exhibition, 'Air Station Farm' and an airship on the village sign.

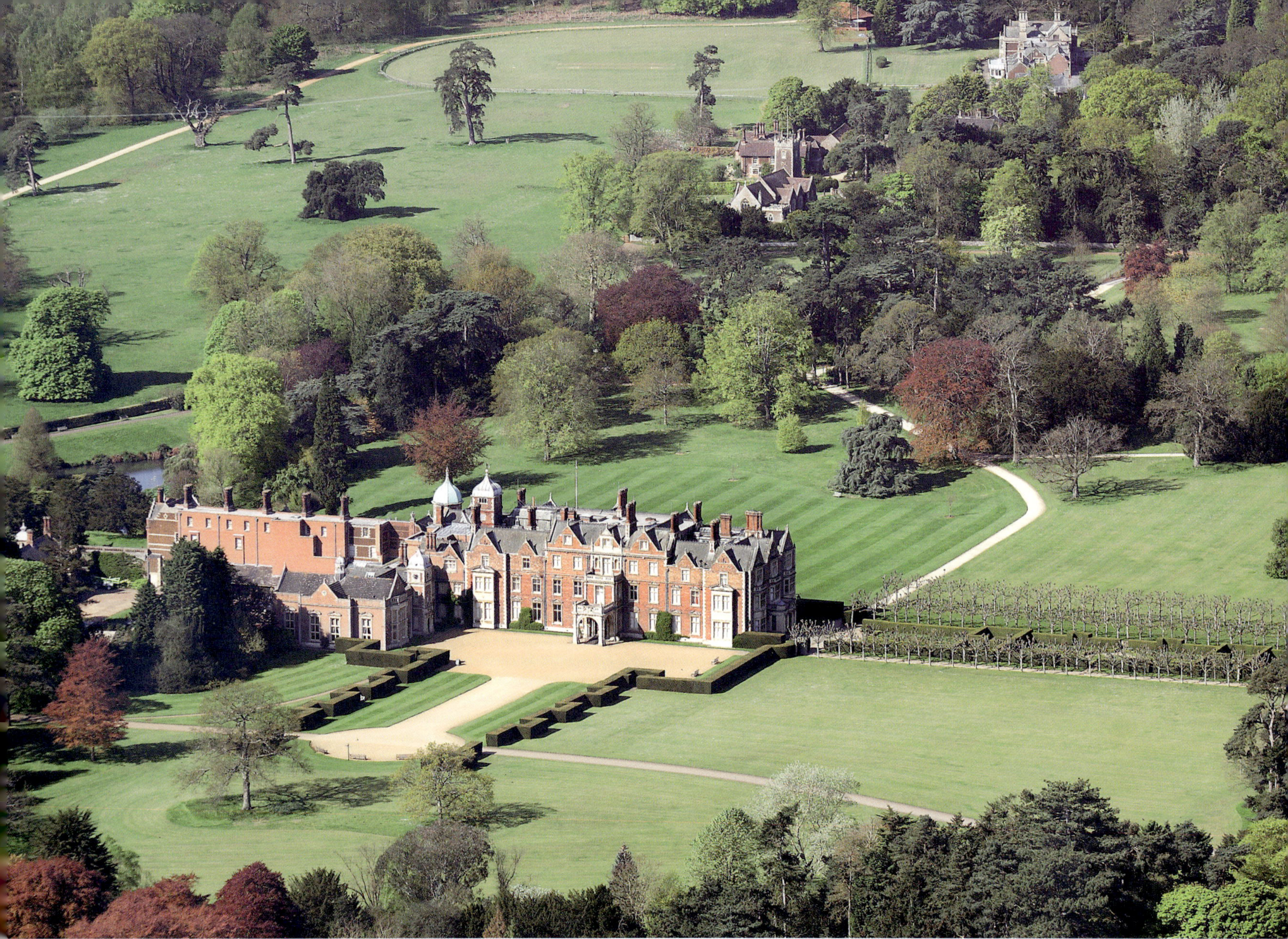

Sandringham House.

Captain Frank Beck 1861–1915

Captain Frank Beck MVO, 5th battalion Royal Norfolk Regiment was an unsung hero of WWI. Land Agent at Sandringham for Edward VII then George V he led the voluntary company of royal staff (gardeners, grooms, farm labourers and household staff) in the 1915 Gallipoli Campaign. After a skirmish the men's bodies were found but not individually identified. They're commemorated on the War Memorial at Sandringham and in West Newton parish church.

Beeston Bump aka Beeston Hump

At 63 metres above sea level Beeston Bump is the highest point on the Norfolk Long Distance Footpath. During WW2 it had a vital role as a 'Y' listening station sending information about German shipping movements back to Bletchley Park. The concrete base of the equipment hut in which members of the Womens Royal Naval Service listened, is still there.

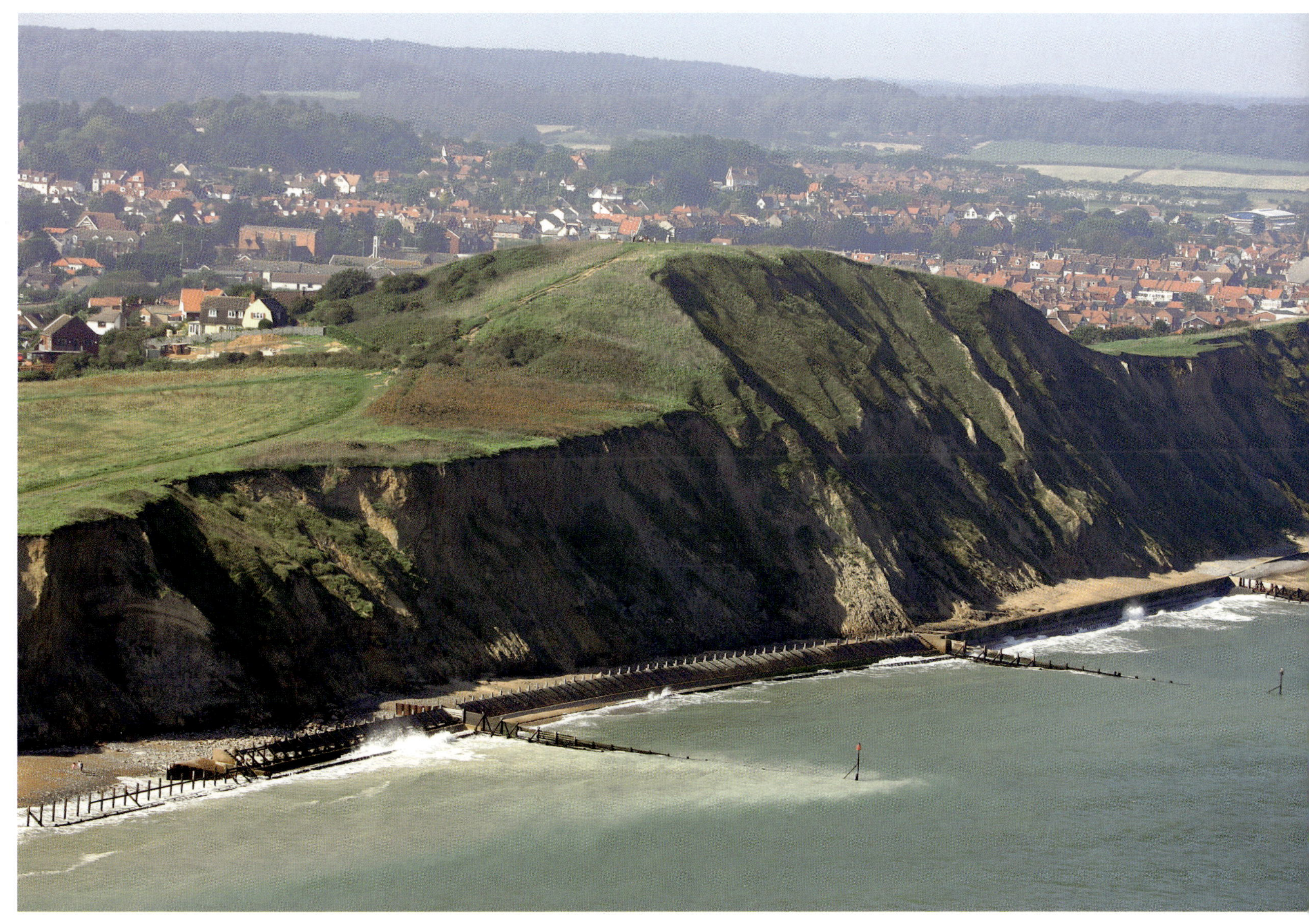

On the beach the wooden revetments are slowing down the rate at which the soft cliffs are being washed away.

Great Yarmouth Harbour

The scene which includes the new harbour has seen much military action. Twice it welcomed Horatio Nelson after triumphant battles and many ships have limped into port for repair making first for the 'spending beach' at the bend in the river. During WW2 the small building at the far end of the pier was used by the Coastguard for observation. The role has been taken over by 'Coastwatch' – a voluntary organisation which records shipping movements along the coast.

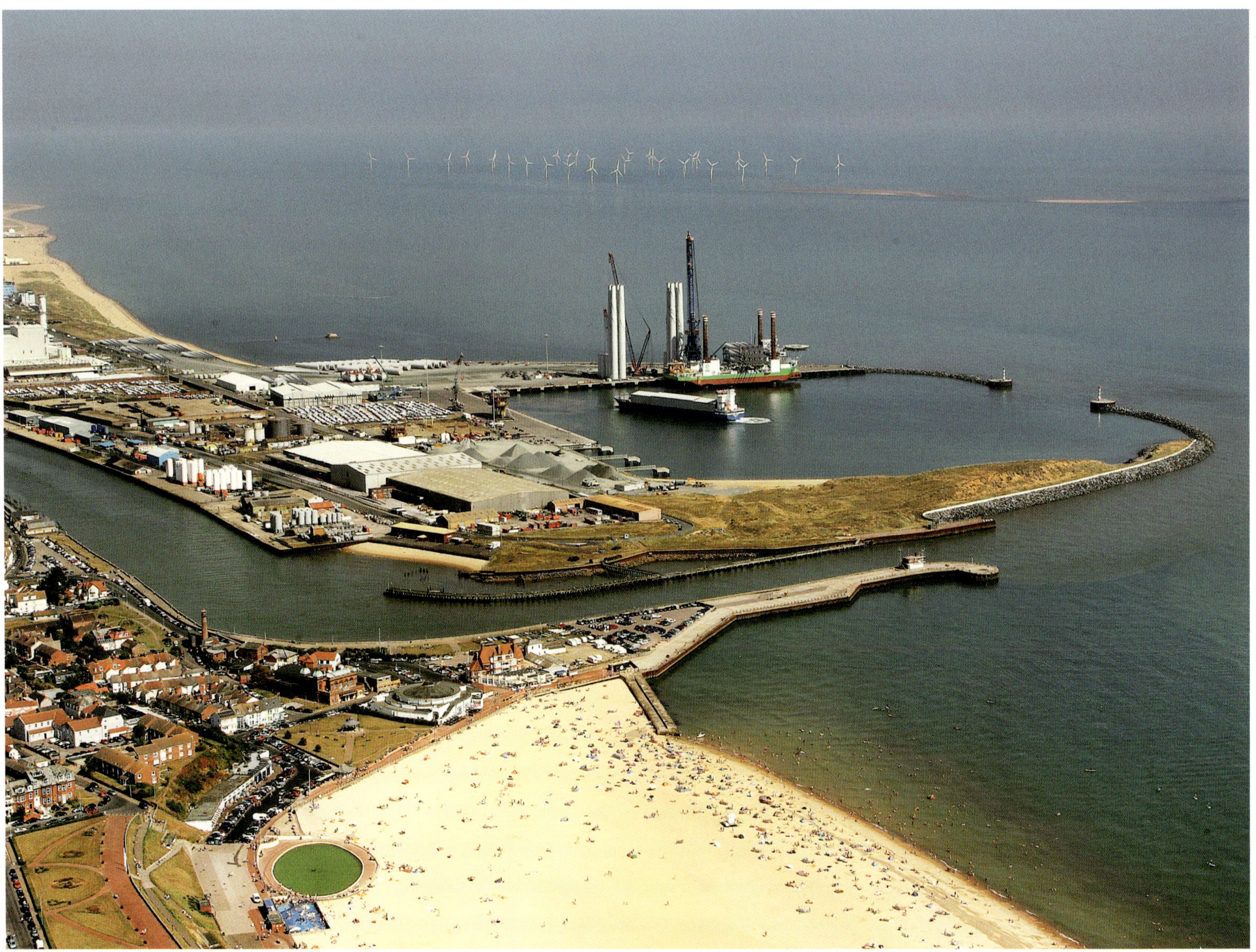

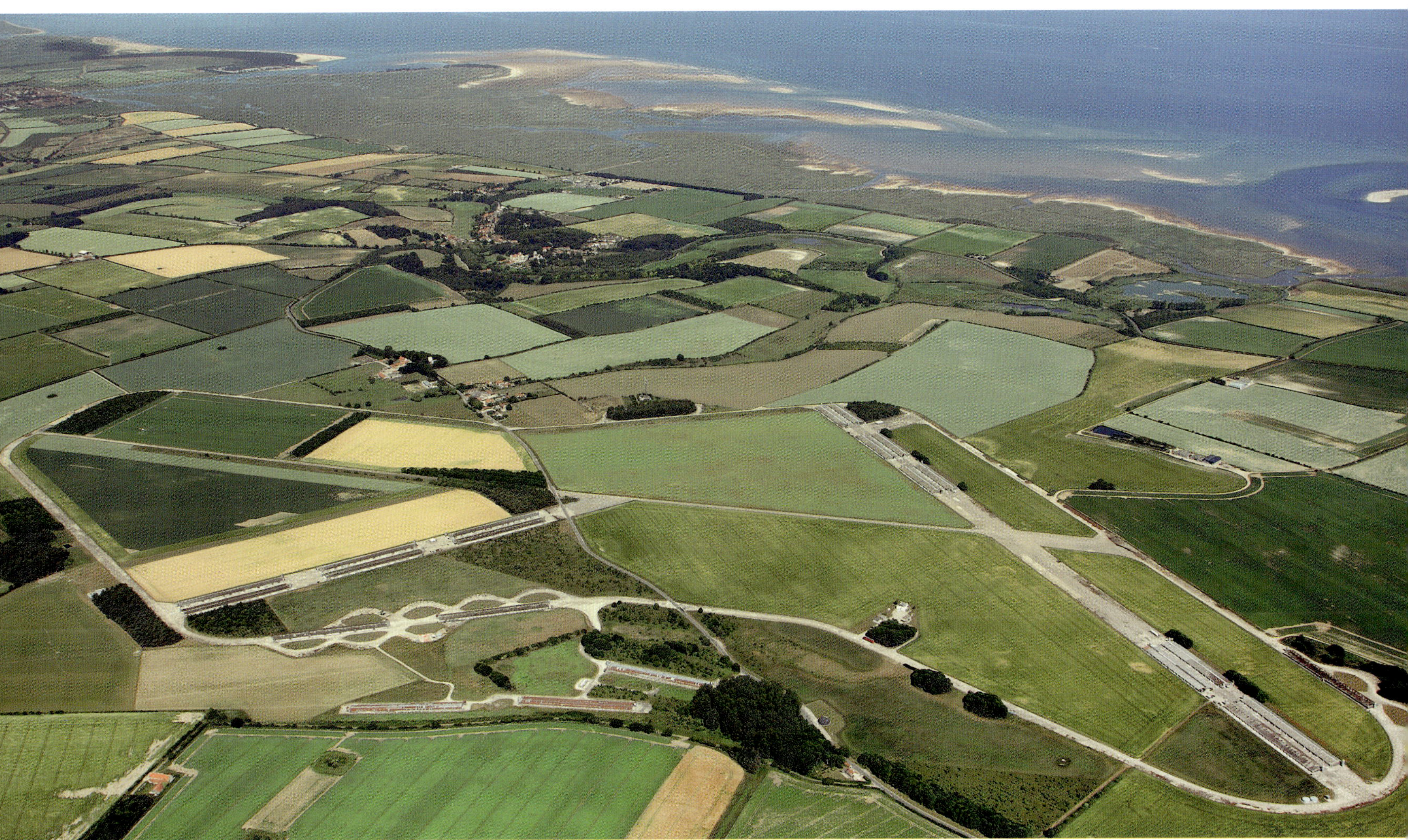

Airfields

The flat terrain and proximity to mainland Europe made Norfolk an inevitable airfield choice in WW2 by both the RAF and the USAAF. Schoolboys living in villages close to airfields used to give graphic accounts of aircraft 'limping' home, pieces hanging off, hardly staying in the air. RAF Langham (Coastal Command) opened in 1940. Langham was closed in 1959 but appropriately an aircraft engineer specialising in the servicing of vintage aircraft (Tiger Moths, Dragon Rapides etc.) is still based there. Turkey sheds occupy what were the taxi ways. The airfield appeared in 'The Dam Busters' film. Blakeney Point is in the distance.

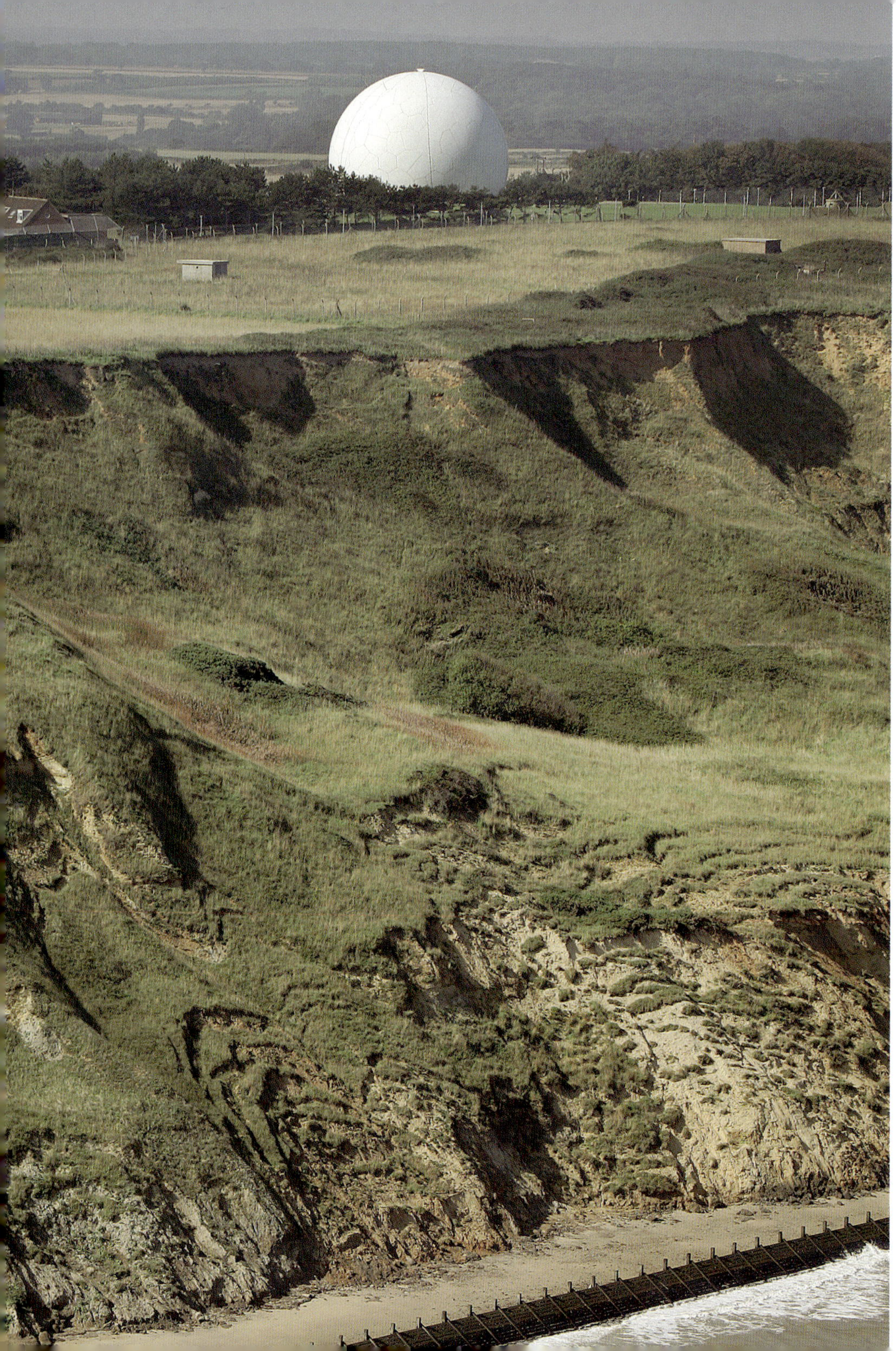

A Golf Ball Becomes a Radar Station

In 1941 RAF Trimingham came into being, detecting enemy activity in the North Sea. Connected to nearby RAF Neatishead the new radar station's purposes were to find both German E boats (motor torpedo boats) and low flying enemy aircraft and to give radar assistance to friendly aircraft in reaching their targets. The dome is constructed from an artificial material called 'Kevlon' in polygonal shapes inside which state of the art radar equipment is housed. Sitting on top of the cliffs as it does it soon became known as the 'Trimingham golf ball.'

Weybourne Hoop or Hope

'He who would England win must first at Weybourne Hoop begin'.

Westwards at Weybourne the cliffs peter out. The beach shelves steeply making a deep harbour close to the shore. This would enable invading ships to anchor close in. The cliffs do not appear again until Hunstanton where they consist of a chalk layer over carrstone (sandstone and iron oxide). The chalk layer is present all the way to the Chilterns.

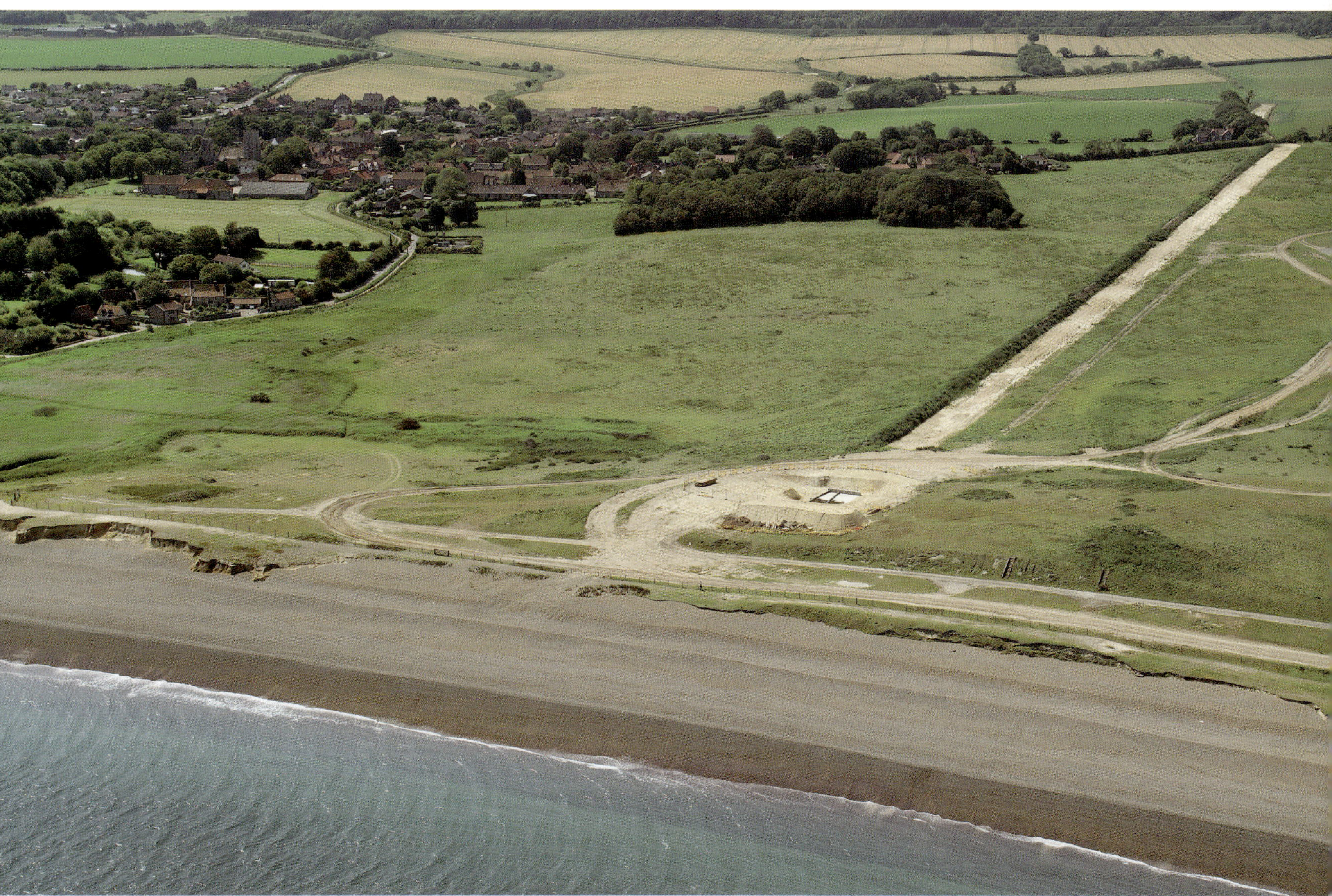

The Muckleborough Collection

The Muckleborough Collection is the largest privately-owned collection of military vehicles and memorabilia in the UK. It is sited at former RAF Weybourne which specialised in anti-aircraft training during WW2. Winston Churchill visited the site in 1941. There's a grass landing strip with two runways still in use today. This with some of the old wartime buildings adjacent to the strip are often used by the Armed Forces for military training exercises.

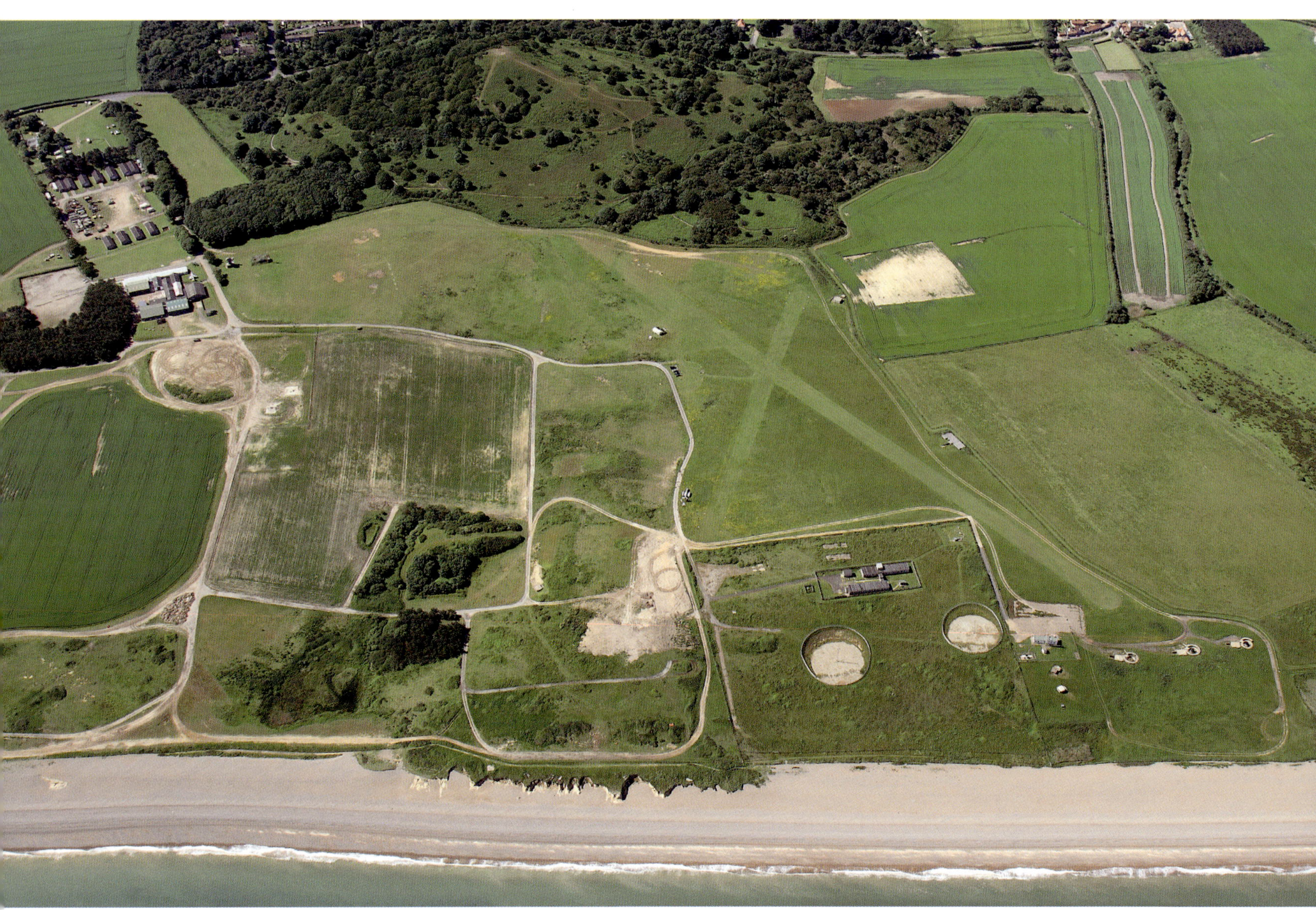

War Tactics

James Hoseason tells that during WW2 boats were sunk across Oulton Broad in Suffolk (one of the larger Broads) to prevent hostile sea planes landing. Lowestoft was particularly vulnerable to enemy attack. It's not known if a similar practice happened on the Northern Broads but redundant wherries were sunk on Surlingham and Ranworth Broads. This slowed up the rotting process and proved a piece of serendipity when millwright Vincent Pargeter and Ted Ellis were searching for fittings during the restoration of wherry *Maud*.

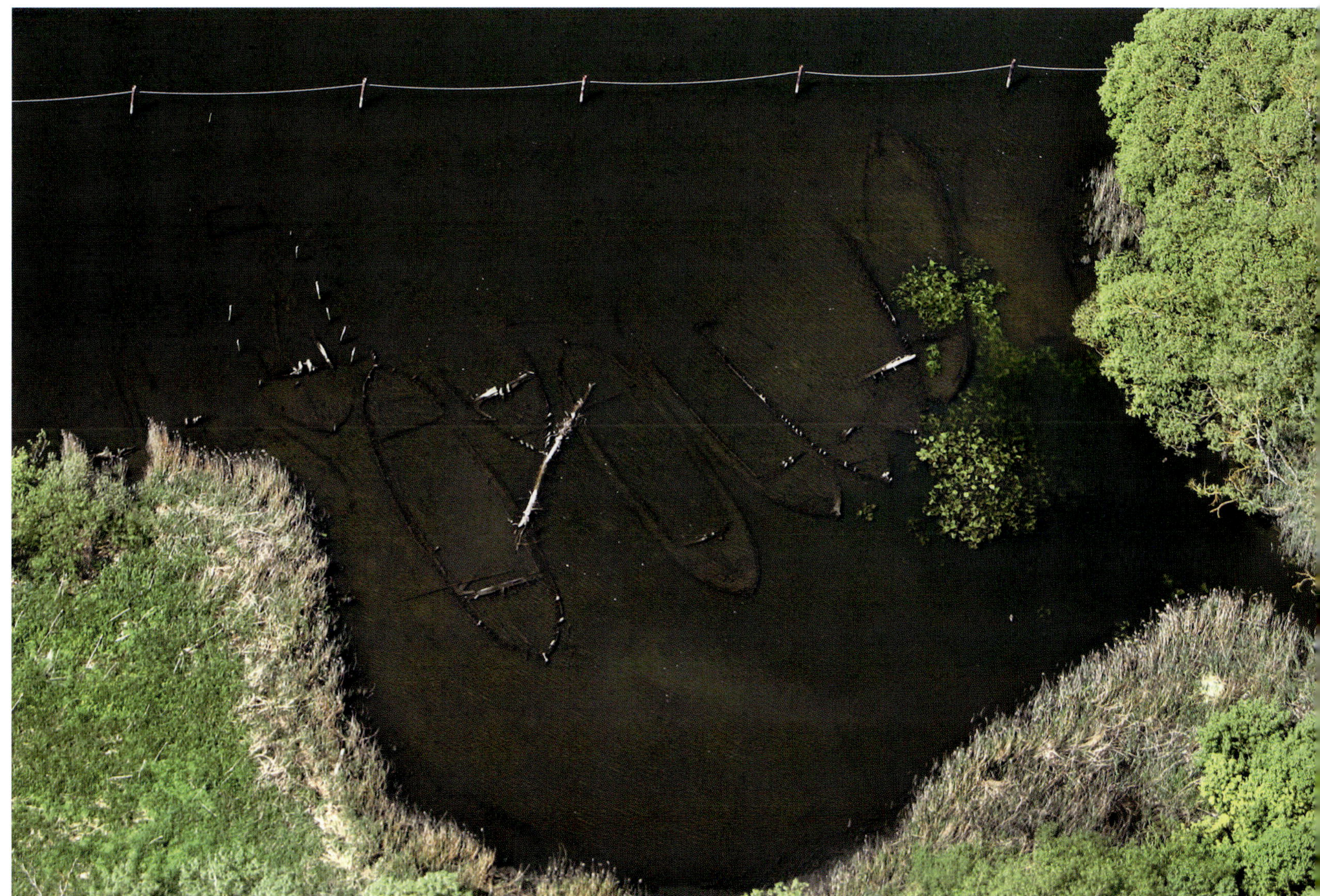

Sunken Wherries on Bargate Broad

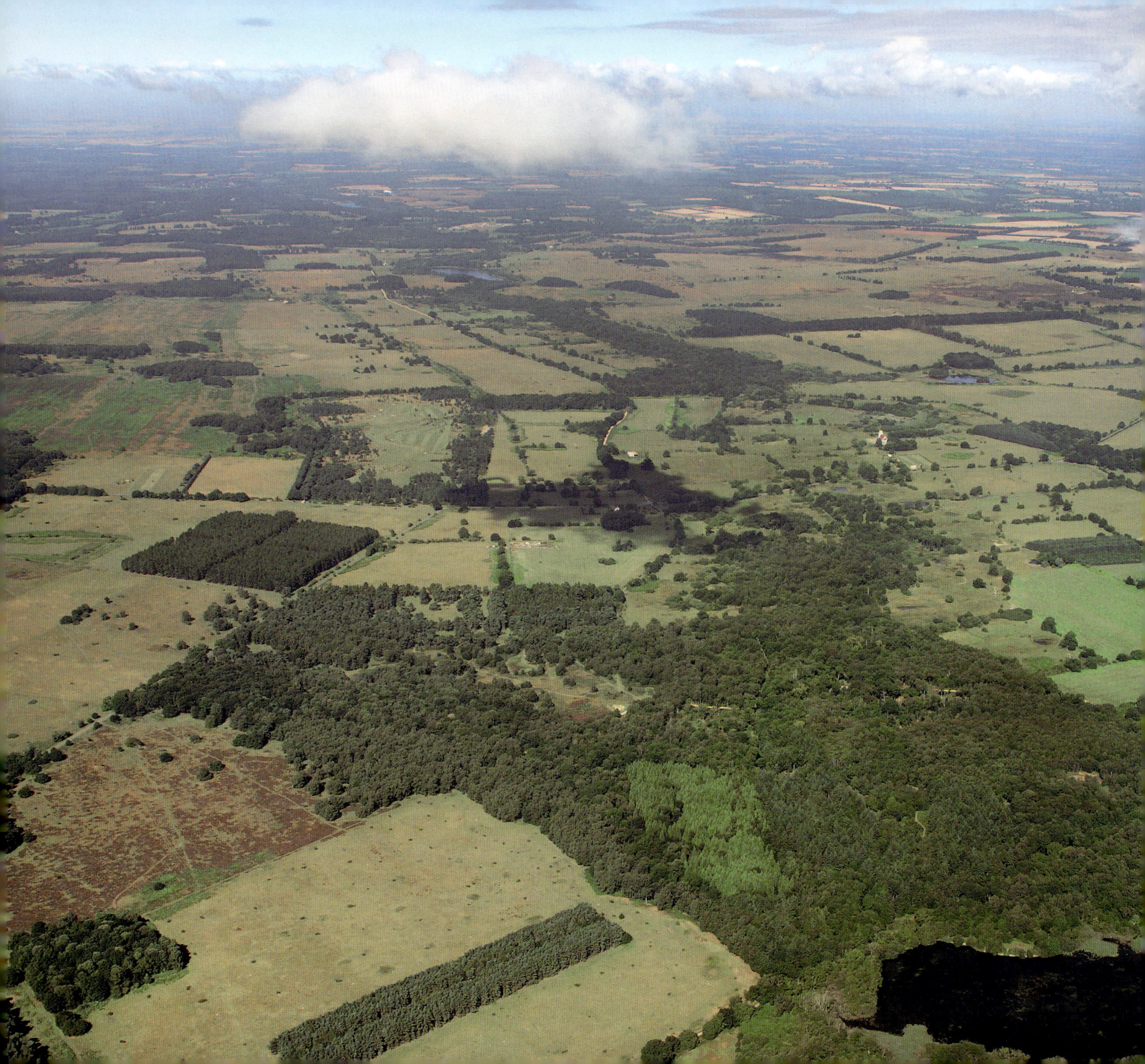

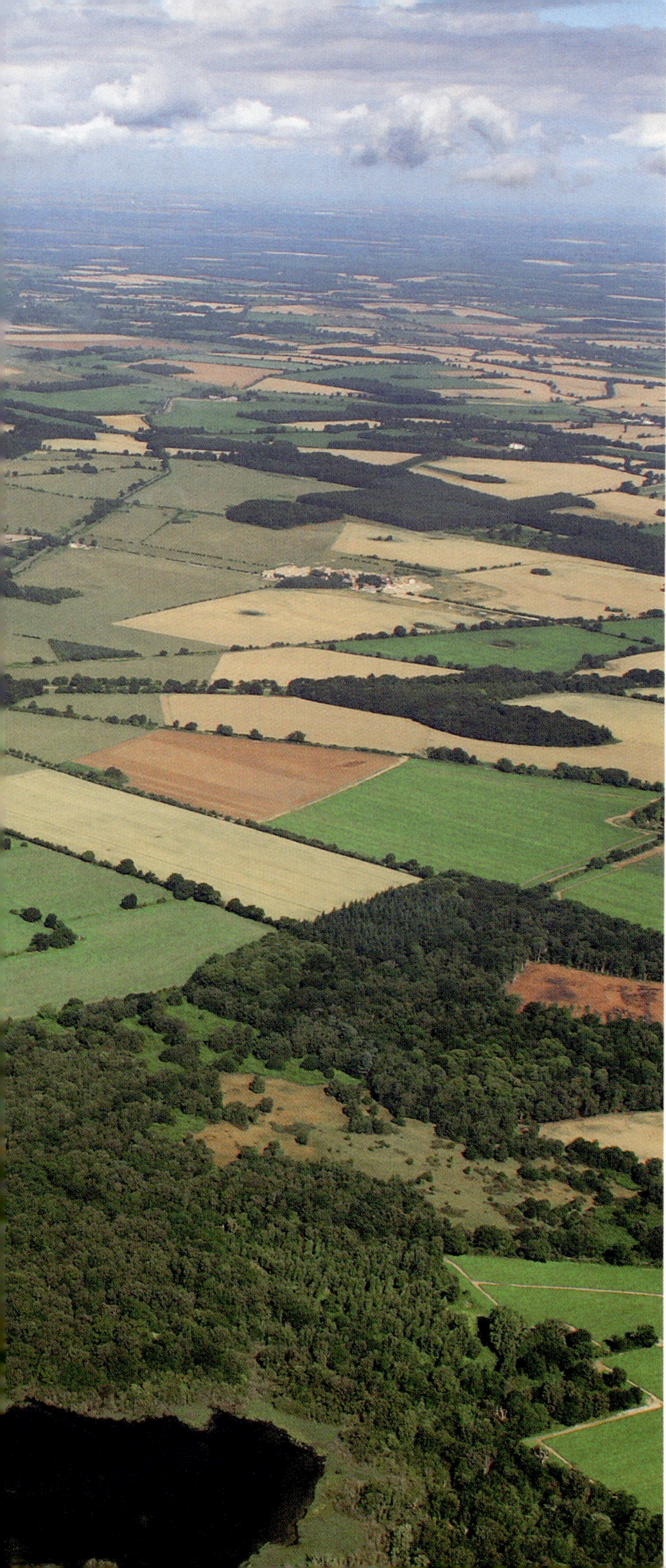

STANTA (Stanton Training Area)

'The battle area' came into being in 1942. The Government needed a troop training area and evicted the inhabitants of four villages and two hamlets near Watton with the assurance that they could return when the war was over. They're still waiting!

Covering several square miles of pine trees, scrub and poor soil (as seen in episodes of 'Dad's Army') access can be gained only with special permission and only in certain areas (there's a lot of unexploded ammunition around).

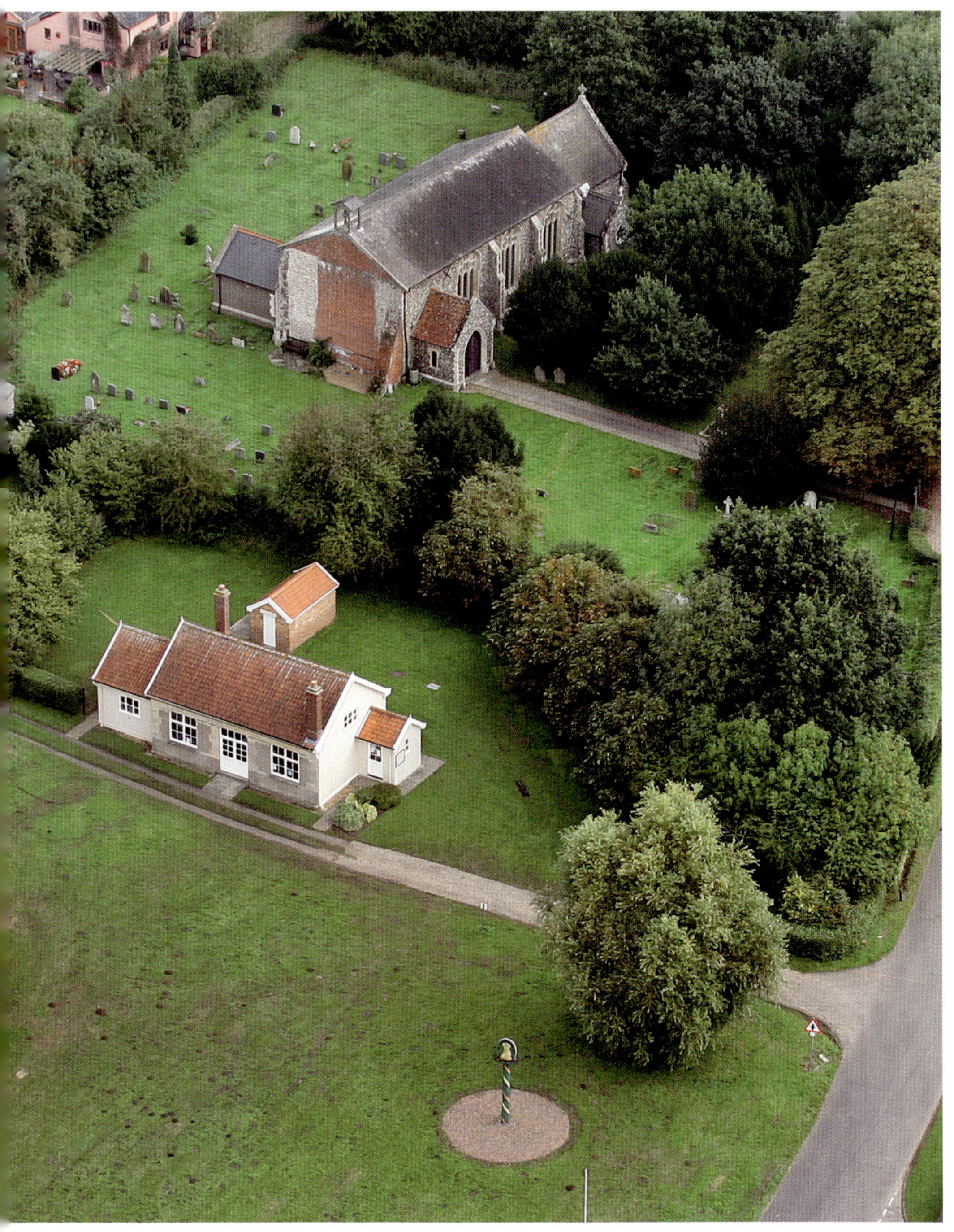

And Wars of a Different Kind

The Burston School Strike 1914–39 – the longest strike in history

Teachers Tom and Annie Higdon, husband and wife, were in dispute with the local school management about the lack of adequate facilities in the village school. The Higdons were dismissed. They continued to teach on the village green and most parents and pupils supported them. With support from the Labour Movement the Higdons set up school in an alternative building. The dispute continued until Tom Higdon's death in 1939. The Strike School is now a museum and a rallying point for Trades Unions who each year hold a celebration on the village green in this (usually) quiet South Norfolk village.

The Battle of Black Horse Broad

In 1949 the scene enacted on Black Horse Broad (aka Hoveton Little Broad) resembled a theatrical farce. The owner wished to keep the broad private. A group of boatyard owners and others led by Herbert Woods considered that all broads should be accessible.
From the *Daily Express* 12 March 1949:

A landing craft with thirty men aboard invaded last night a stretch of the Norfolk Broads claimed as private. Stakes and chains guarding the entrance were pulled up with a winch. The expedition cost £60. The invaders, under Mr Herbert Woods, leader of the movement which claims all broads should be open to the public, were met by an agent, a policeman and a solicitor in rowing boats. The policeman took names. [Chances are the policeman had been at school with most of them.]

A compromise was reached. The public were to be allowed access to the broad from Easter to September.

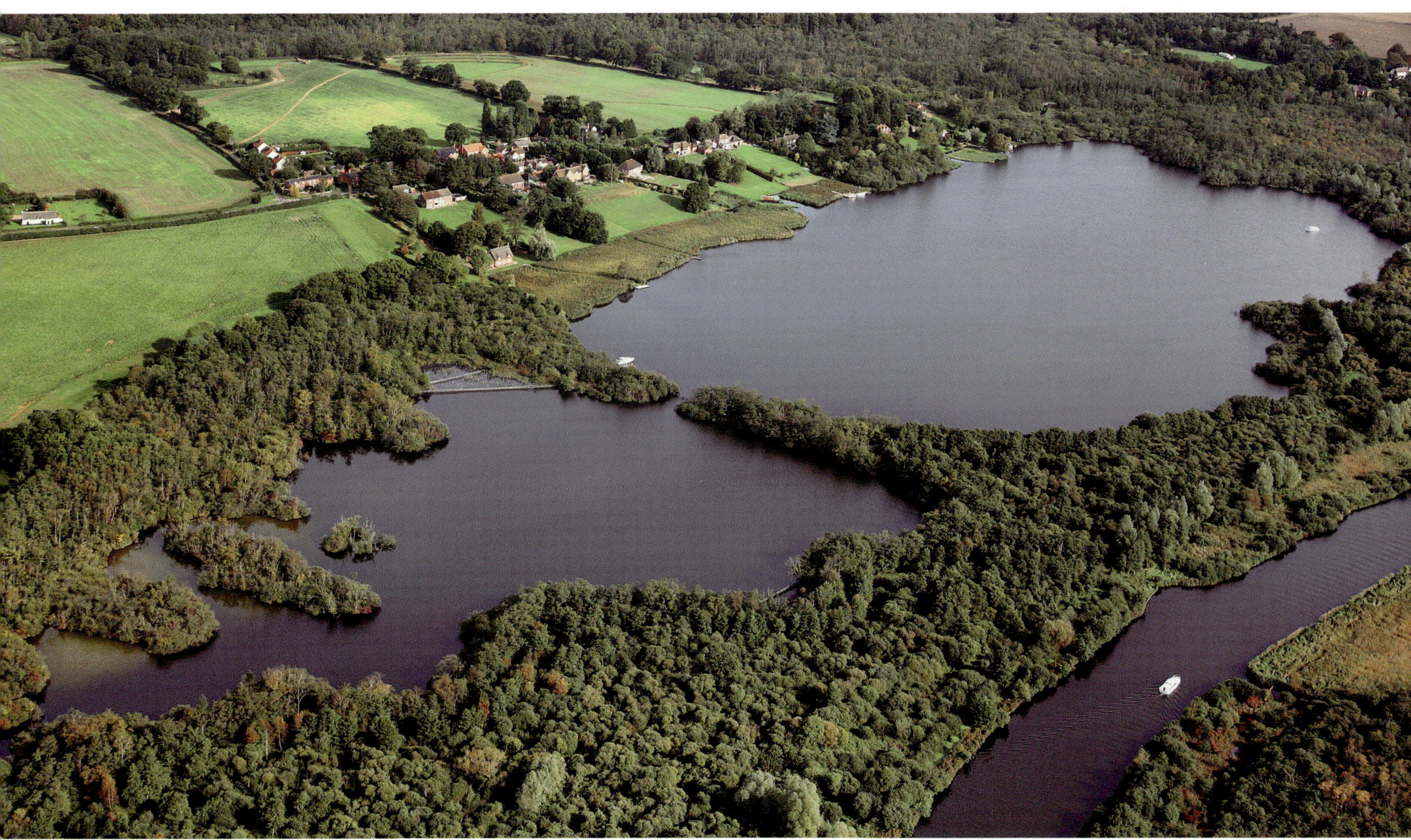

Chapter 7

Norfolk Connections

Melton Constable Hall and *The Go Between*

The book by LP Hartley was made into a very successful film over forty years ago. The title role is played by a young boy who's a house guest of wealthy Norfolk people. He's drawn into the love affair between the daughter of the house and a tenant farmer on the estate, delivering letters between the two (he's the Go-Between). The story is told by the boy in his old age. It all ended unhappily. The book's opening sentence will be familiar:

'The past is another country. They do things differently there.'

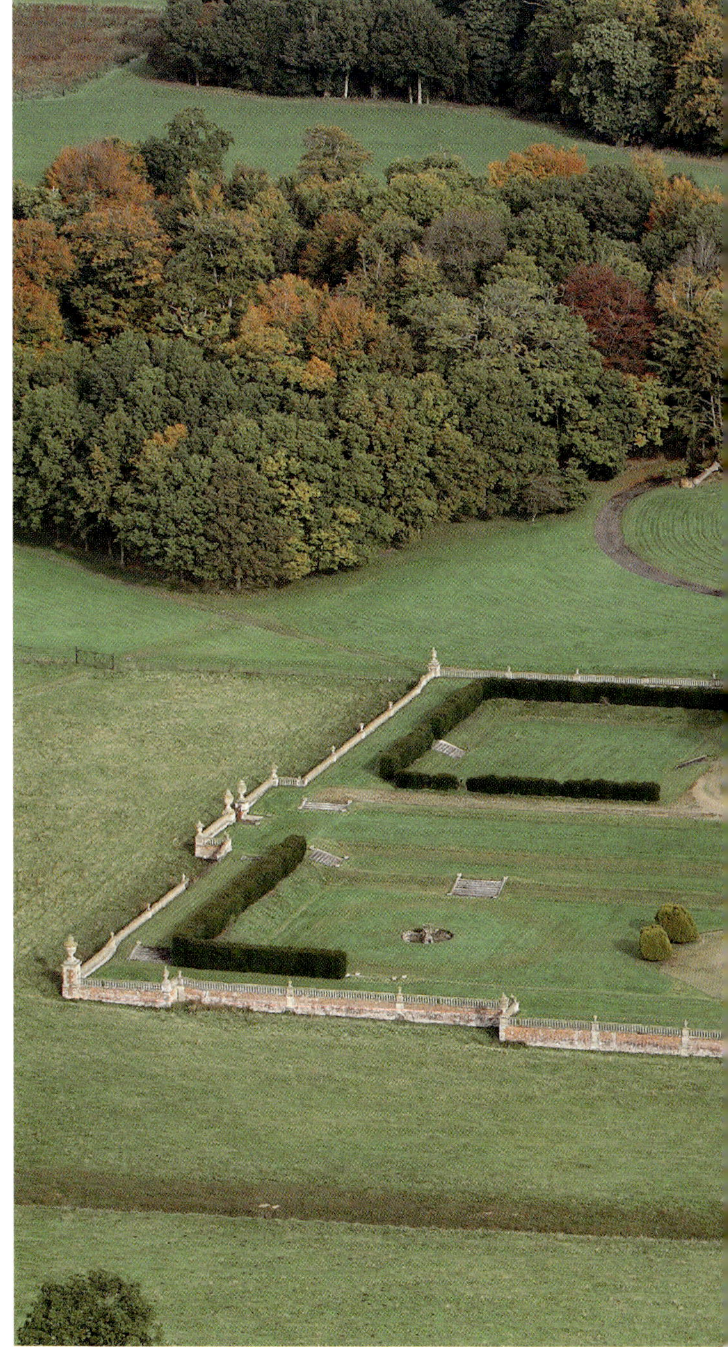

The house has been subjected to several attempts at renovation. The Capability Brown landscape is magnificent.

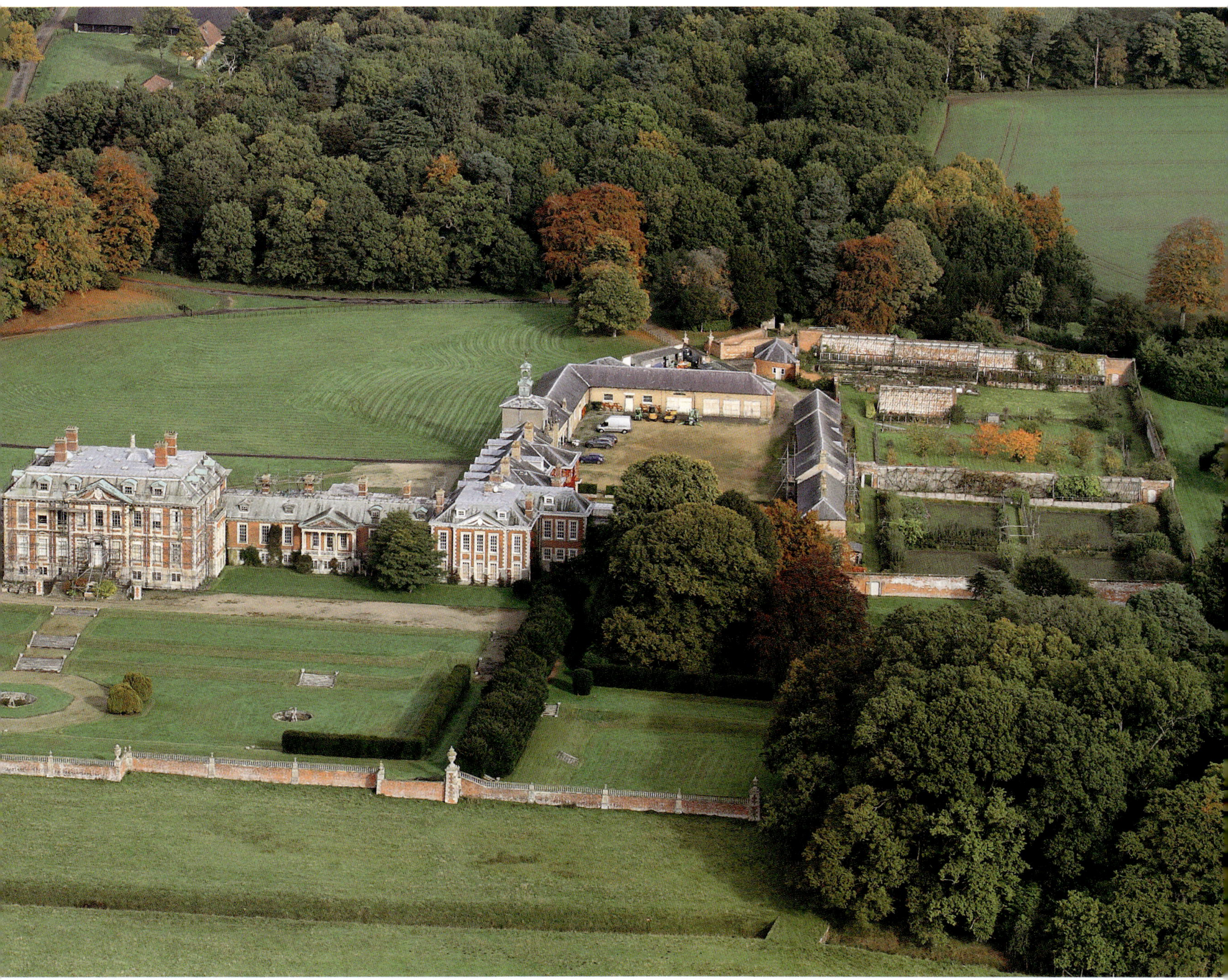

Kimberley Hall and Hunstanton Hall

The Wodehouses (pronounced Woodhouse) have had Kimberley connections for centuries but it's at Hunstanton Hall where family member P G Wodehouse, as a guest, spent many of his days writing his Jeeves stories. The stories were only a part of his considerable literary output.

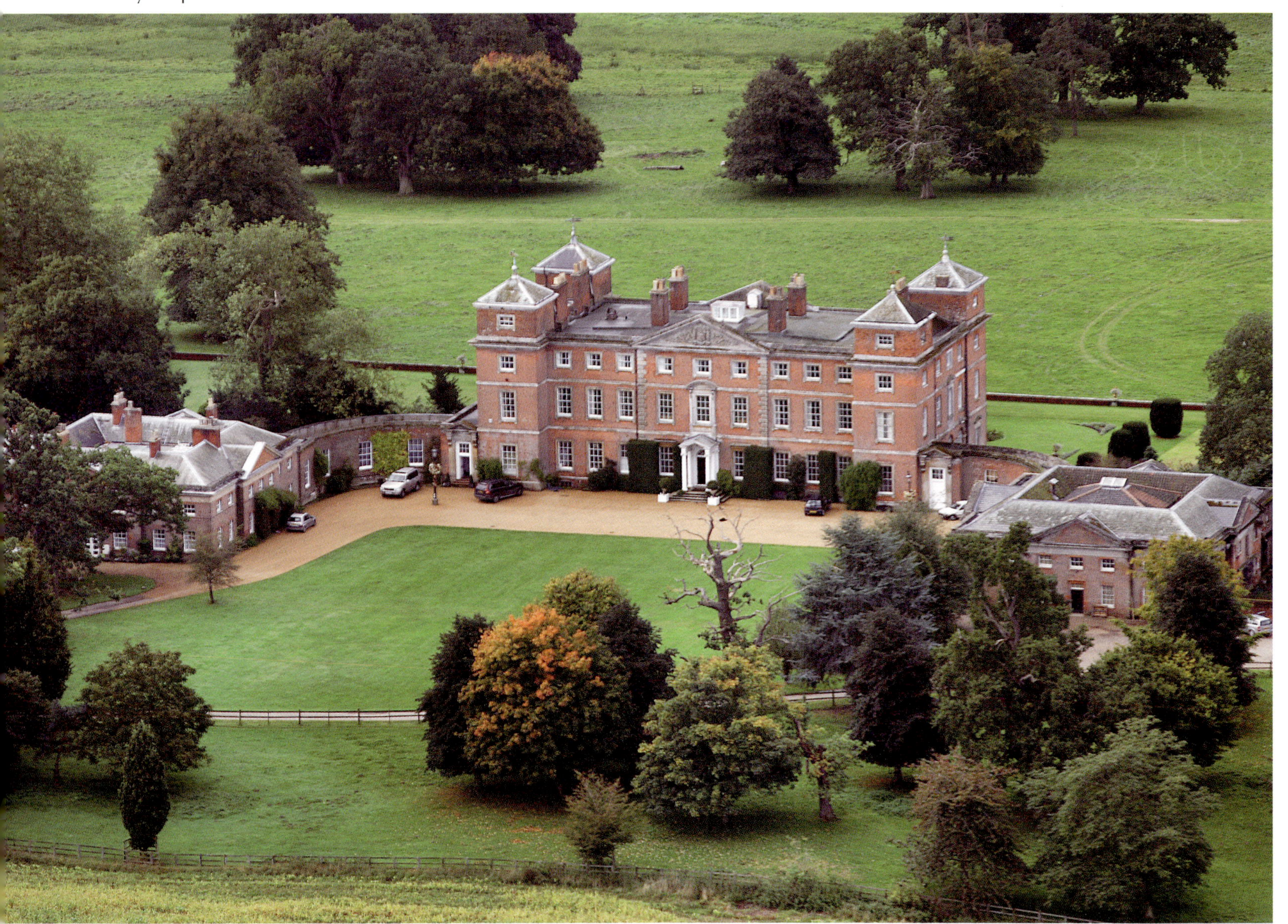

Kimberley Hall was subjected to much misuse by the Army during WW2 during requisitioning. Built in 1712, it has regained its elegance.

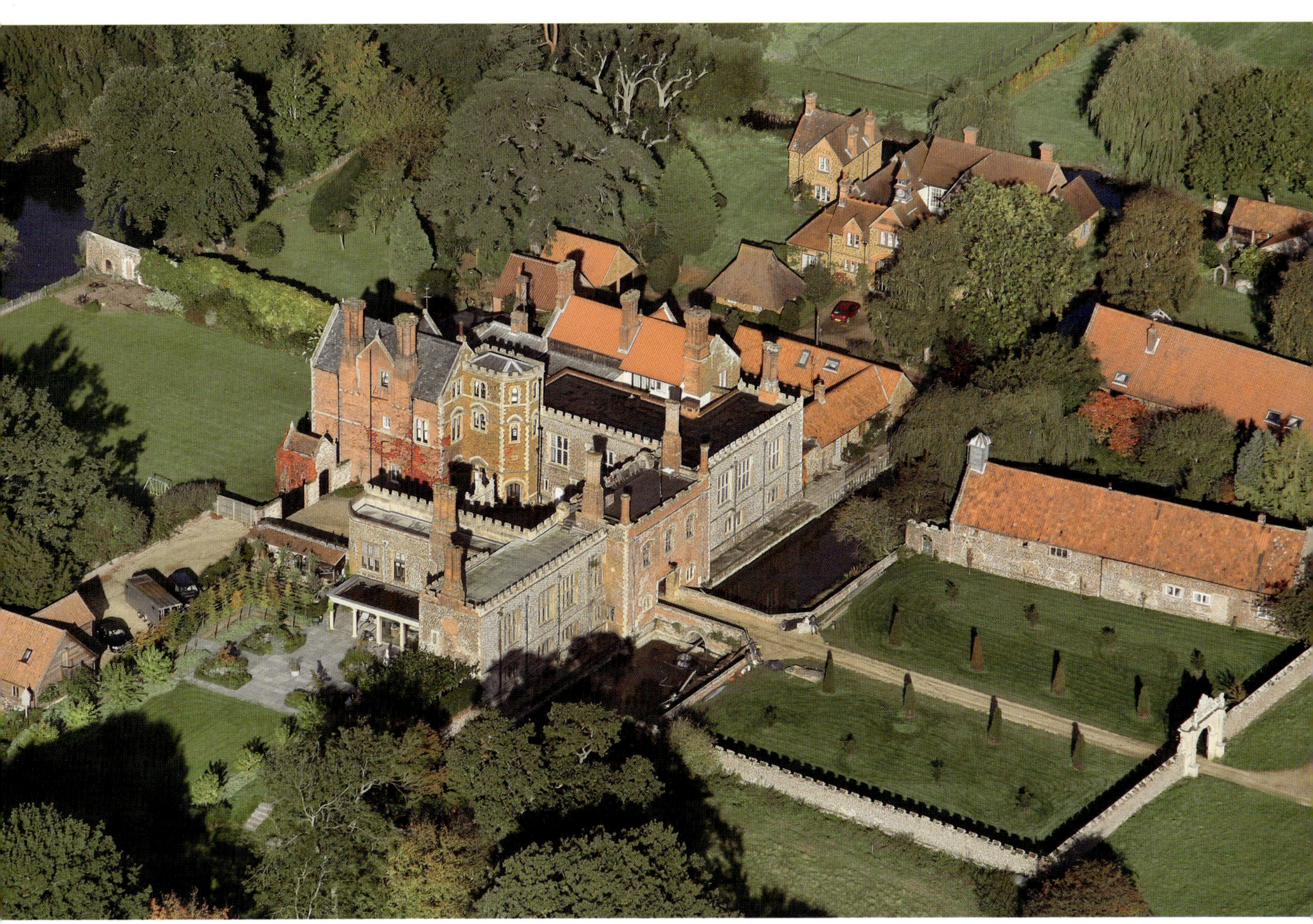

Moated Hunstanton Hall was begun c1500 but altered and added to many times. The house always has belonged to the LeStrange family.

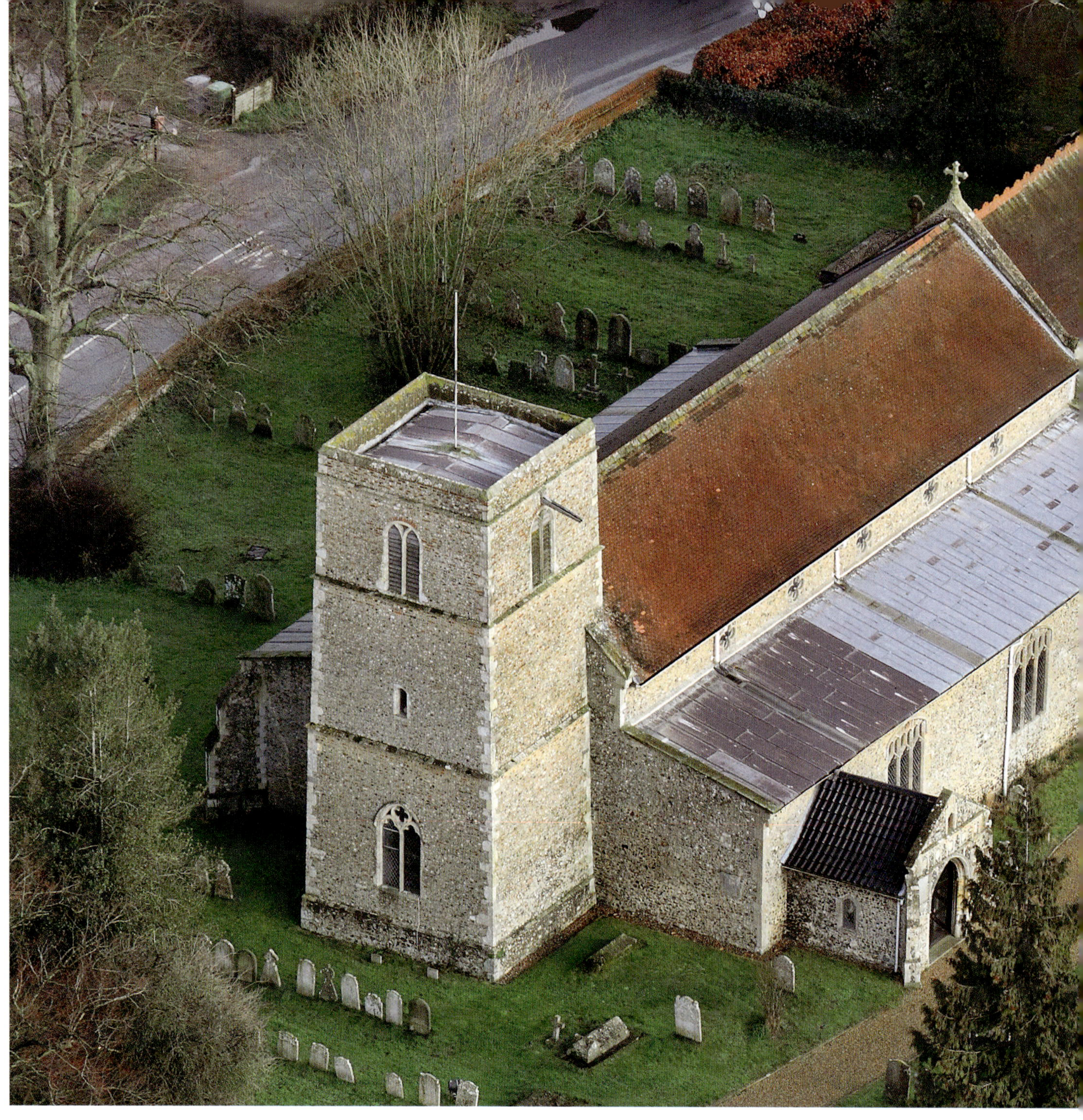

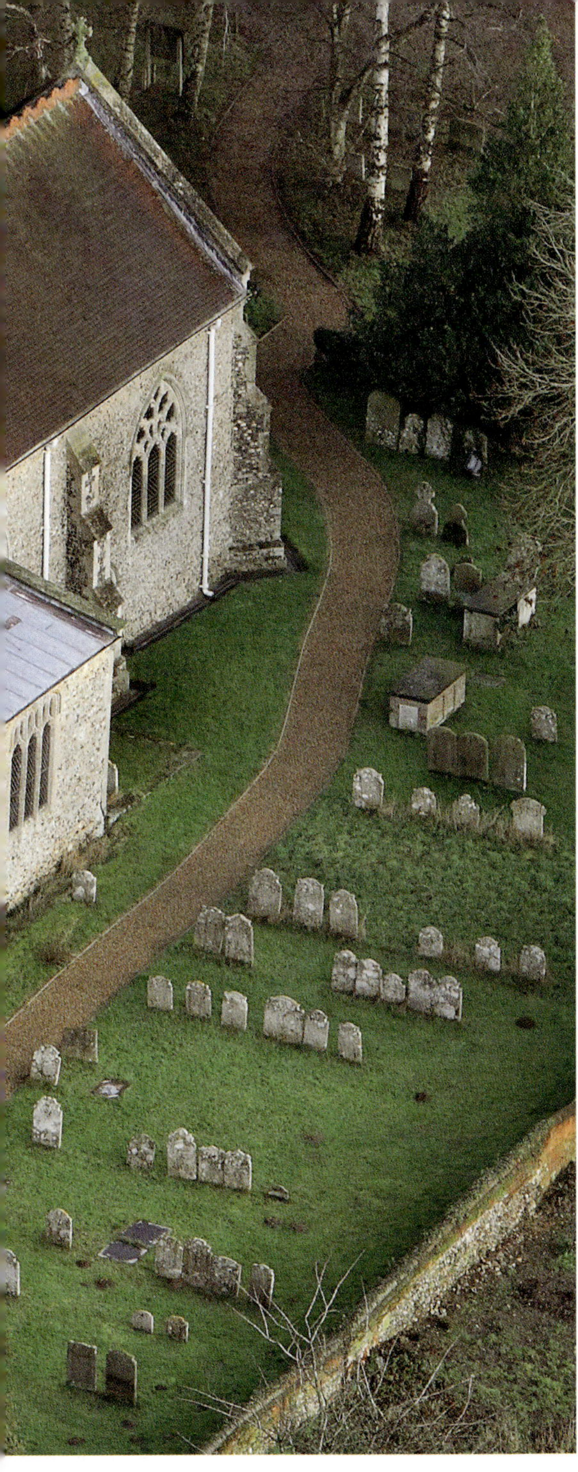

Weston Longville and the Reverend James Woodforde

Parson Woodforde (1740–1803) was doubtless a kindly, conscientious parson but for what do we remember him? His love of food! His diary of 1776, the date of his arrival in the parish of Weston Longville, tells not of world events nor even happenings in his rural parish but of the meals he ate both as host and guest.

First course: pike, large piece of boiled beef, peas, soup [unusually he fails to mention what kind] stewed mutton and goose giblets.

Second course: a brace of partridges, roast turkey, baked pudding [presumably savory], lobster and scalloped oyster tartlets.

Pudding: black and white grapes, walnuts, almonds, raisins, damson cheese and golden pippins.

All washed down with Madeira wine and port. And that was just lunch.

His diaries were first published in 1924 by the Reverend Christopher Woodforde (a descendant of James Woodforde's brother).

Roman Camp and Noel Coward

Line from the stage play *Private Lives*: 'Very flat, Norfolk.'
Perhaps someone should have walked Noel Coward up to Roman
Camp in West Runton at 103 metres above sea level (338ft).

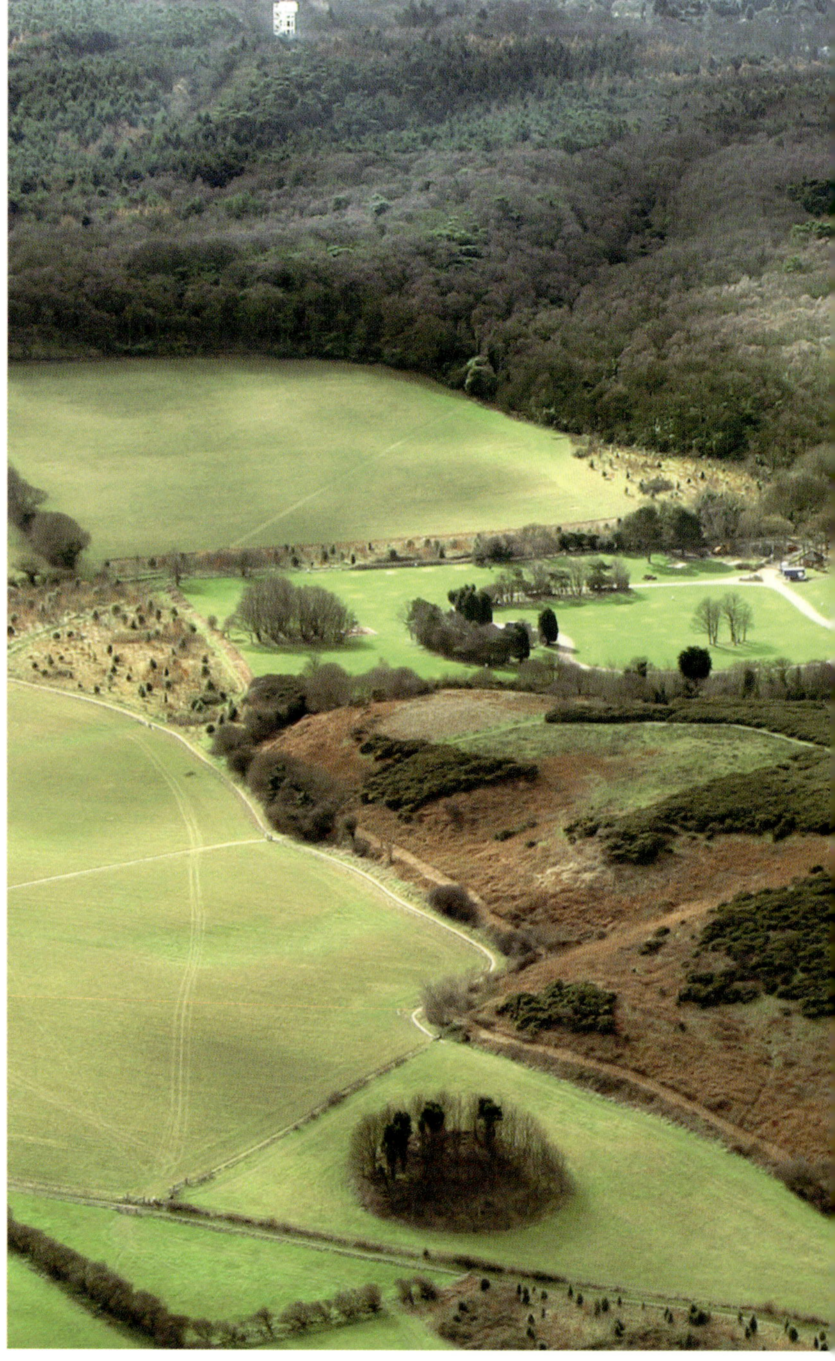

Seemingly the Romans never came here; the origin of the name is a mystery.

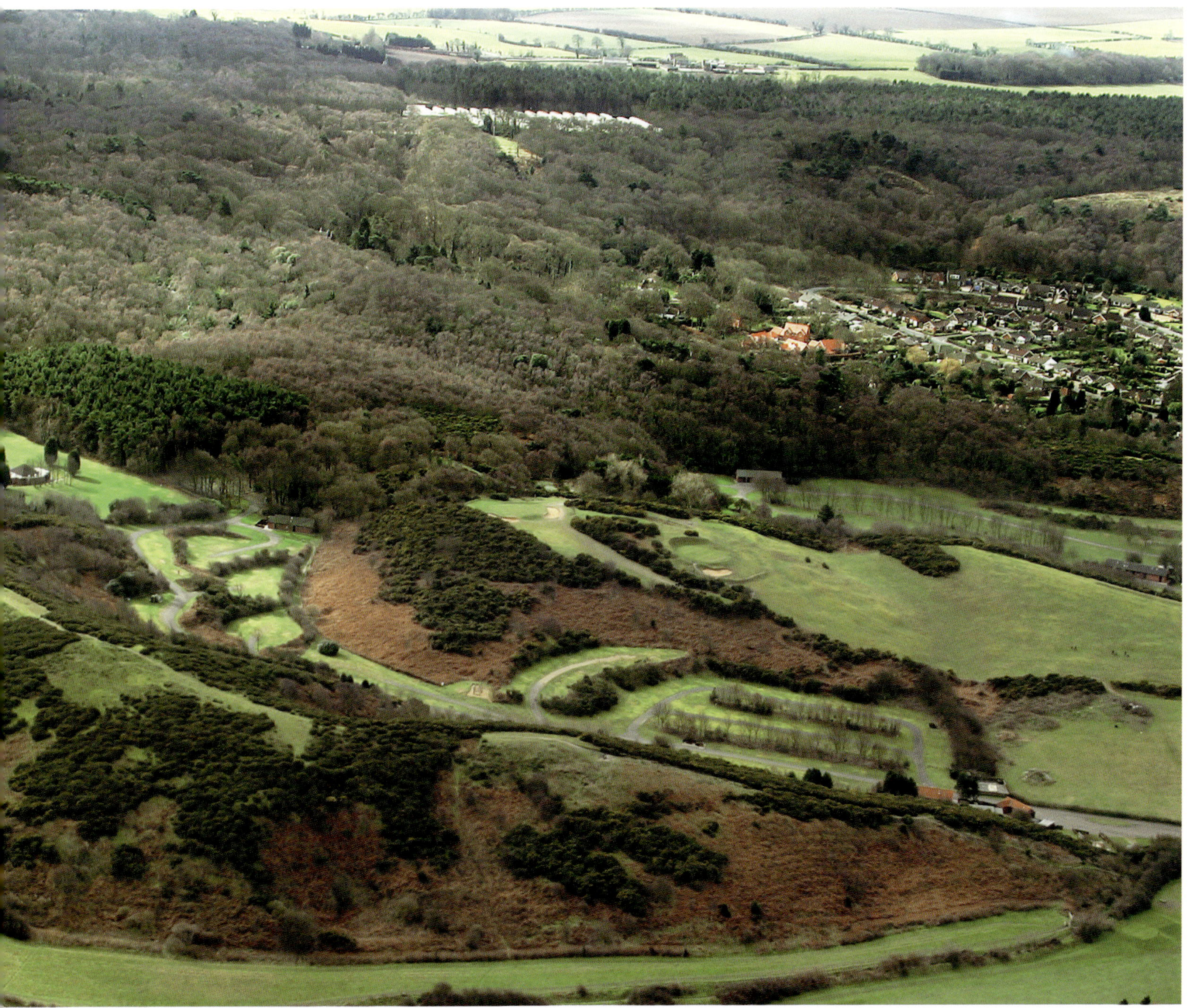

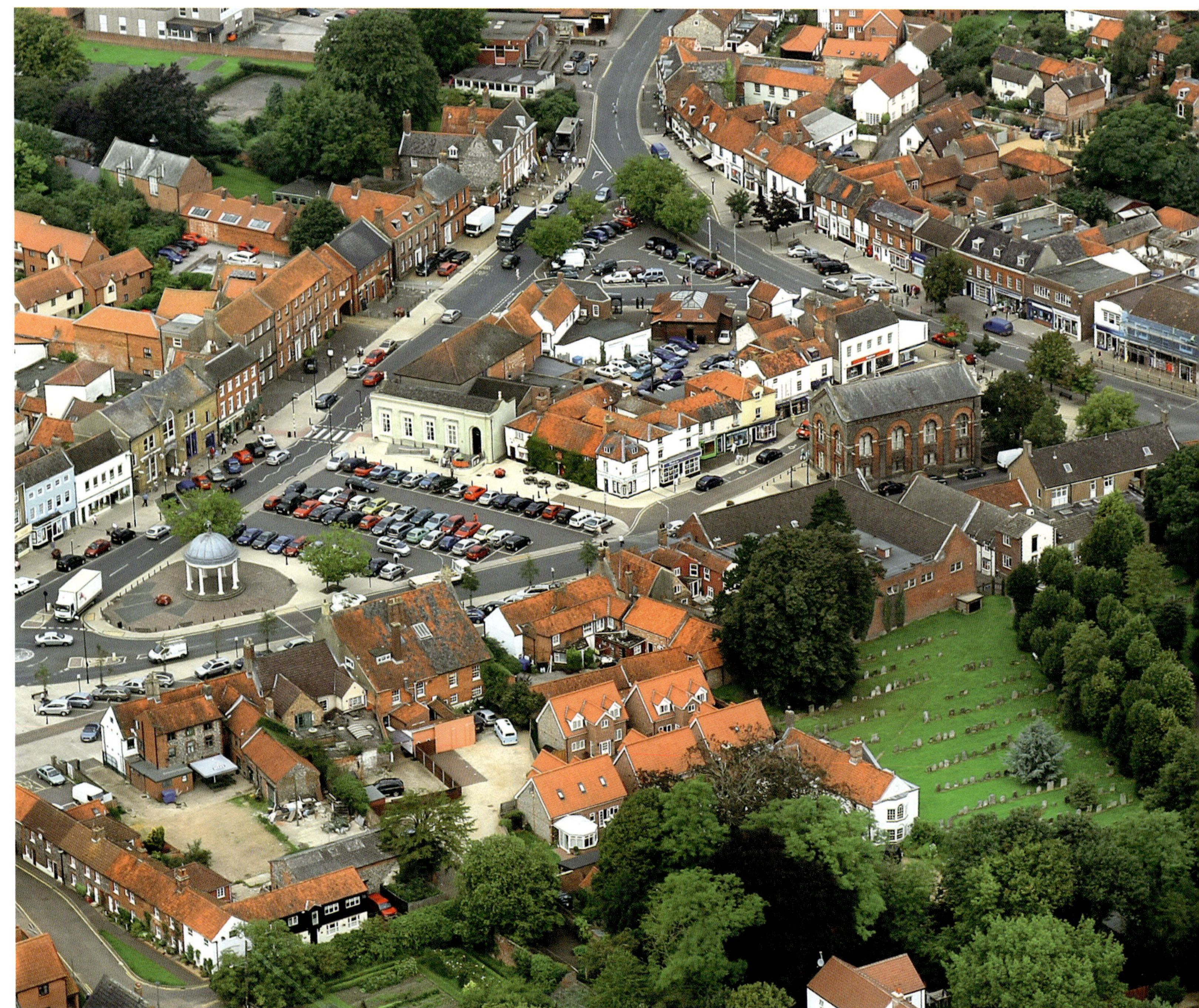

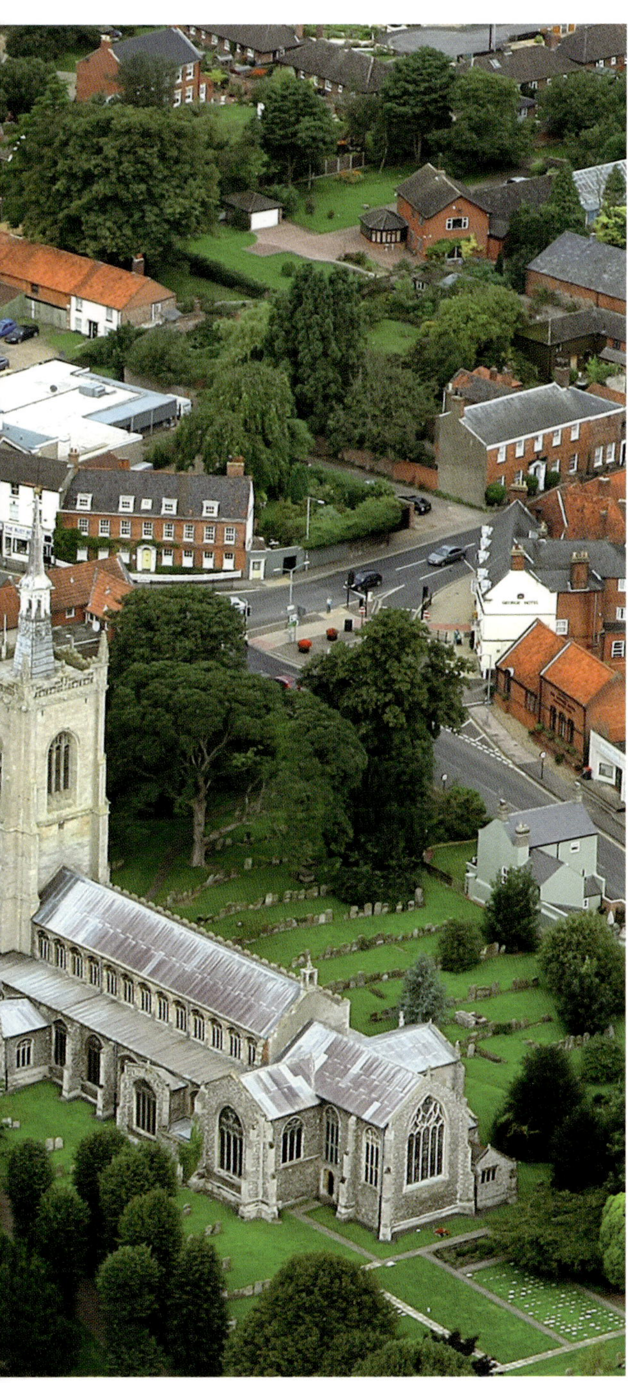

Swaffham and The Pedlar

In Swaffham parish church the bench ends on the first row of pews in the nave have beautiful carvings of the pedlar and his dog.

A pedlar from Swaffham was told in a dream to go to London Bridge where he would find his fortune. Nothing happened there except he was told by a stranger that he too had had a dream telling him to go to Swaffham and dig under an apple tree where he would find his fortune. The pedlar returned and dug under the apple tree in his garden where he found a bag of gold coins.

There are many versions of this story but suffice it to say that John Chapman (a travelling pedlar selling ribbons and stuff) made a fortune and enriched the church by adding a north aisle.

Swaffham St Peter and St Paul church.

The Wind on the Heath and George Borrow

George Borrow (1803–1881) associated with gypsies particularly with those on Mousehold Heath. His book *Lavengro* is a semi biographical account of his time spent in gypsy company and particularly with Jasper Petulengro who taught him the Romany language. To posterity Borrow has left phrases such as 'the wind on the heath' and of Norwich 'a fine city'.

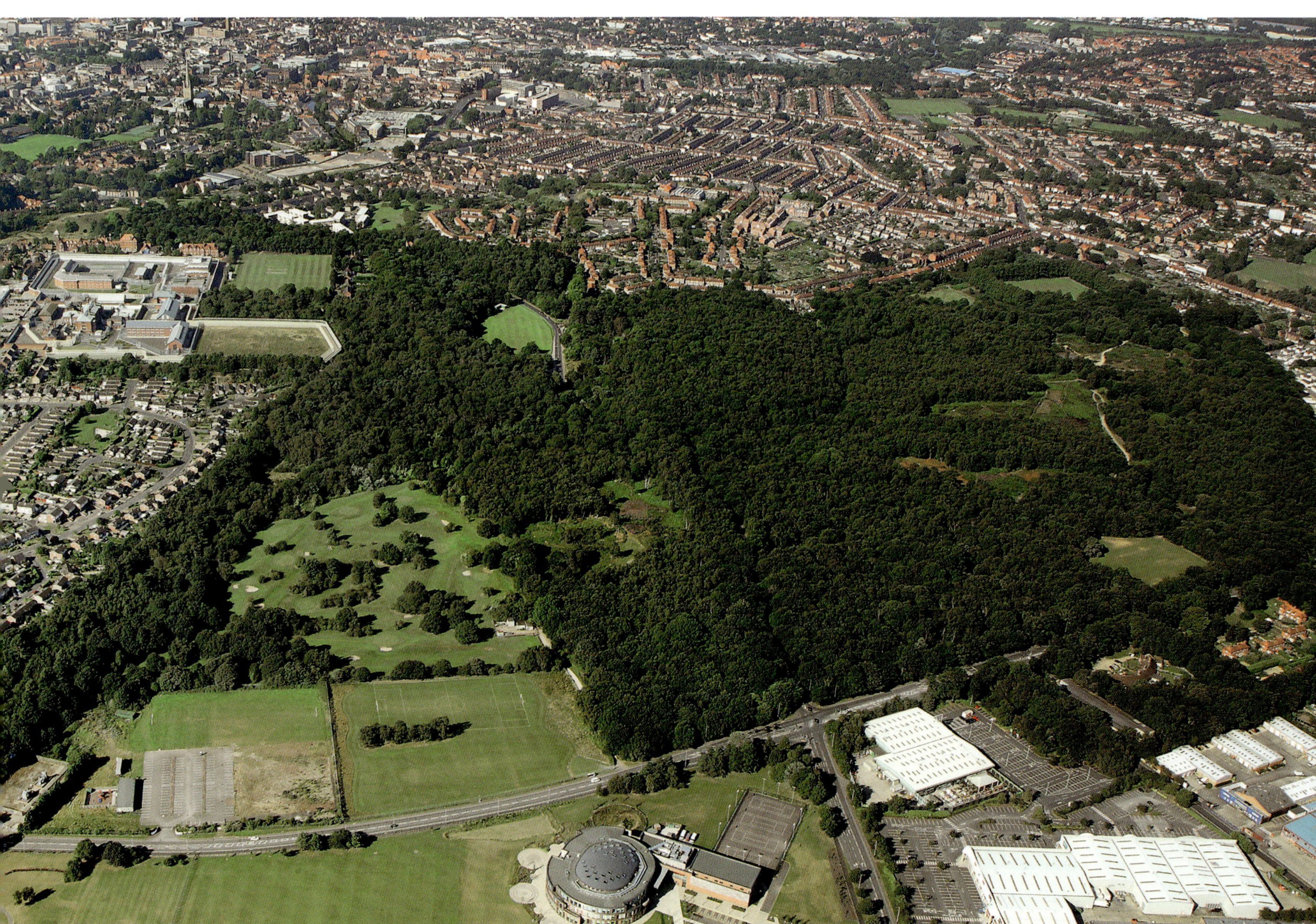

Geoffrey Chaucer and the Reeve's Tale

In *The Canterbury Tales* Geoffrey Chaucer (born 1340s) created a plot in which thirty or so pilgrims meet at The Tabard Inn in Southwark to make a pilgrimage to the shrine of Thomas Becket in Canterbury Cathedral. To keep their companions amused the pilgrims in turn tell a story. The Reeve (a Land Agent) from Bawdeswell (Baldeswell) in his tale refers to the Holy Cross of Bromholme (Bromholme Priory near Bacton). The fortunes of the Priory improved considerably when it claimed to have a piece of the True Cross which pilgrims travelled to see.

There were two Bawdeswell churches prior to the one illustrated. Built in colonial style this last one (1950) was a tribute to the two American airmen who in 1944 were killed when they crashed onto the previous church when returning from a raid over Germany.

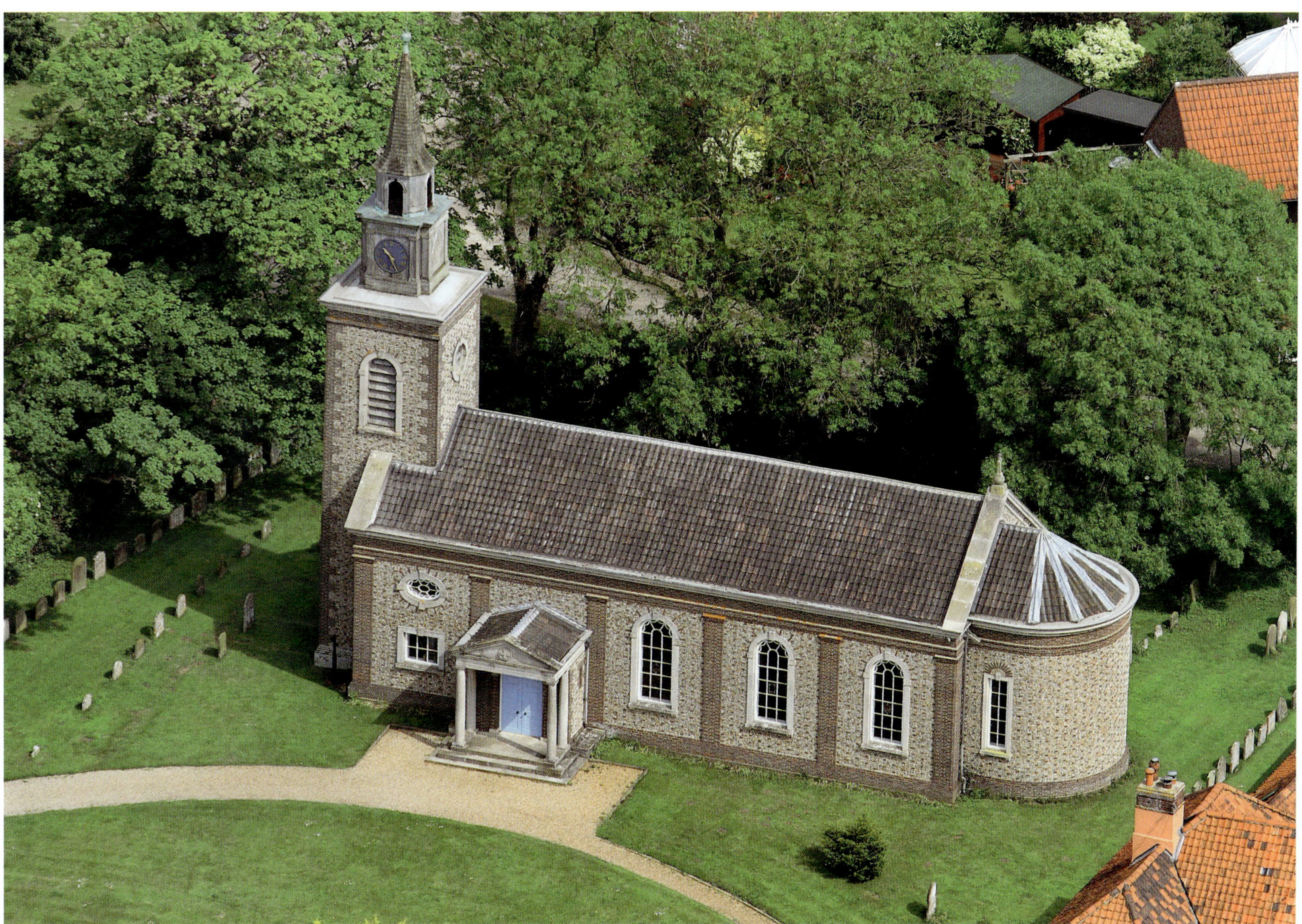

Dorothy L Sayers (1893-1957) was one of the first crime writers whose work was broadcast by the early BBC. Her mystery, *The Nine Tailors* was named after a fictitious peal of bells in a fictitious Fenland church.

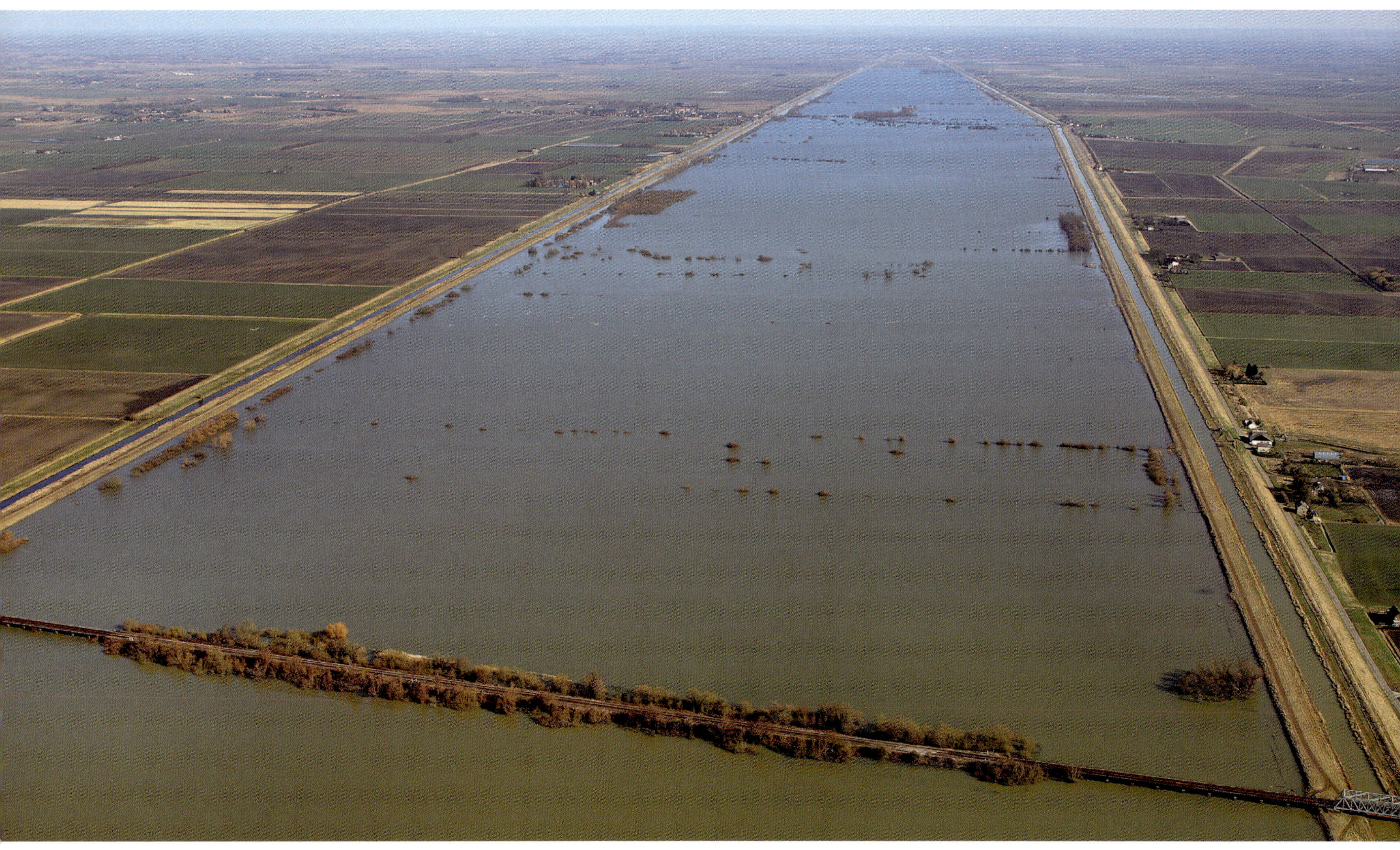

Pictured are the flooded Ouse Washes. Top left to the north would be Outwell and Upwell. Bottom of picture running east to west, the March to Ely railway line. On either side of the Washes the Old Bedford River (left) runs parallel to the New Bedford River (right).

Hymns and William Cowper

William Cowper 1731–1800 (alternative pronunciation 'Cooper') was a deeply religious man who suffered from depression, although some of his hymns are surprisingly upbeat, for example 'God moves in a Mysterious Way' and 'Sometimes a light surprises the Christian while he Sings'. Of him it was said that his was a 'crushed gentle spirit escaped from a world in which it had known naught but sorrow'.

There's both a Cowper Memorial church in East Dereham's Market Place and a wonderful window in the parish church where he's portrayed with his pet hares. In St Nicholas' churchyard there's a spring attributed to St Withburga. It's claimed that Cowper drank from the well every day in the belief that it would cure his melancholy.

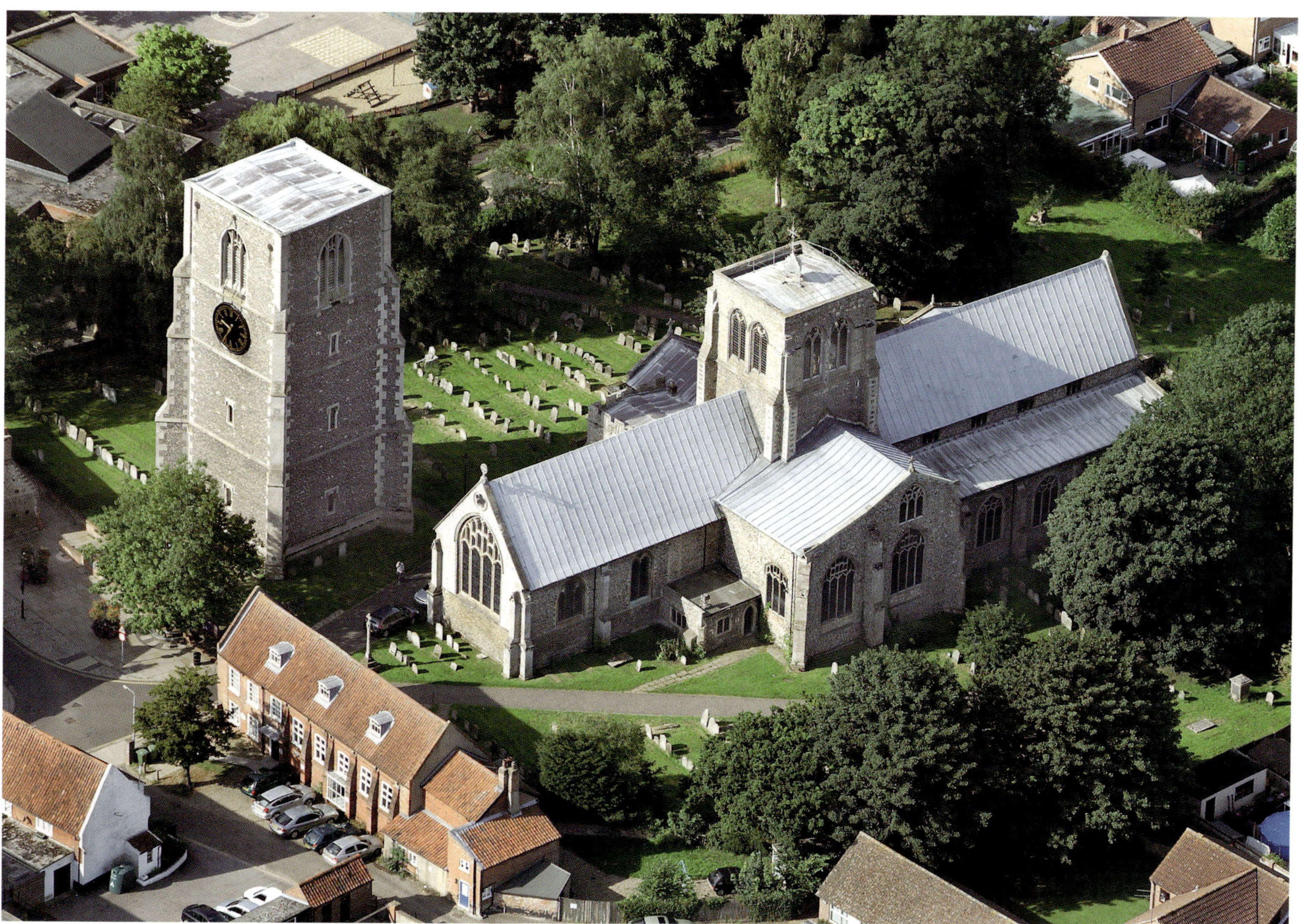

Biggles and The Sanitary Inspector

WWI pilot Captain W E Johns (1893-1968) was a one-time Sanitary Inspector (today would be called Environmental Health Officer) in Swaffham. At the start of WWI he enlisted in the Norfolk Yeomanry and served at Gallipoli. His basic flying training was at Thetford. In 1932 he began writing the Biggles books which at the time of his death amounted to over a hundred. They told the story of Air Ace James Bigglesworth as he progressed through the ranks of the RAF being awarded a DSO and an MC en route.

W E Johns wrote other aviation-based material and was also an air correspondent.

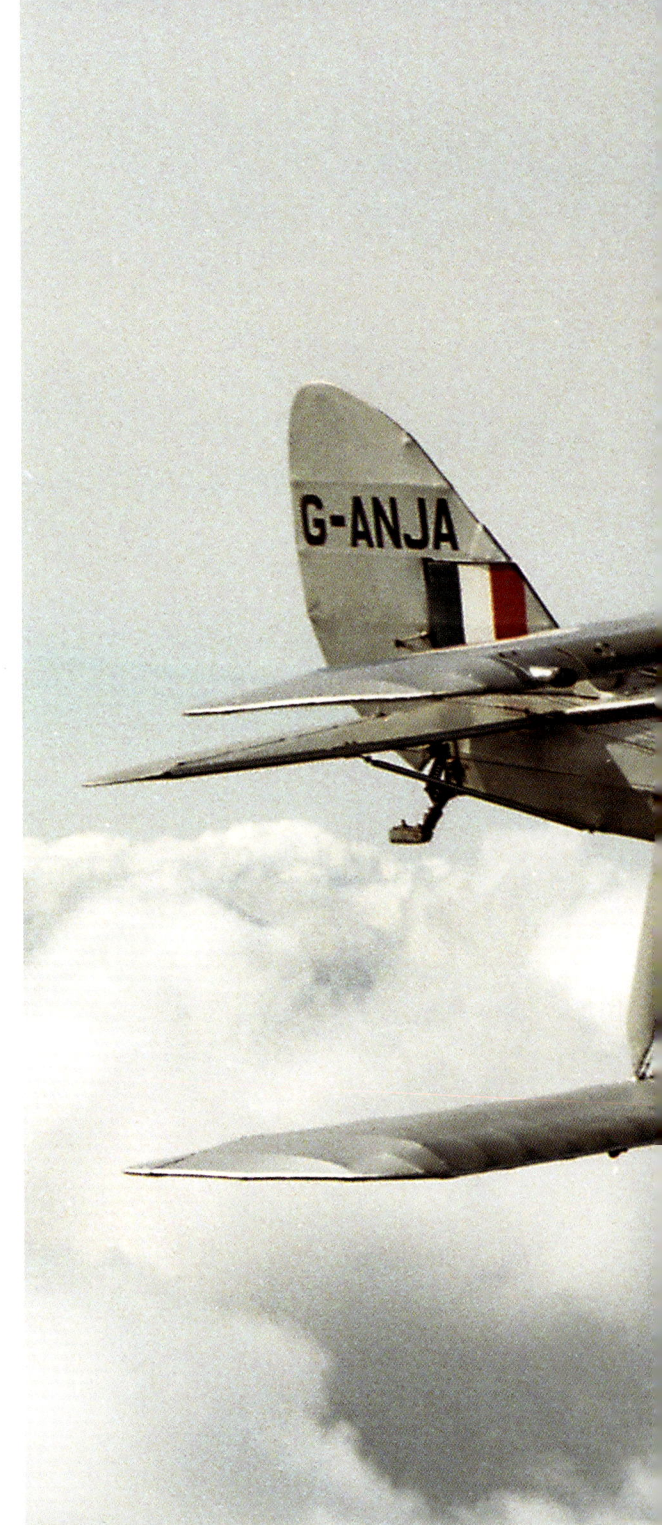

De Havilland Tiger Moth.

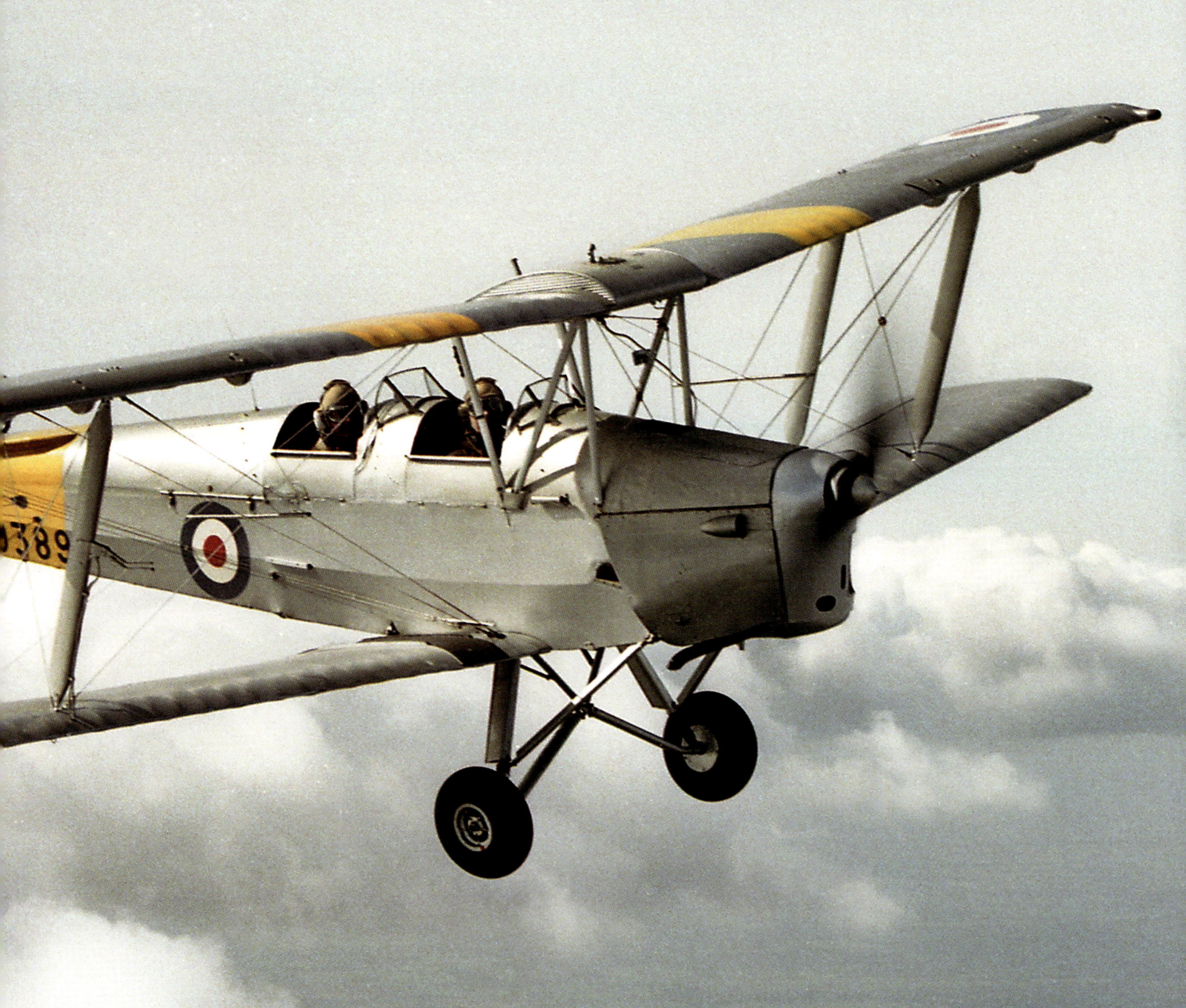

Sarah Glover and The Sound of Music

Remember 'Doe a deer, a female deer'? How could you forget it? Sarah Ann Glover (1785–1867) lived in Norwich's Colegate and gave music lessons. She invented the *tonic sol-fah* system whereby each note was related to the next within an octave. She claimed it made music easier to learn. The scale runs 'doh, ray, me, fah, soh, lah, tee, doh'.

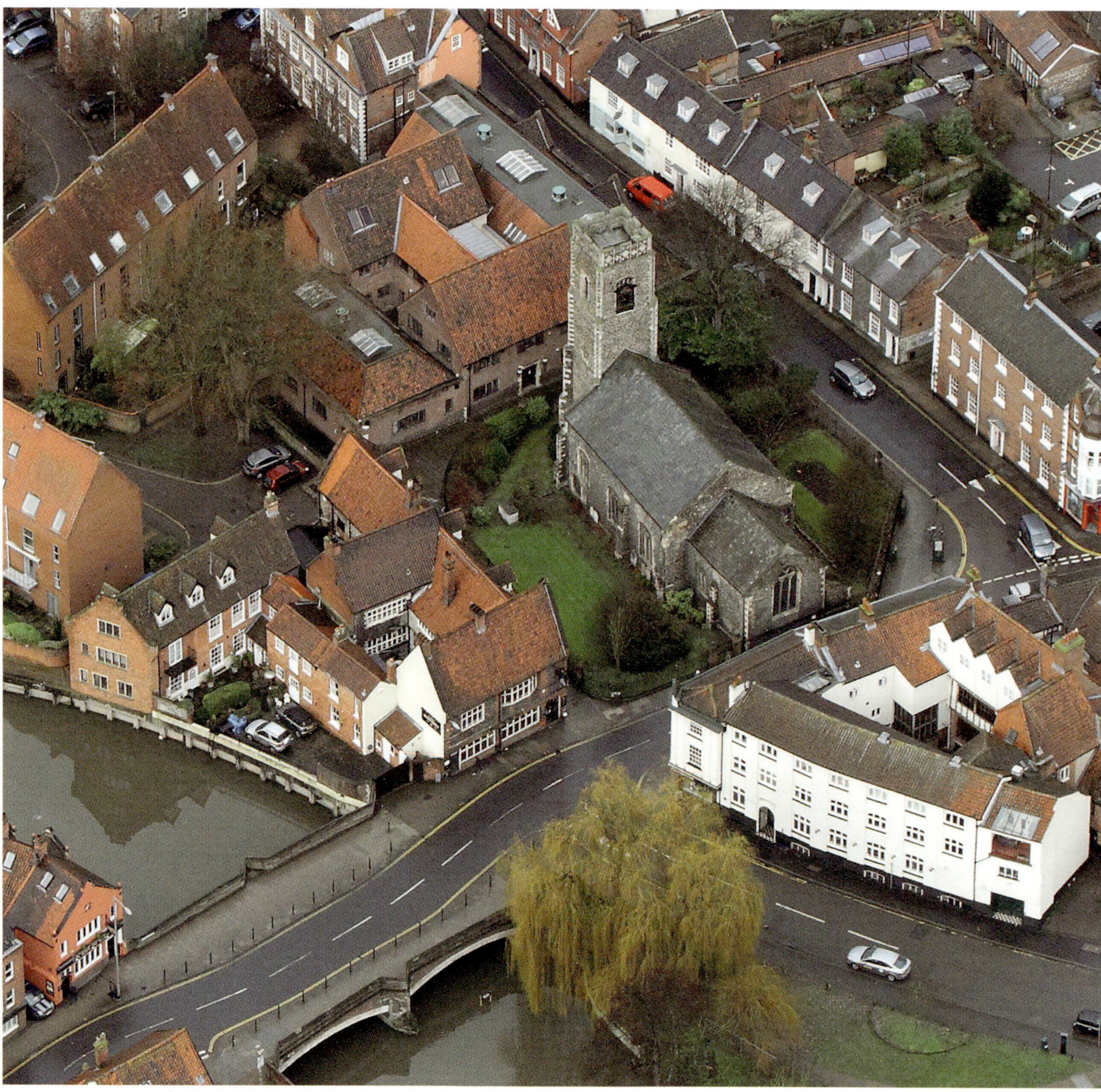

Norwich's Colegate runs right to left mid picture. The River Wensum is crossed via Fye Bridge.

Blame it on the Railway and Clement Scott

In 1883 the *Daily Telegraph* journalist Clement Scott, fancying a holiday, took the train from the recently opened Liverpool Street Station to Cromer (via Norwich) on the new railway. He found lodgings at Mill Cottage, Sidestrand. He was enchanted by the miller's daughter and even more so by the surrounding area christening it 'Poppyland' because of the abundance of poppies in the fields. He came to regret writing so enthusiastically about the area. Holidaymakers flocked by train to stay at the new hotels being built along the coast. But the damage had been done, the area was spoiled. Incongruously, along the Cromer to Overstrand Road, there's a horse trough (now planted with flowers) in his memory.

In 1840 the round tower of Sidestrand church collapsed and tumbled over the cliffs, the remainder of the church followed shortly after.

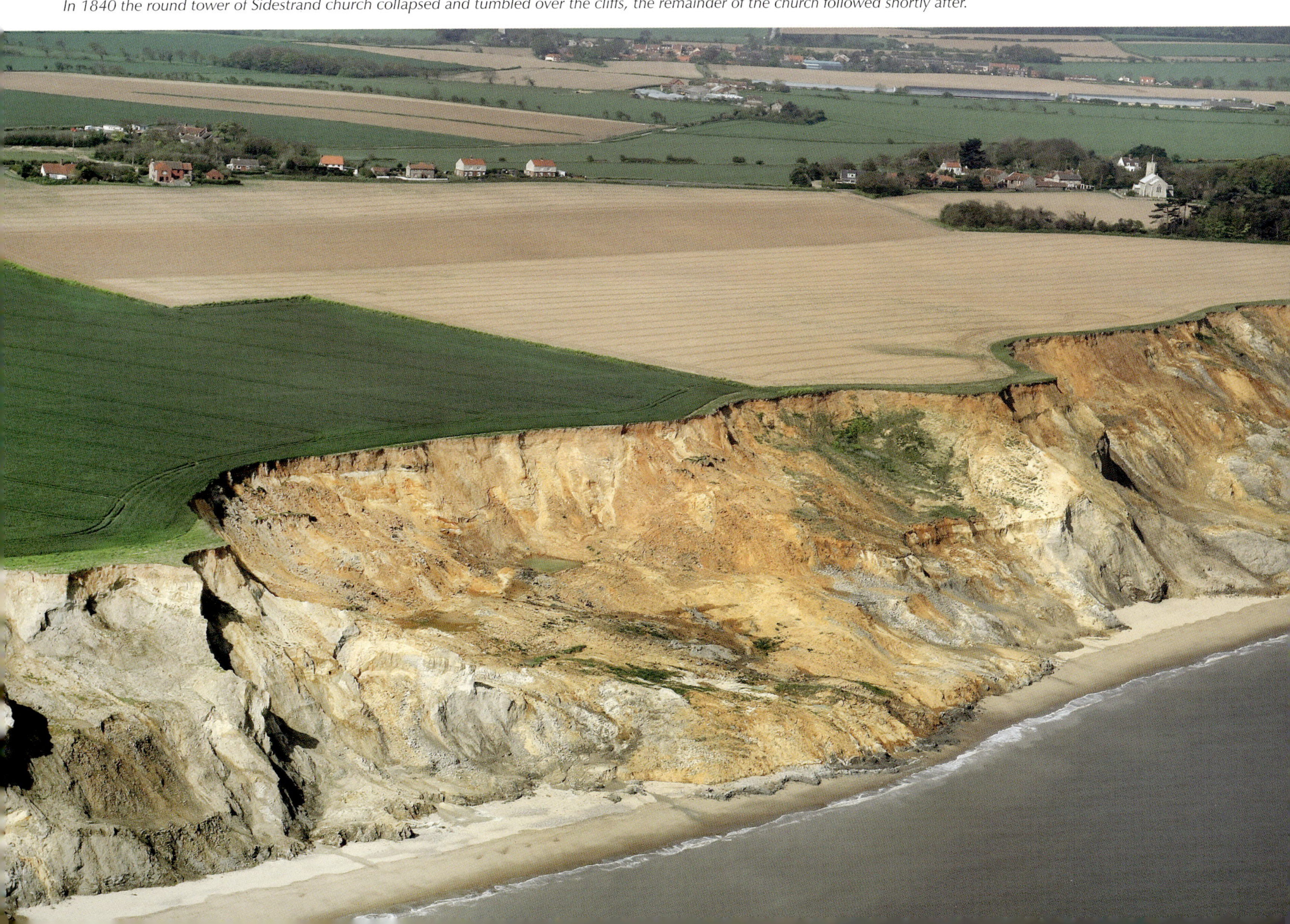

Chapter 8

Do Different (an old Norfolk saying)
(People who put Norfolk on the map by doing just that)

Billy Bluelight

He was definitely an odd ball. For many summers he made a living racing the pleasure steamers as they plied between Bramerton's Woods End pub and Norwich's Carrow Bridge. The route is now part of the Wherryman's Way footpath. Dressed in knee-length cricket shorts, long stockings, plimsolls and a cricketer's cap he sang

'My name is Billy Blue light, my age is forty five

I hope to get to Carrow Bridge before the boat arrive.'

Passengers would cheer him on, throwing coins when they reached Carrow Bridge. Born in 1859 he remained forty-five for many years. On the green at Woods End there's a half size statue of Billy, real name William Cullen. The statue is one of a series along the River Yare at riverside villages where a river-related skill such as boat building was carried out.

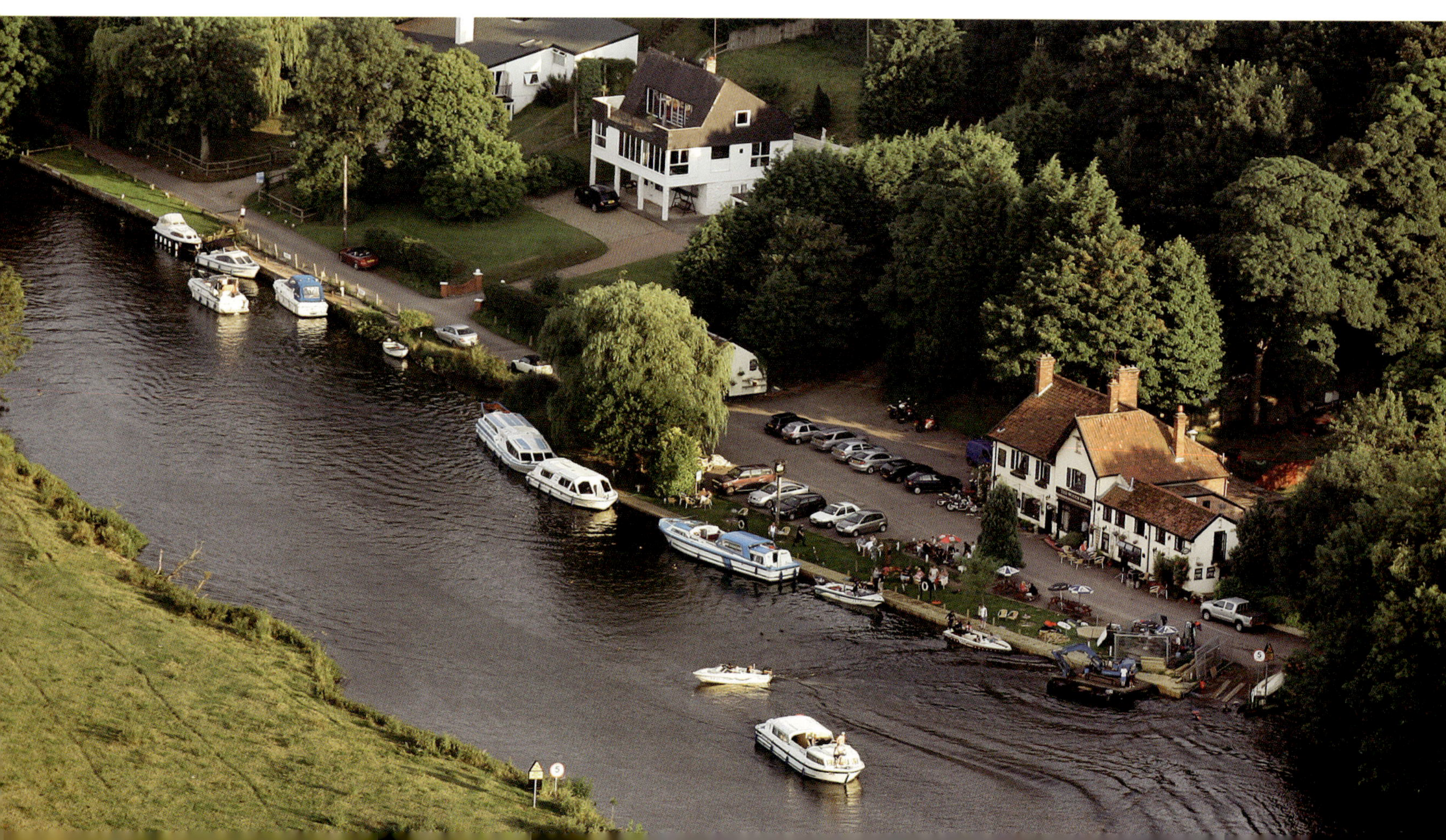

Henry Blogg 1876–1954

He's the most highly decorated lifeboatman ever and his awards include the George Cross. Henry Blogg became a lifeboatman when he was eighteen. He served as coxswain for over fifty years saving the lives of over nine hundred souls. He neither drank nor smoked and in common with many fishermen couldn't swim. When he died the Cromer pavements were lined several people deep as they paid their respects as his cortege slowly went past.

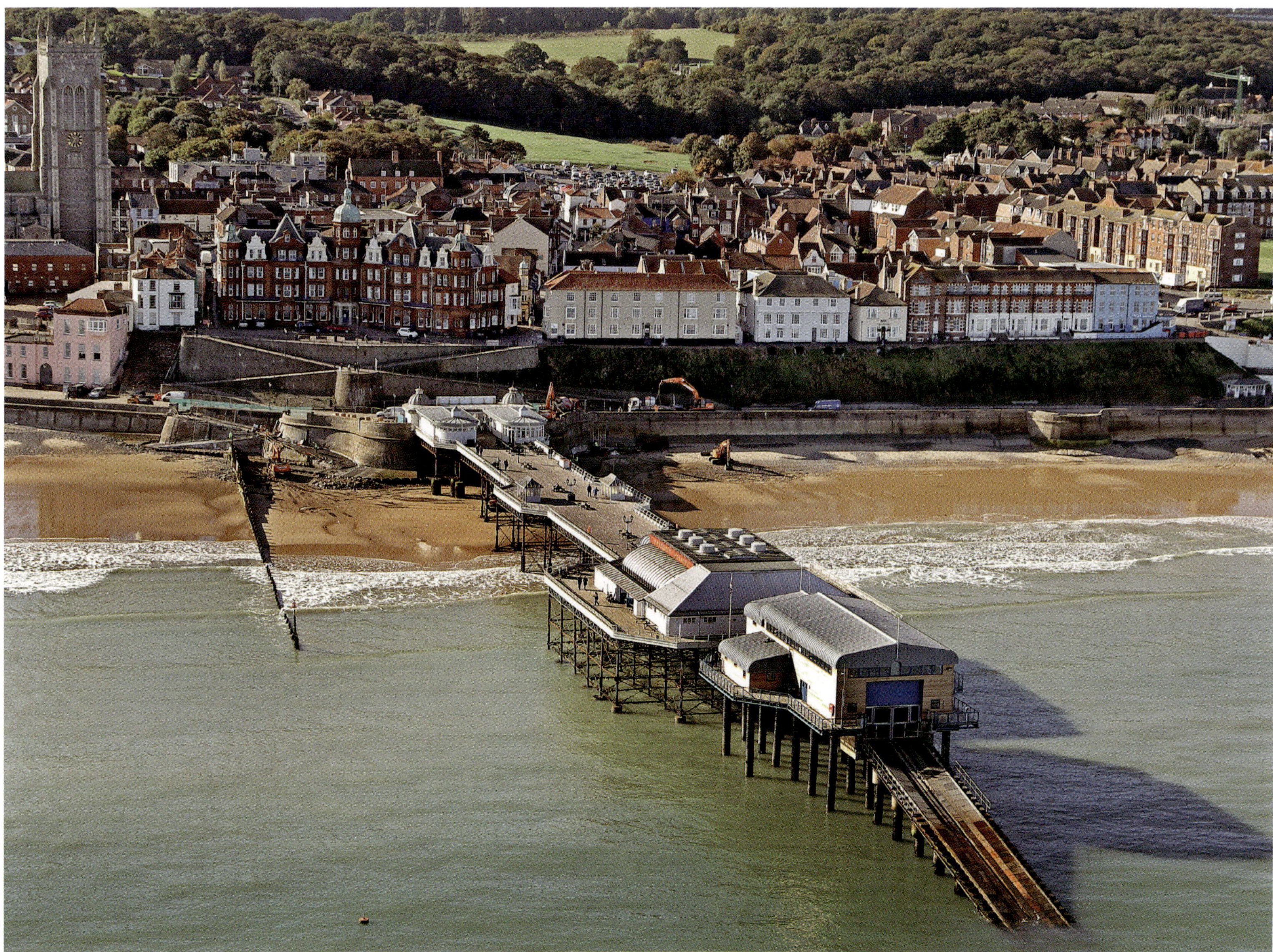

Cromer.

Thomas Paine: The Rights of Man

It took over 200 years for the Working Class Movement to adopt Tom Paine's philosophies and whilst his early years were full of promise he died a pauper in America. Born in 1737 into a Thetford Quaker family he had a firm grounding in pacifism and believed that humanitarianism was an end in itself. During his visits to America he had conversations with Ben Franklin and in Norfolk with Horatio Nelson during Nelson's 'wilderness years'. Tom Paine's philosophies were set out in *The Rights of Man* which he wrote during his visits to Thetford. But suspicions of his motives were rife, the French Revolution was still uppermost in some minds and he was regarded as seditious. Now he qualifies for a statue at his birthplace – and a hotel named after him!

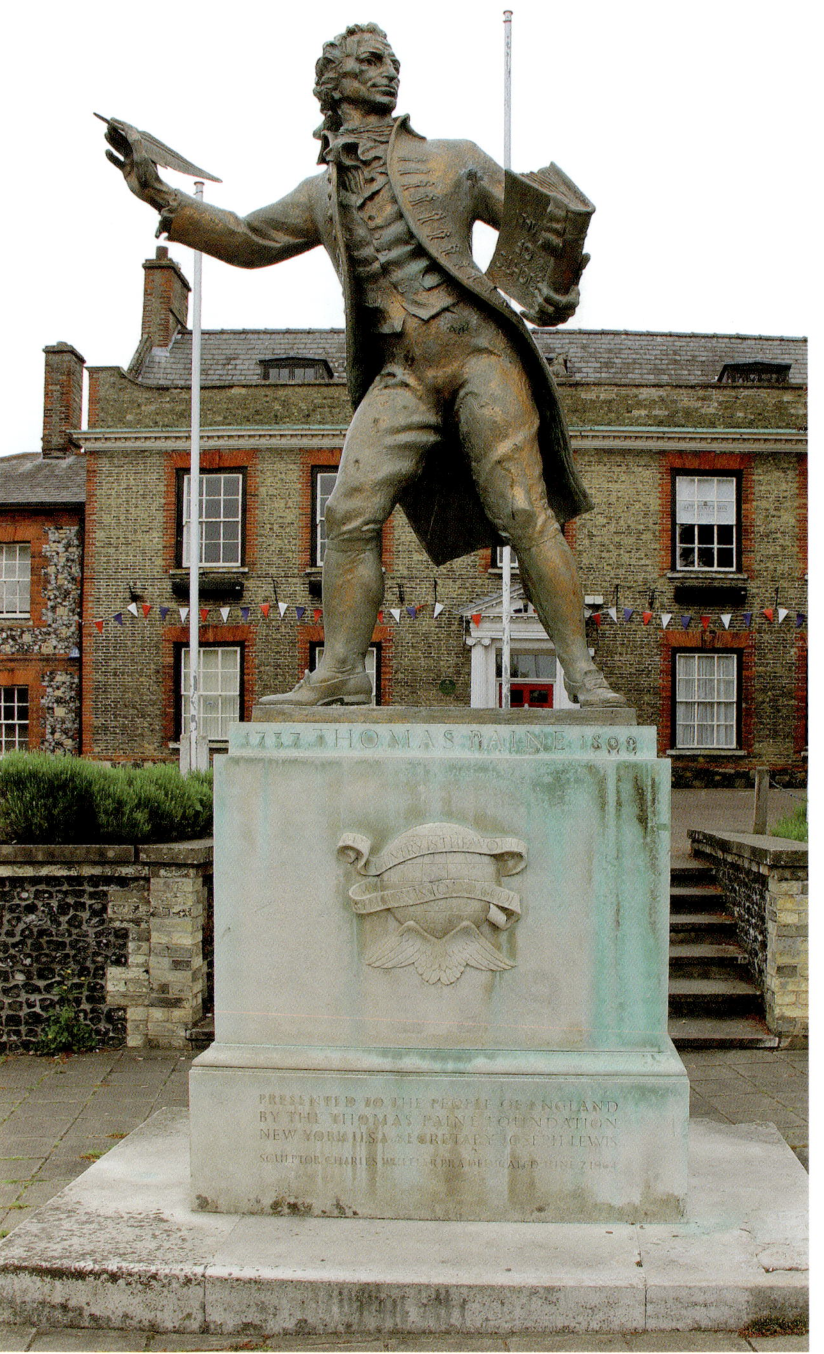

The Thomas Paine statue in Thetford.
© Tim Ball

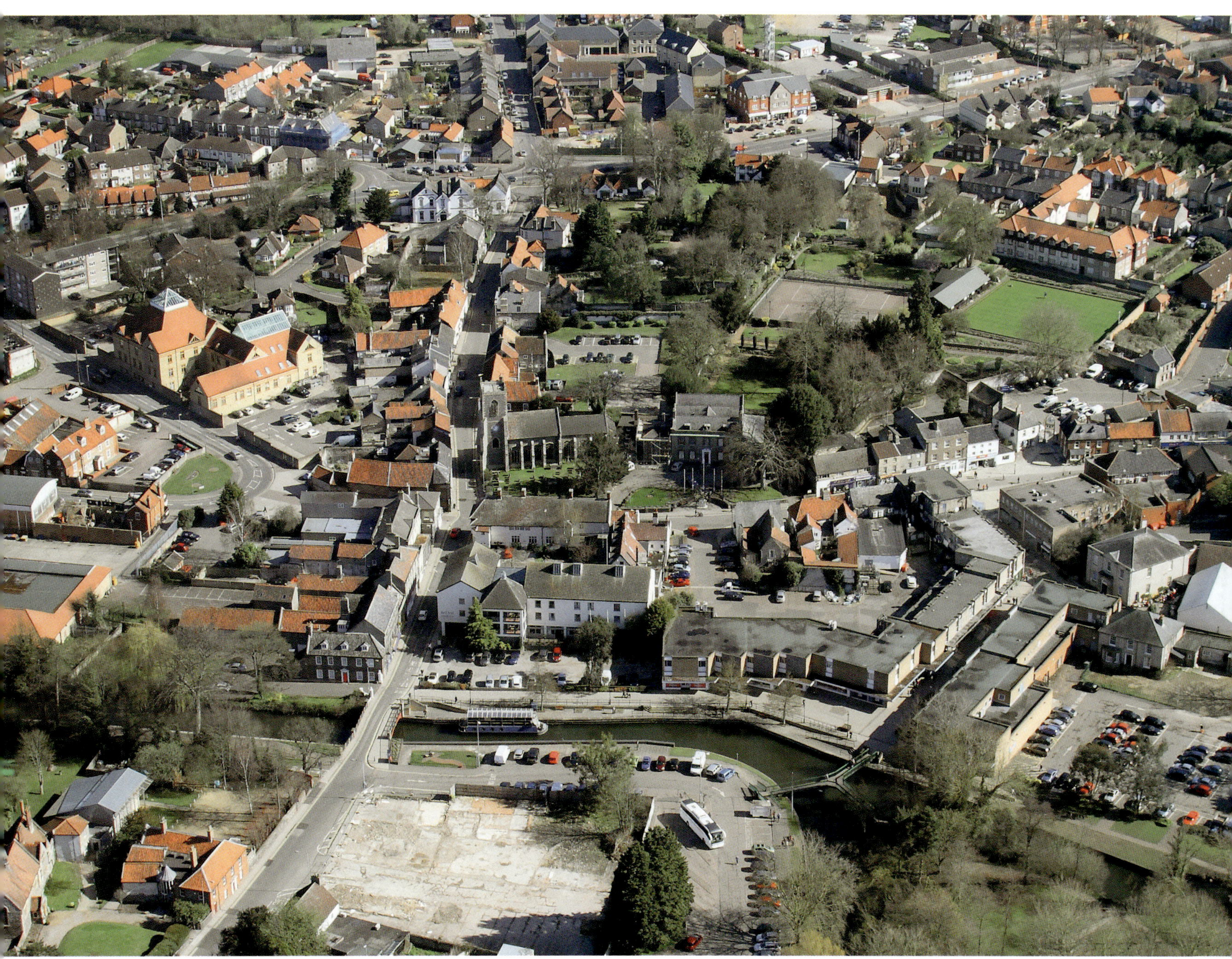

How would Thomas Paine have reacted to having an hotel named after him in the town? (The hotel is towards the top middle of picture.)

Bernard Matthews

Just about anyone who has a mind to it can raise a few turkeys but to become 'The Turkey King' takes courage, enterprise and probably an inventive advertising agency. It was a clever idea to use both Bernard Matthews' Norfolk accent and Bernard Matthews in person speaking on TV to sell 'bootiful' turkey meat thus providing jobs for many and a mansion for himself. Successful entrepreneurs acknowledge the role that luck played a part in their success. Perhaps his luck was that at the end of WWII there were empty Norfolk airfields with unused concrete hard standing – just the place to put up a few turkey sheds.

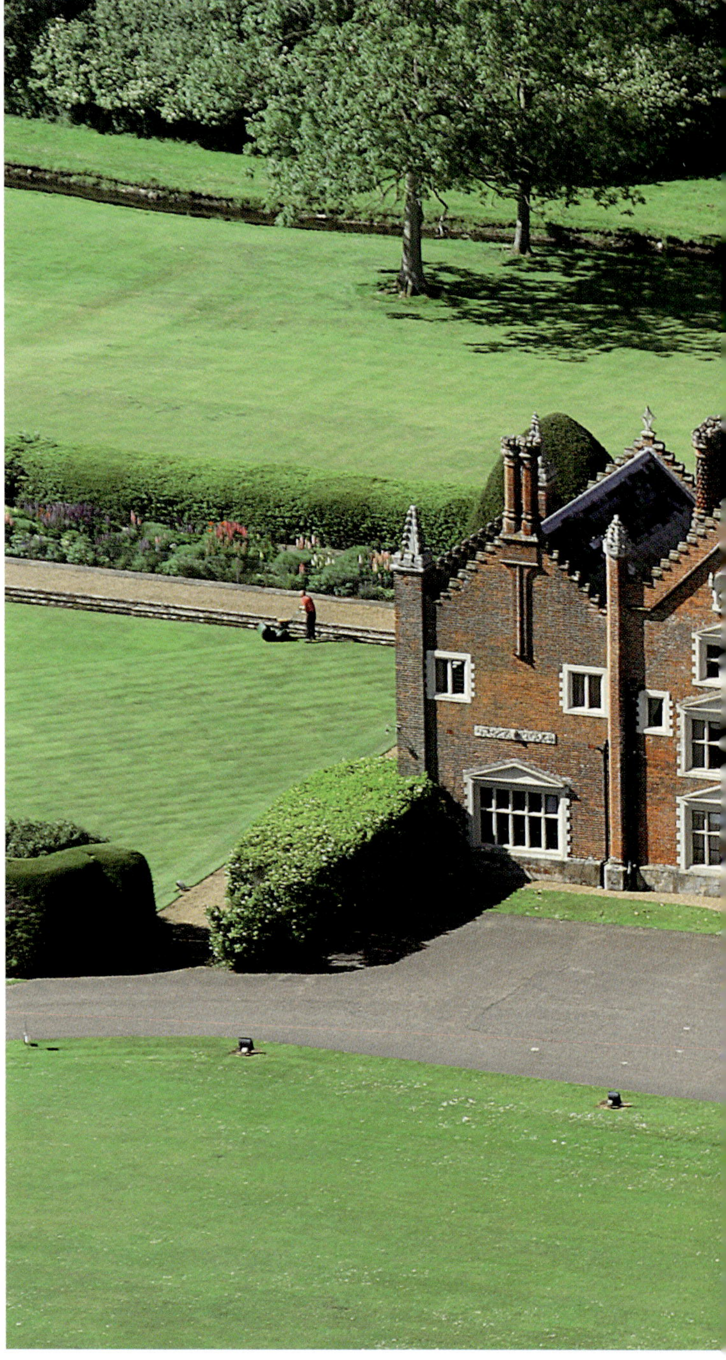

Great Witchingham Hall. According to Pevsner the front is Elizabethan but the rest is substantially Victorian.

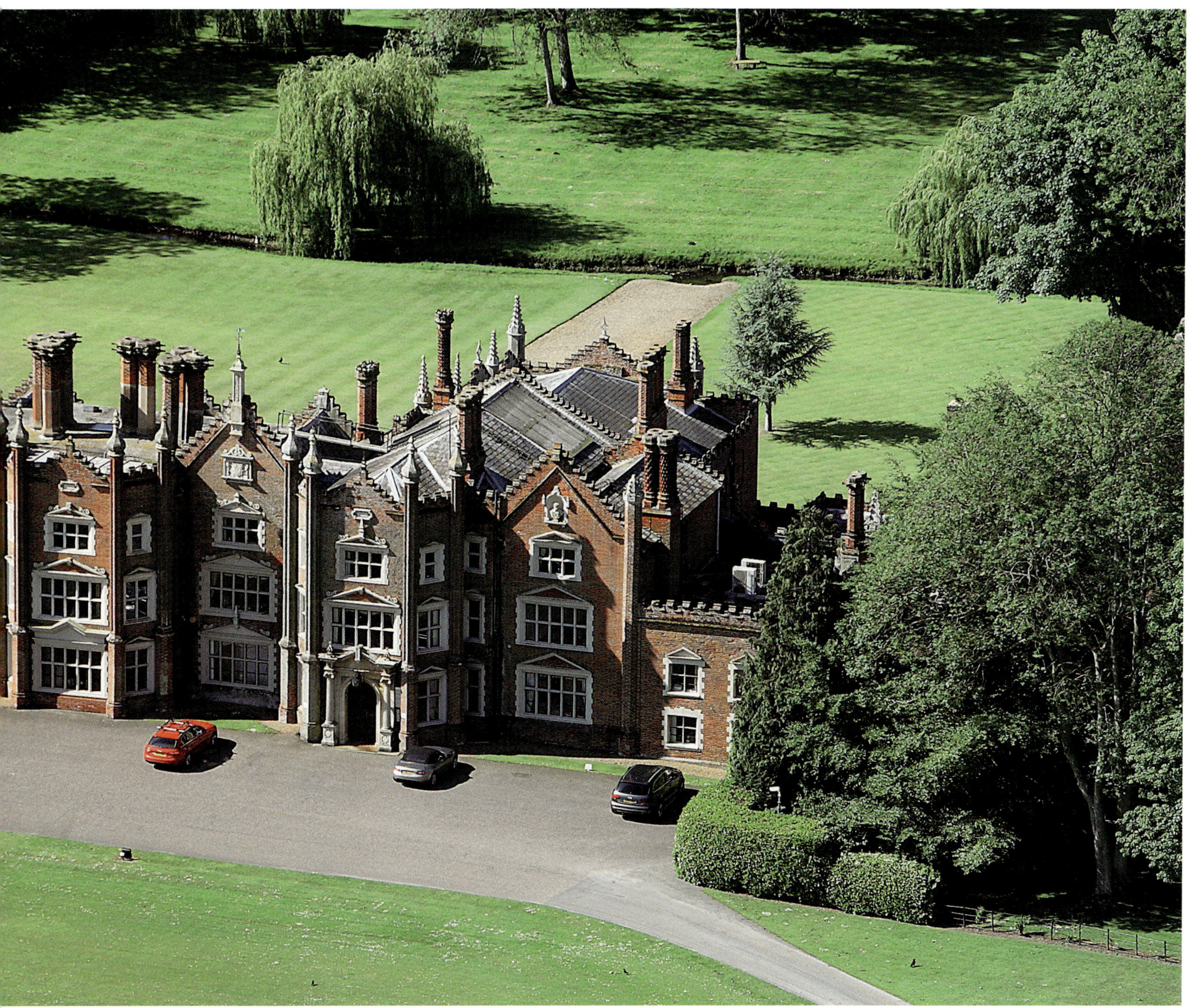

Captain George Manby 1765–1864

Born at Denver on the edge of The Fens and educated at Downham Market, Gearge Manby, as a young person, witnessed a shipwreck which changed his life for ever. He saw two hundred lives lost from HMS *Snipe*. In 1808 he contrived a method of shooting a rope over a stranded vessel, securing the rope then enabling a sailor in a breeches buoy (a life buoy with a pair of breeches with shortened legs attached) to be hauled across to safety.

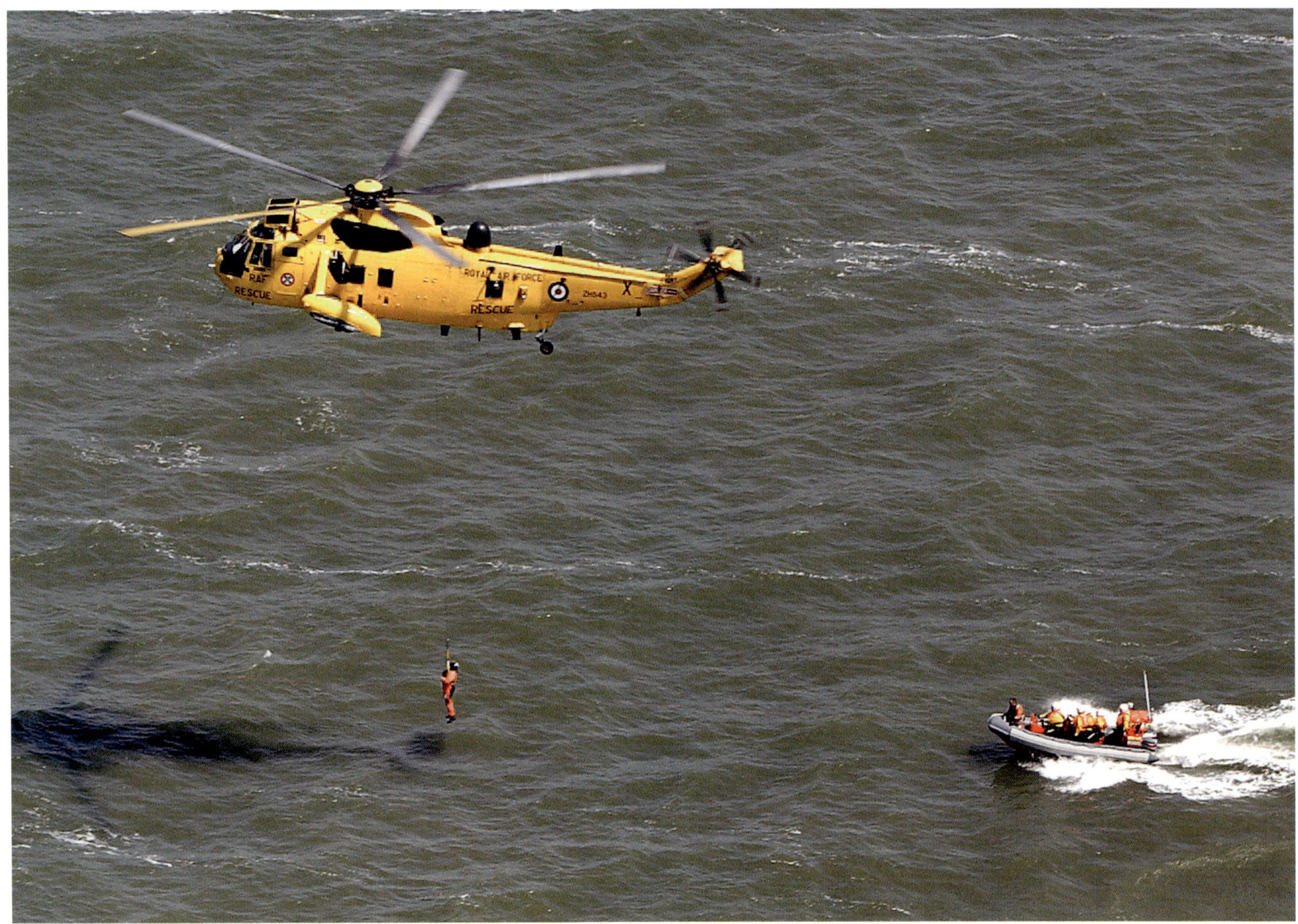

This picture taken during an exercise. The modern version shows the winchman attaching a harness and a rope to the rescued person who is then winched up to safety. The principle of the breeches buoy remains the same.

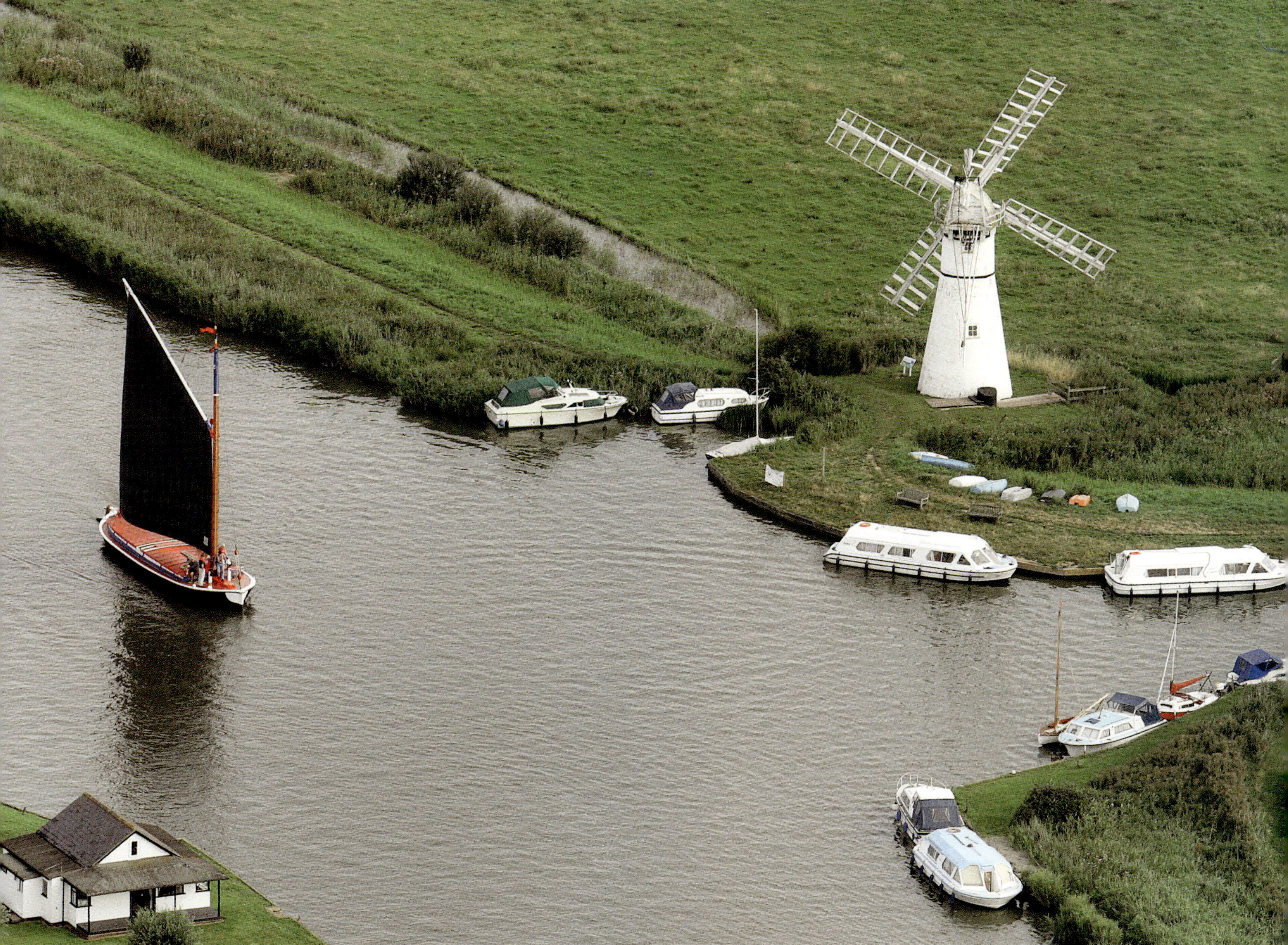

Bob Morse 1924–2007

Described as 'a pioneering conservator of all things mechanical' the late Bob Morse rescued Thurne Mill in the late 1940s. Built around 1820 the mill was 'tailwinded' in a gale and the cap and sails crashed to the ground in the 1930s. It's also known as 'Morse's Mill', quite a tribute. There is a unique collection of Morse's wind engines, pumps and memorabilia on display at the Wind Energy Museum in Repps with Bastwick, Norfolk.

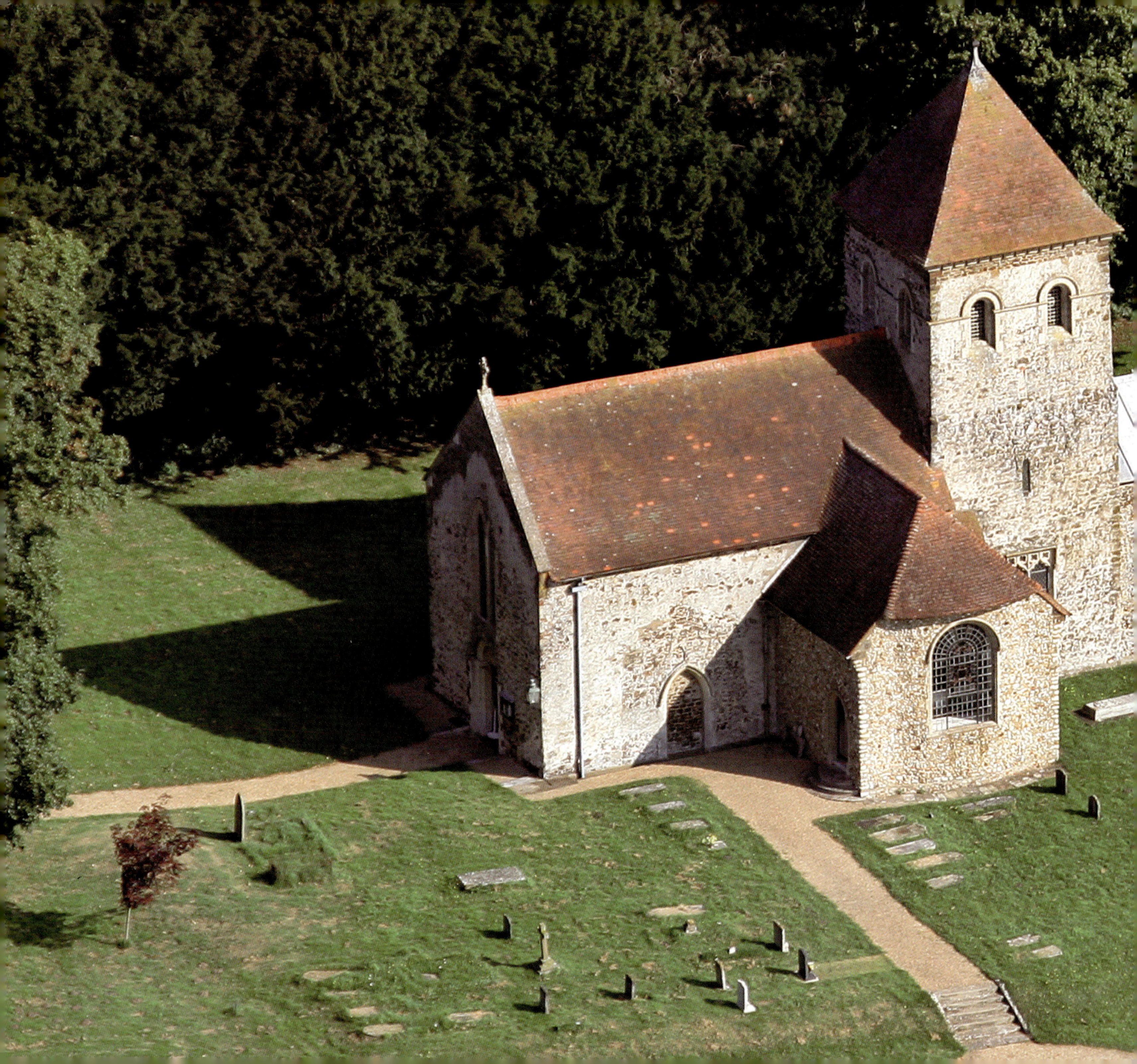

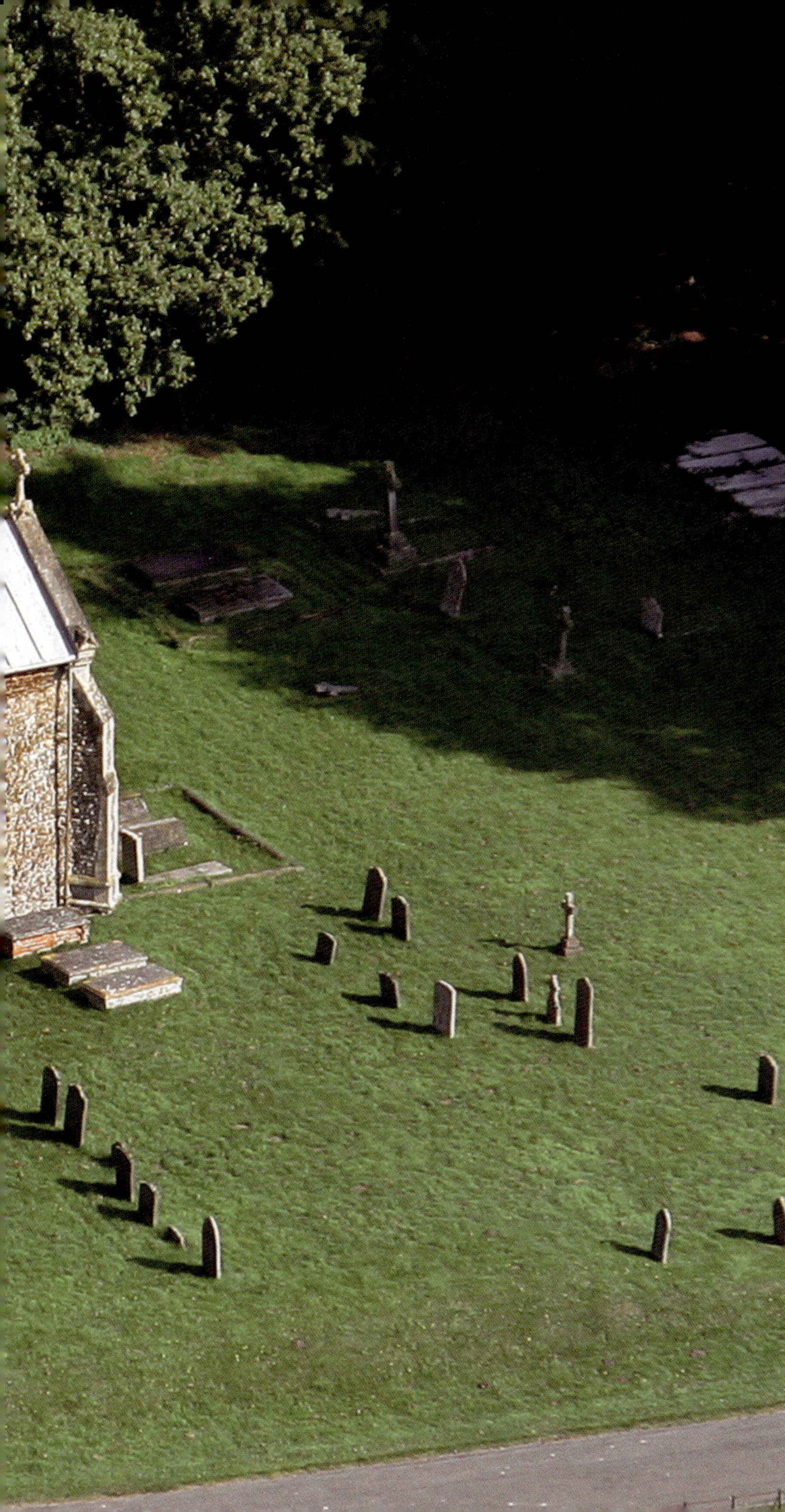

Melton Constable Church – Jacob Astley

Melton Constable was home to generations of Astleys. Jacob Astley (Lord Hastings) was one of the Royalist leaders in the Civil War Battle of Edgehill in 1642 (the result was inconclusive). His prayer before battle was

'O Lord, thou knowest how busy I must be this day.
If I forget Thee, do not Thou forget me'.

A visit to see the rather grand Astley pew is worthwhile. It has stairs!

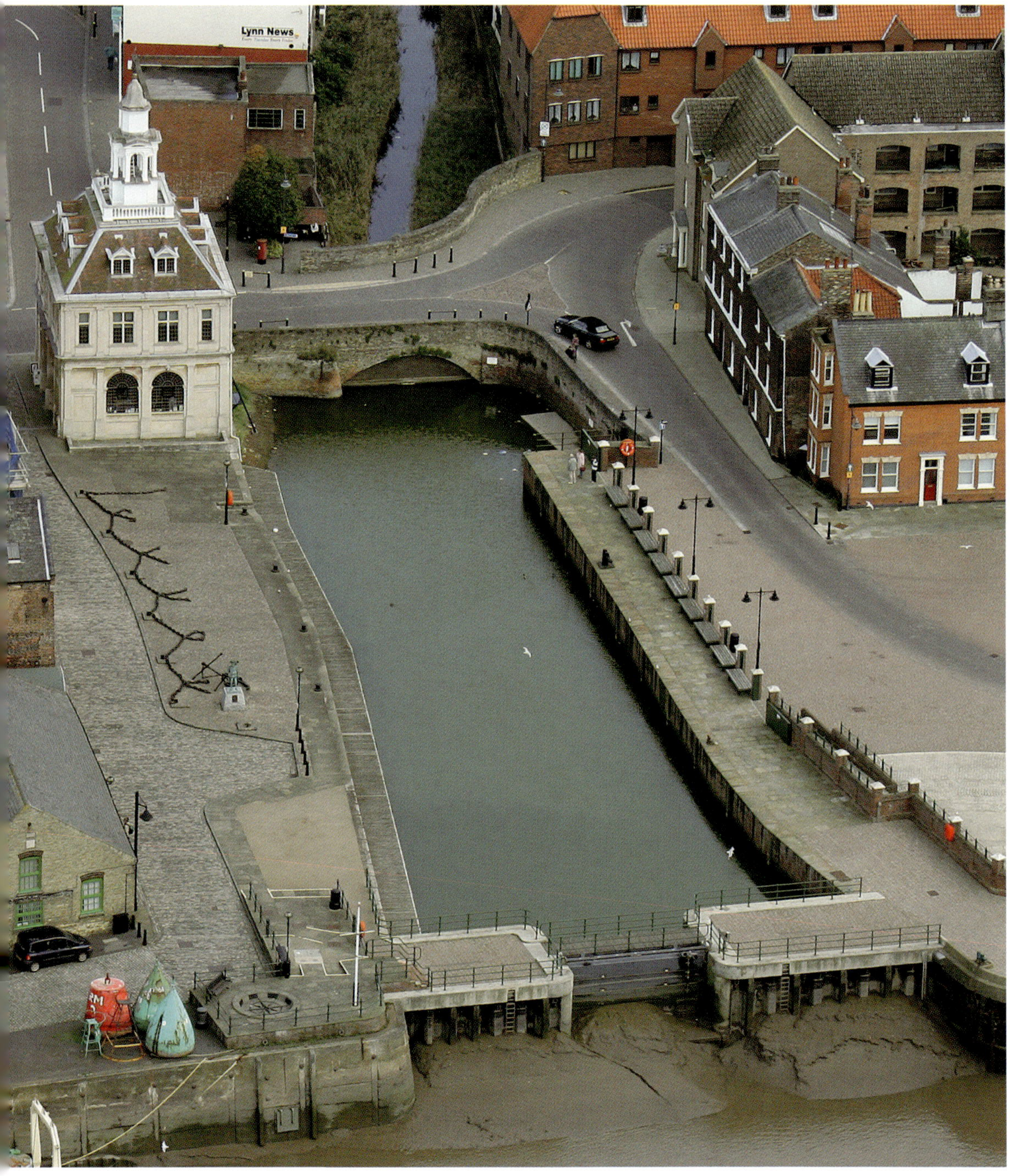

Kings Lynn Custom House with the George Vancouver statue.

George Vancouver

Explorer and navigator Captain George Vancouver (1757–1798) was born in Kings Lynn. He learned his seamanship sailing under the command of Captain James Cook. He would have been familiar with the Custom House (1683) on the Purfleet Quay in front of which his statue stands. The beautiful building had been built less than a century earlier. It was where the Hanseatic League Traders discussed their business with Germany and the Baltic countries. But George Vancouver's interests were westwards and the city of Vancouver was named after him.

Norfolk Architects George Skipper and Edward Thomas Boardman

They both made a difference to the look of Norfolk addressing the new architectural styles of Art Nouveau and the Arts & Crafts movement.

George Skipper 1856–1948

Skipper's buildings were executed in several parts of the country but Norfolk and Suffolk are well represented by Norwich's Royal Arcade, in Cromer by the 'Hotel de Paris' (described as 'Loire Fantasy') and most exciting of all by the Norfolk and Suffolk Yacht Club in Lowestoft.

The Royal Norfolk & Suffolk Yacht club (1902) – painted cream mid-left picture (Skipper).

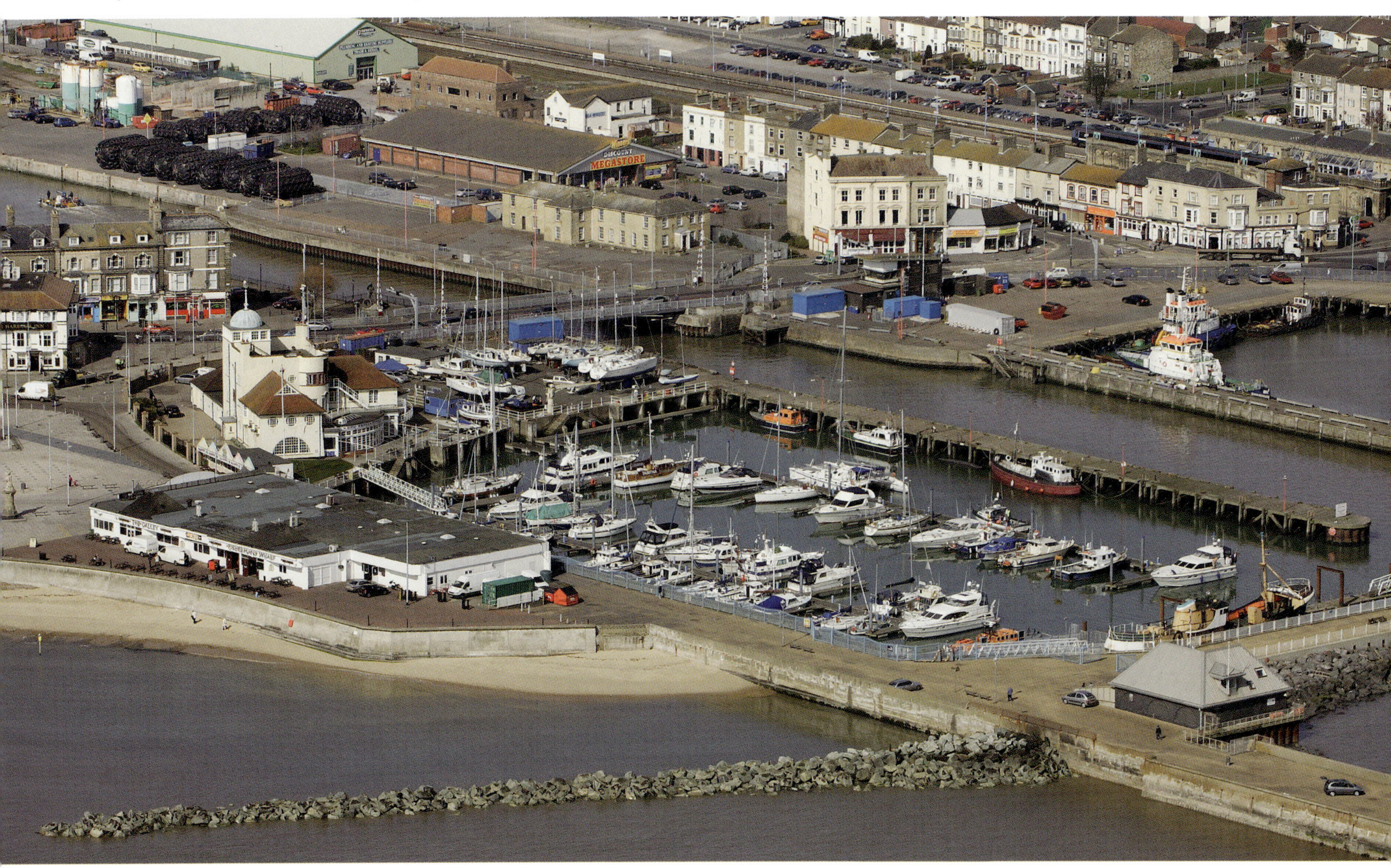

Edward Thomas Boardman 1861–1950

Boardman was a 'comfortable' architect whose buildings didn't excite, they were traditional but with some artistic flair. His window treatments pointed the way towards Art Deco whilst the carved door surrounds and roof treatment harked back to mediaeval craftsmanship.

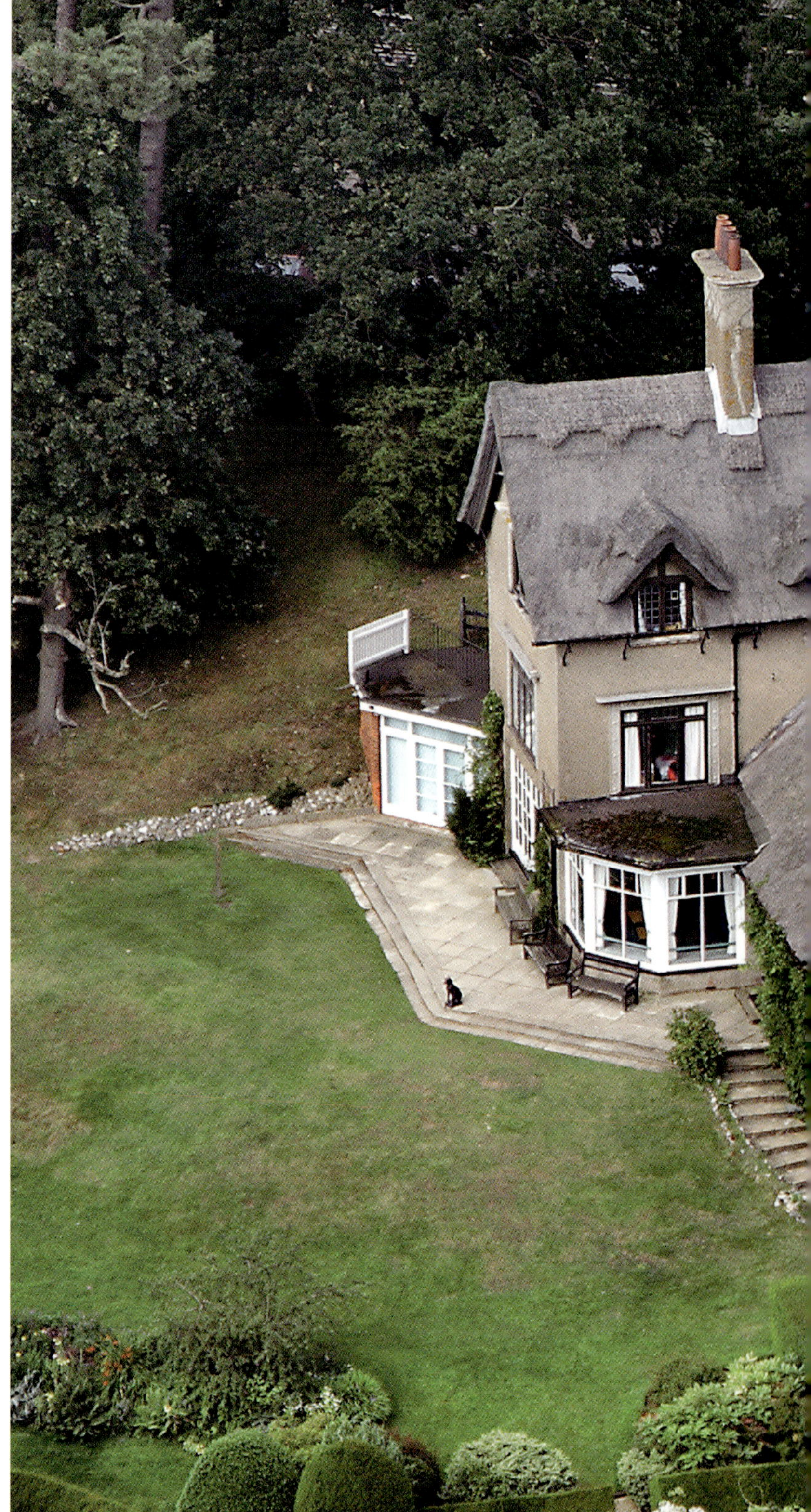

How Hill House 1904 (E T Boardman).

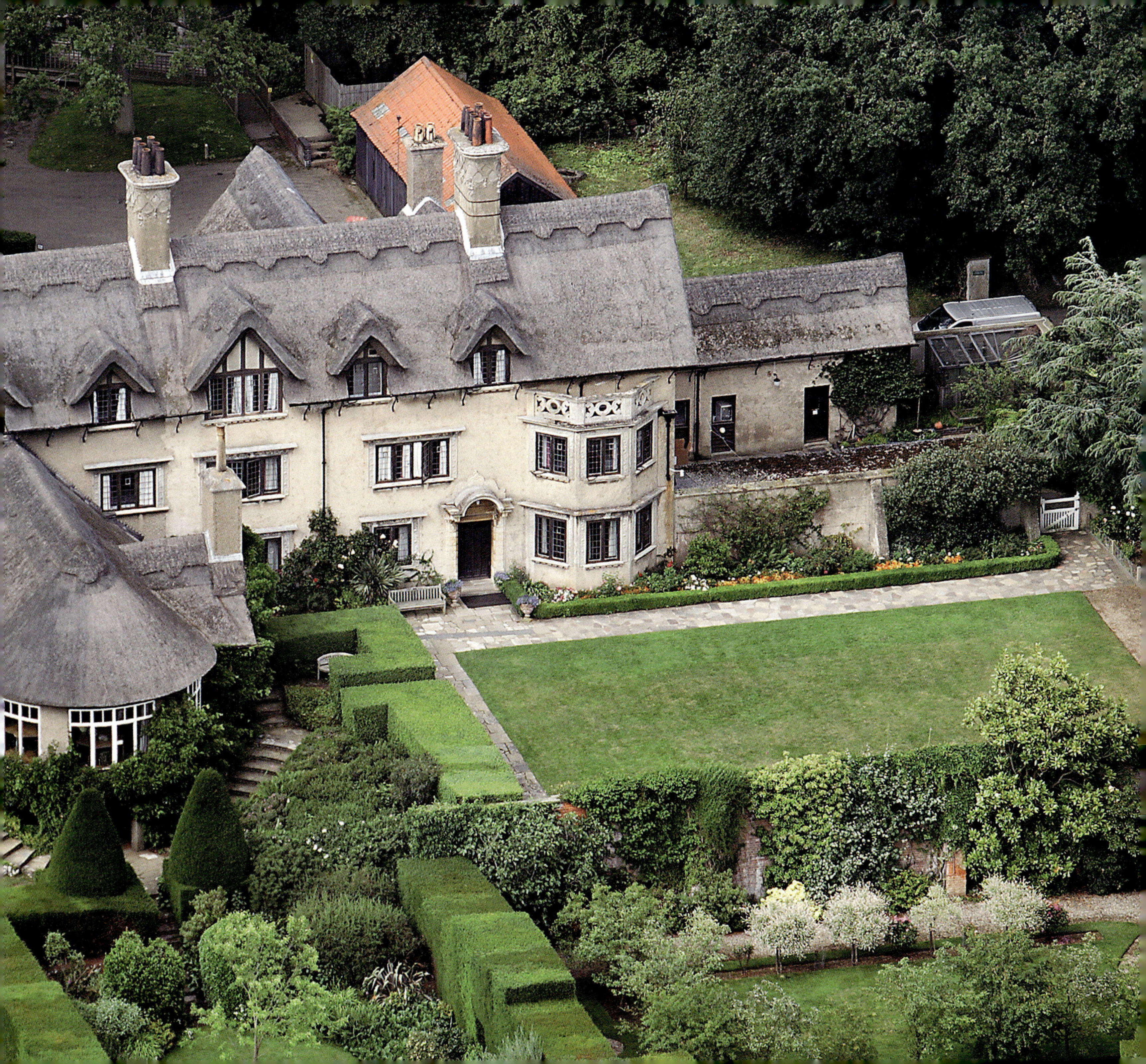

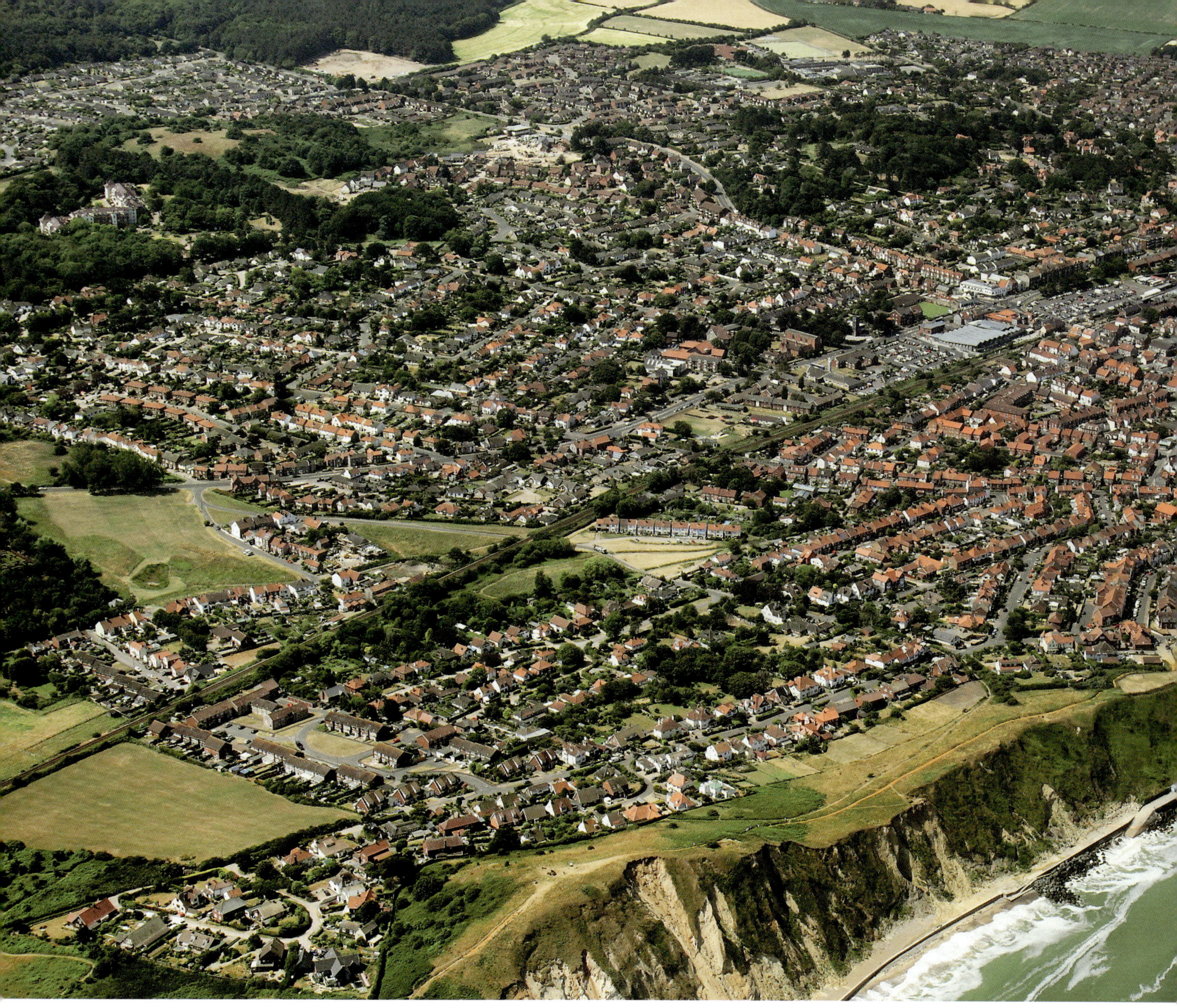

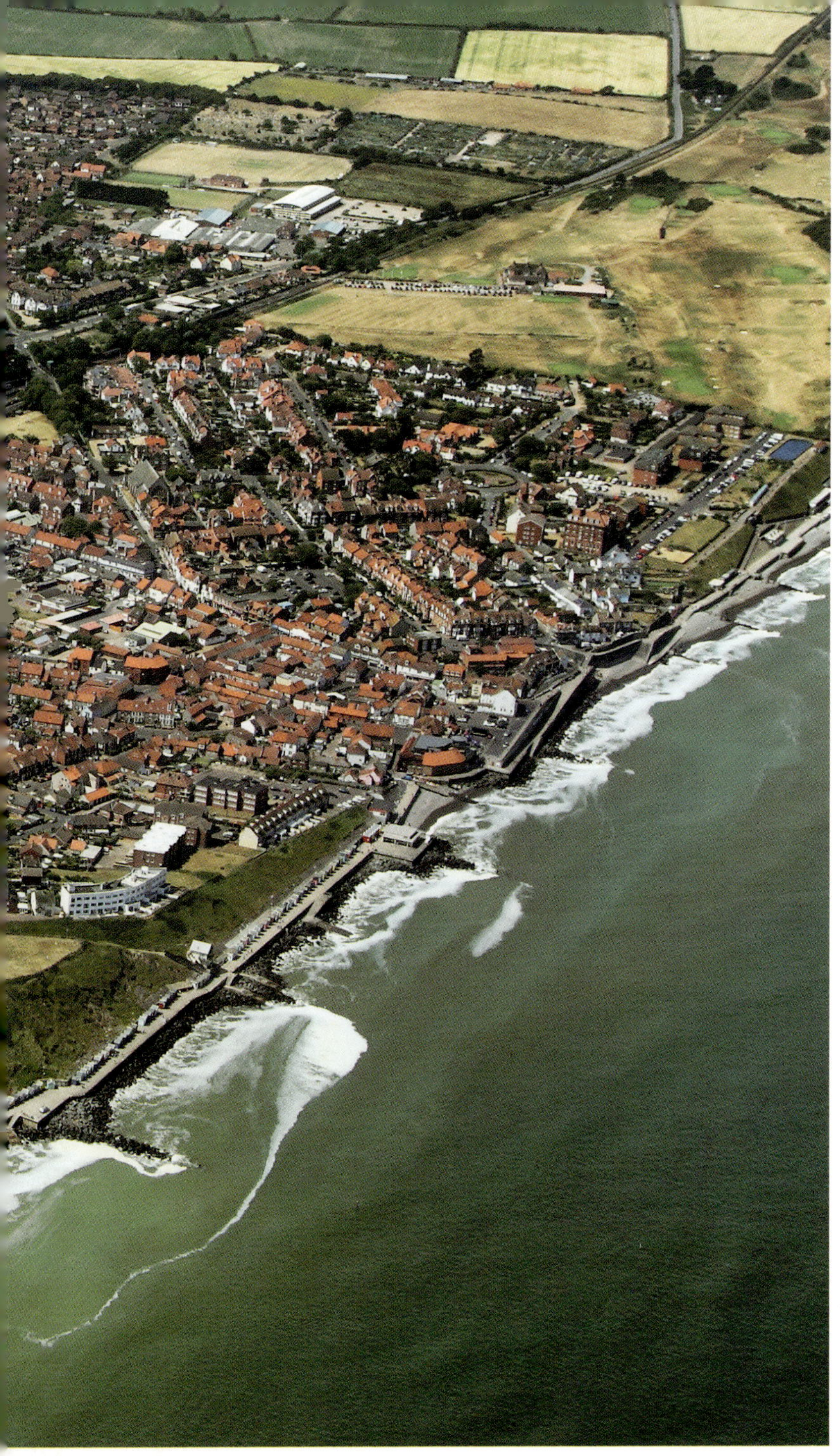

The Singing Postman

Born Allan Smethurst in 1927 in the Midlands, his family moved to Sheringham when he was two years old so he's an honorary Norfolk man with a Norfolk accent. His singing act was characterised in the Norfolk way – verbs in the present tense and upwards inflections at sentence ends. His most popular song was 'Hev you got a loight, boy'? It tells of Molly Wimbley ('she smoke loike a chimbly') but stage fright and alcohol got to him and he ended up a derelict alcoholic dying in 2000.

Sheringham – home of the Singing Postman.

Mrs Elizabeth Woodhouse of Breckles Hall

During the reign of Elizabeth I it didn't pay to be different but Elizabeth Woodhouse seems to have got away with it – there are no tales of her being burned at the stake. Breckles Hall is a beautiful Tudor mansion between Watton and Thetford. Elizabeth I came to the throne in 1558 and was a staunch Protestant. Elizabeth Woodhouse built her house mid 1500s and was a devout Catholic. Her religious inclinations seem to have been widely known and that included the making of a Priest's Hole where Catholic priests could hide to escape detection. There's one on view at Oxborough too so perhaps it was blind eyes all round.

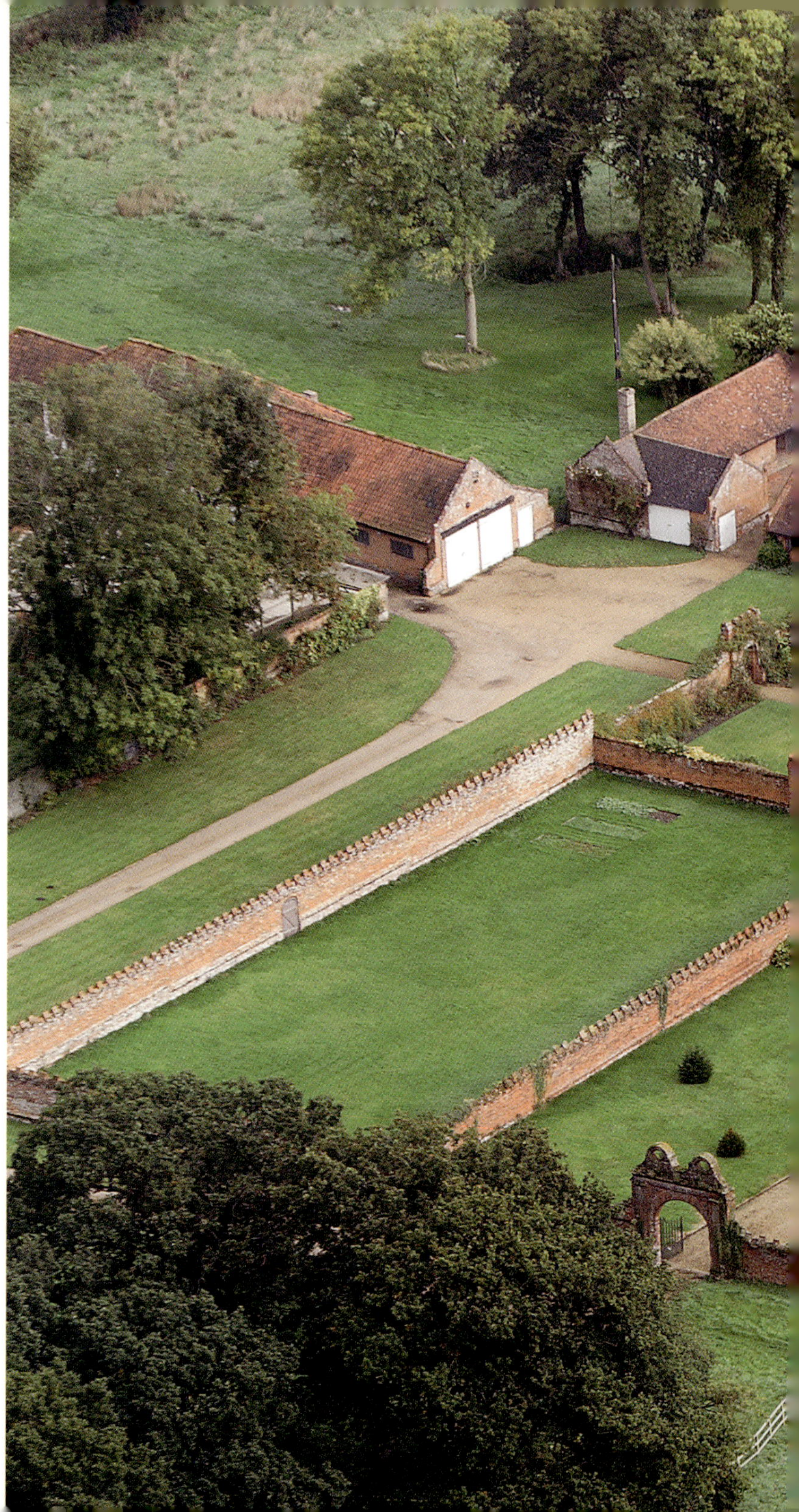

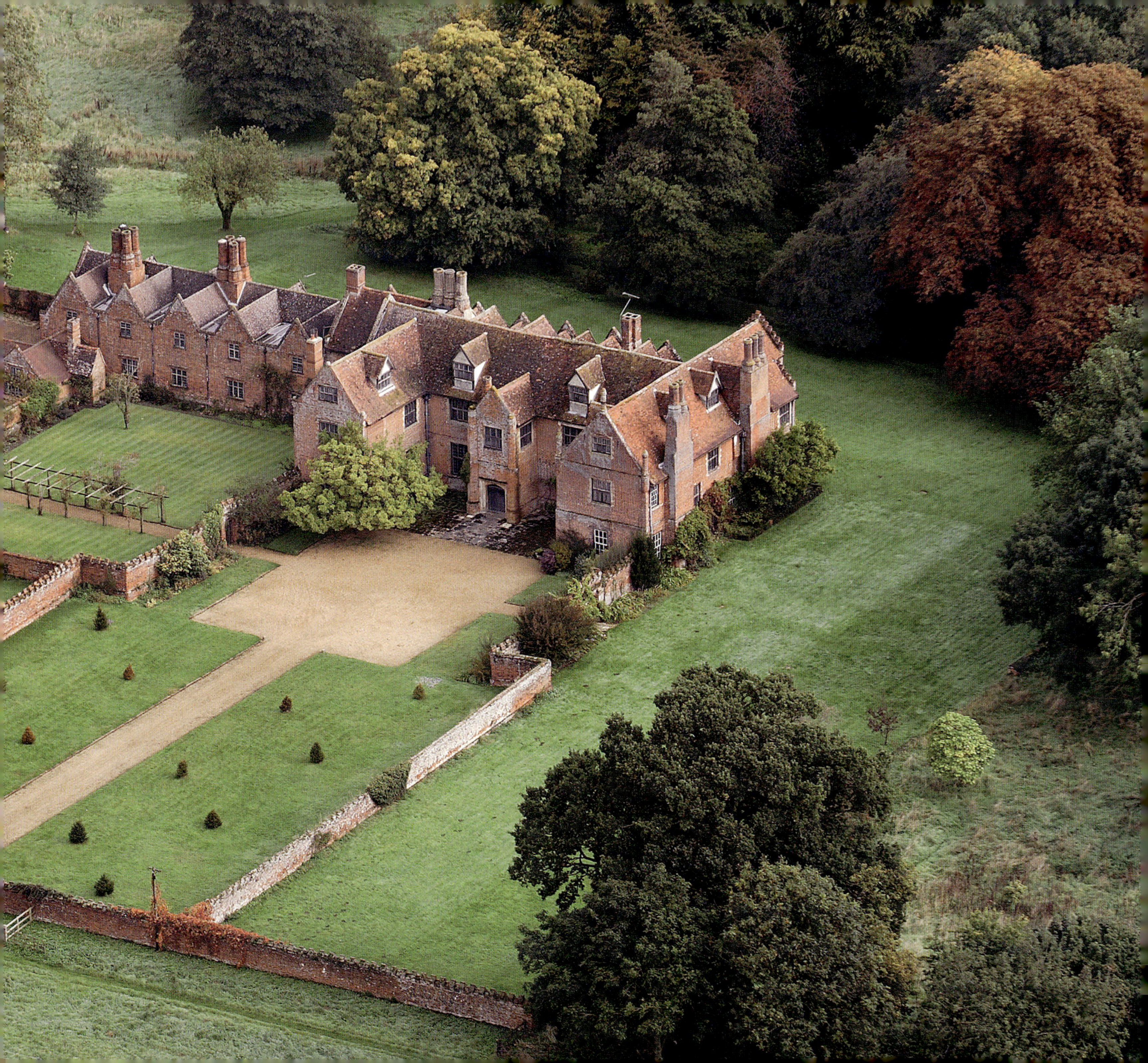

John Innes 1829–1904

Imagine the satisfaction of going to a Garden Centre and buying compost with your name on the bag, an unusual achievement. John Innes left funds and royalties, from making his fertile growing medium, for plant research. The John Innes Institute moved to Norwich from Cambridge, being constructed in 1967. It is a world renowned Biological and Biotechnical Research Centre, forming part of the Norwich Research Park, which includes food research, part of the UEA and medical research.

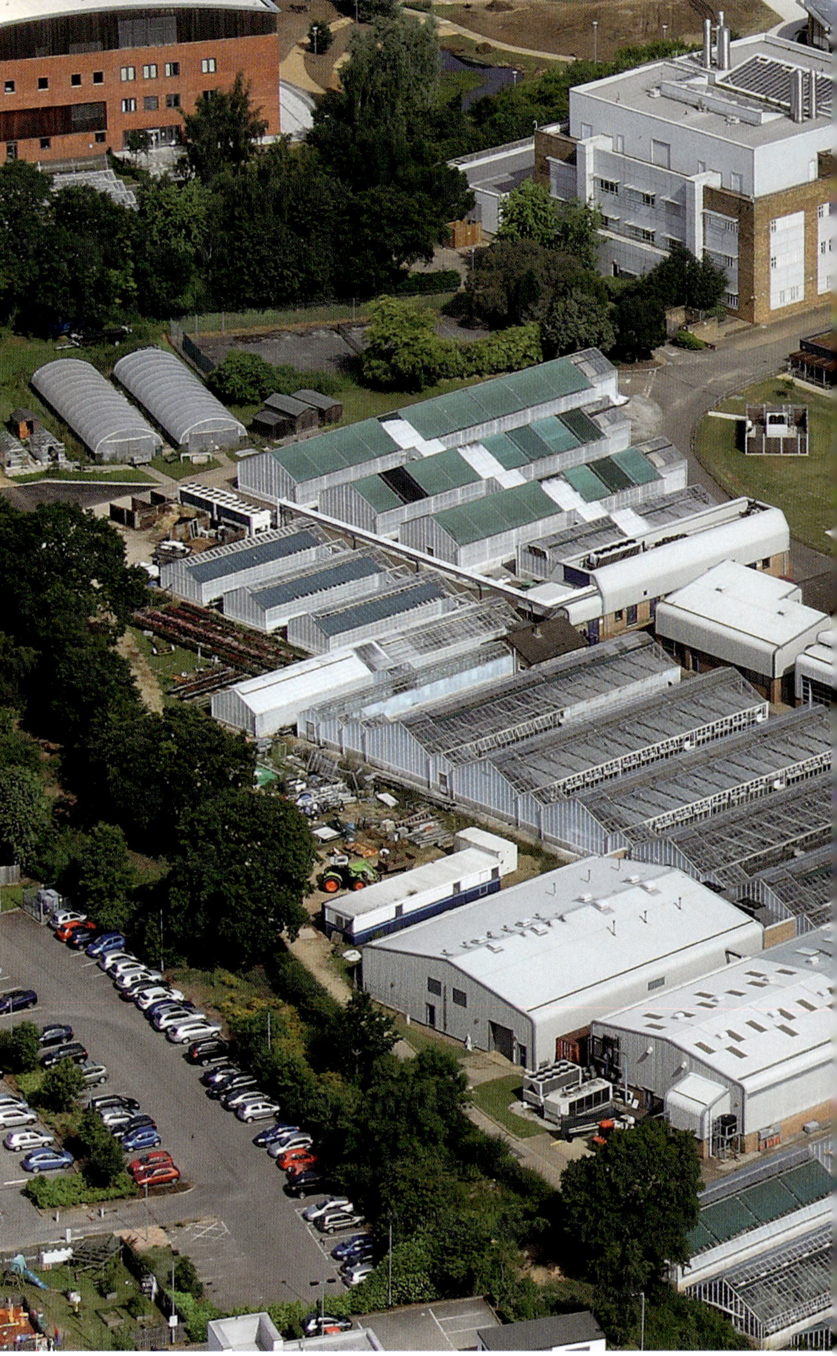

The John Innes Centre, part of the Norwich Research Park at Colney on the outskirts of Norwich.

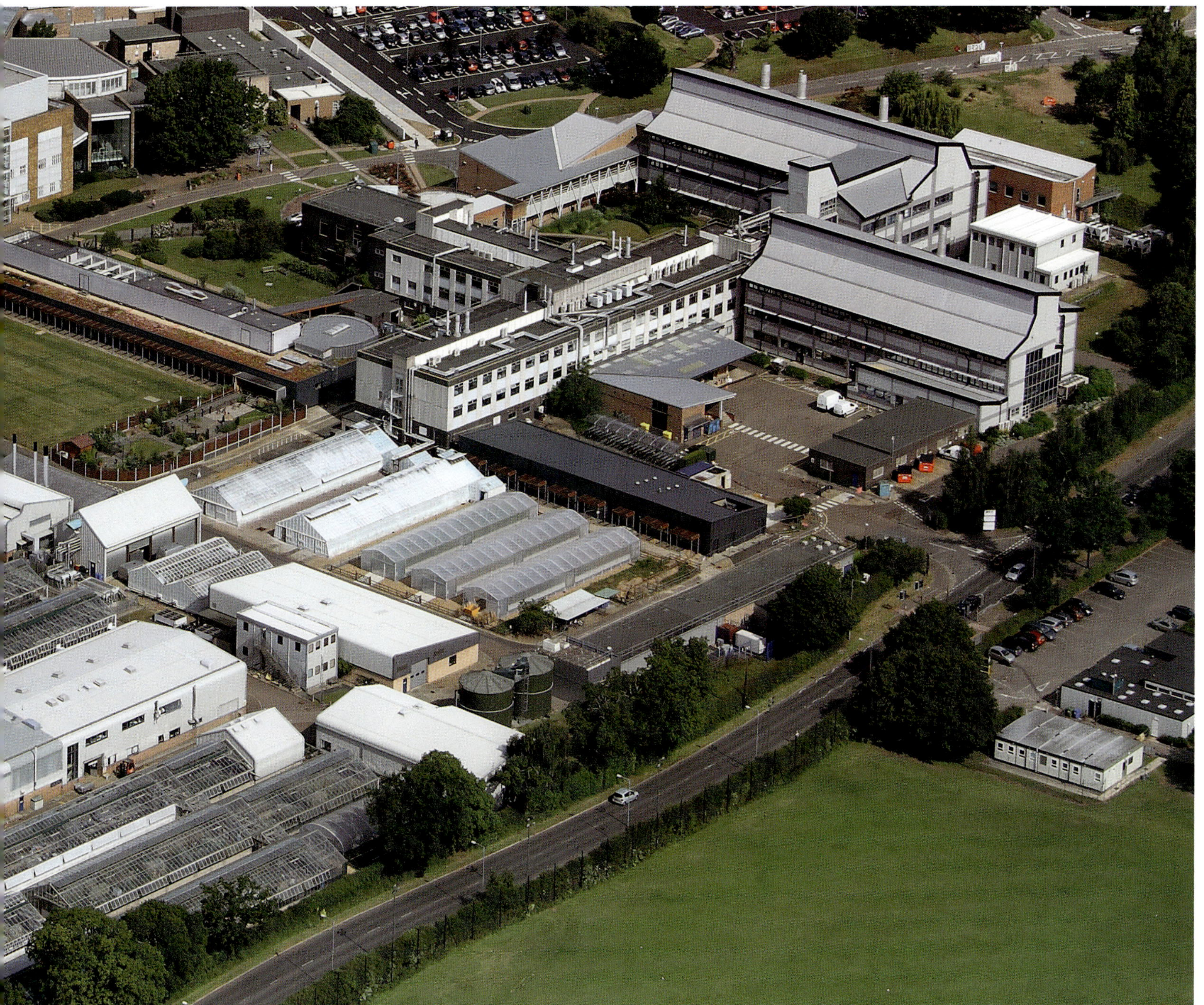

John Betjeman

If anyone earned the title of 'Honorary Norfolk man' it was John Betjeman who sang the praises of Norfolk churches loudly and in print and latterly on TV.

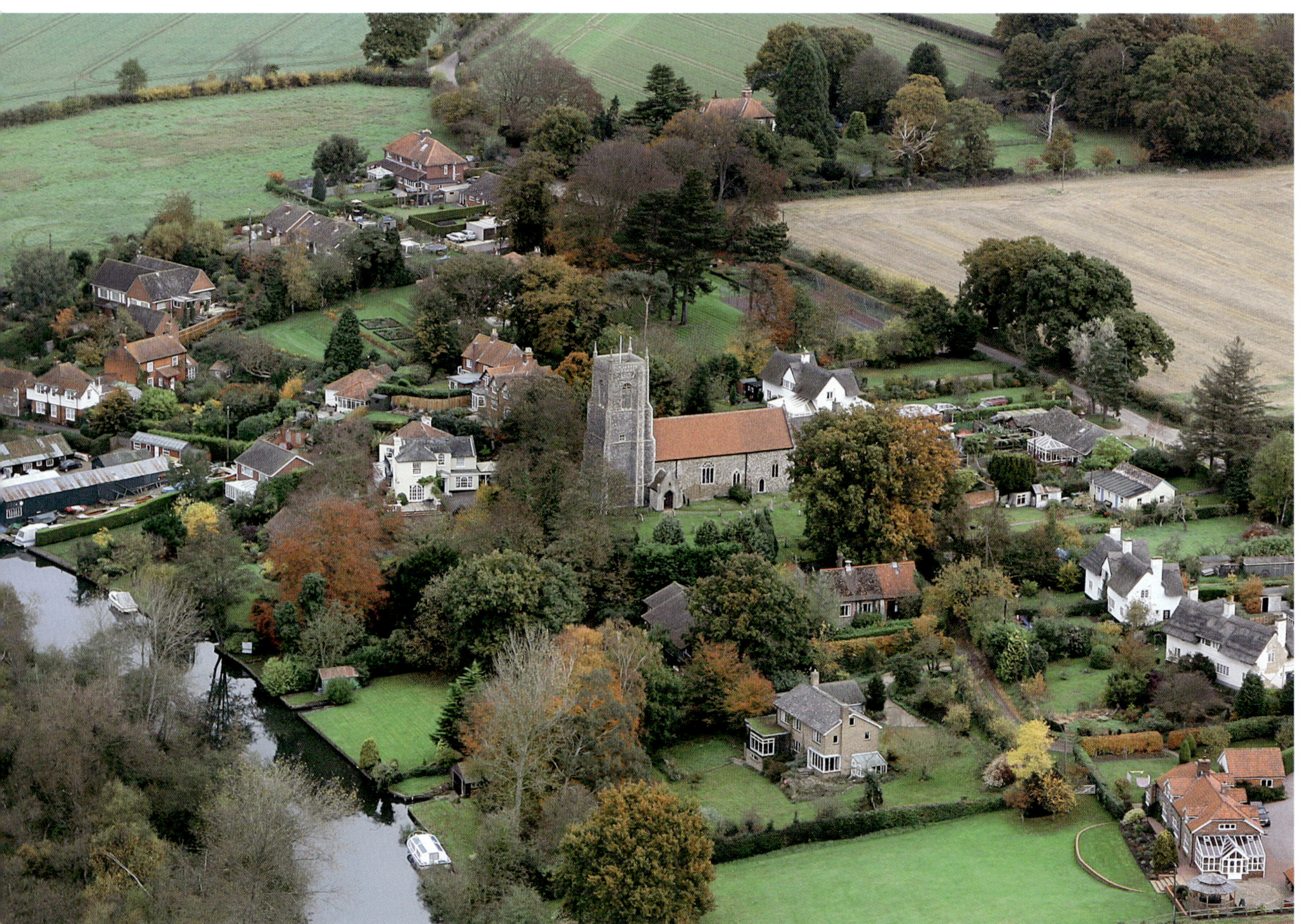

Belaugh church on the River Bure.

Caistermen Never Turn Back

Beachmen were the forerunners of lifeboatmen. They made their living from what they could salvage from the sea. In 1791 they organised themselves into the Caister Beach Company which in turn became the Norfolk and Suffolk Shipwrecked Mariners' Association. In 1852 the RNLI took over from them.

Events in 1901 gave the lifeboat service their motto 'Never turn back.' The Caister lifeboat *Beauchamp* was a heavy boat needing many men to launch her. A signal from a vessel in distress was received from a ship aground on the Barber Sands off Great Yarmouth. The lifeboat was launched with difficulty but later, cries could be heard from the *Beauchamp*. She was found upturned on a beach with the crew trapped inside. Only three seamen were rescued alive. A former coxswain, James Haylett, when questioned about the wisdom of going out in such appalling conditions said 'Going back is against the rules when we see distress signals like that.' This in turn became 'We never turn back'– a motto adopted by the RNLI. Subsequently the independent Caister Lifeboat proclaimed 'CAISTERMEN NEVER TURN BACK'.

The RNLI station closed in 1929 and the independent Caister Lifeboat Service took over. They have the only independent fully-sized lifeboat round these shores. Bernard Matthews was a generous supporter and has a lifeboat named after him.

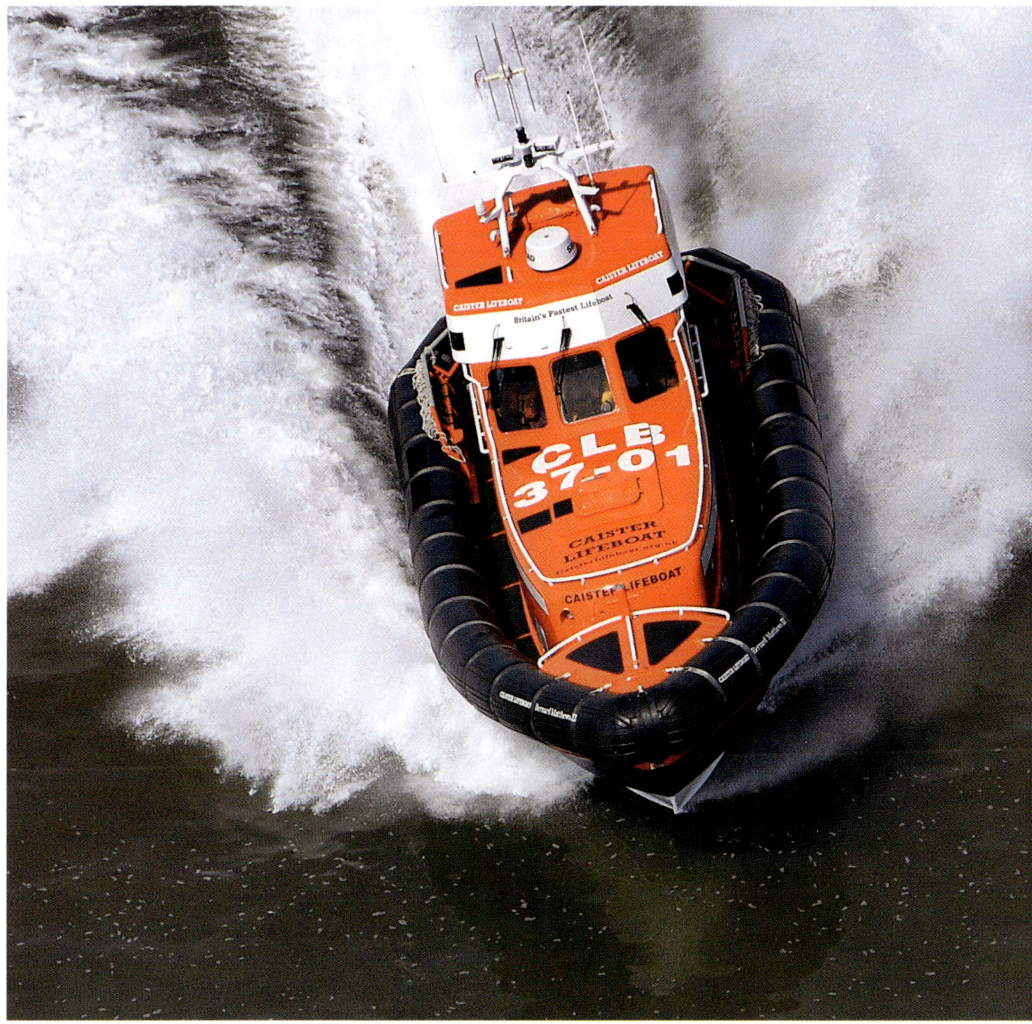

There are currently two lifeboats at Caister: The Bernard Matthews 2 *(illustrated) and the inshore rib* Fred Dyble *introduced in 2019.*

Turnip Townshend and Coke of Holkman: Agricultural Pioneers

To be an innovator takes confidence, less so perhaps when you're the owner of thousands of acres of Norfolk soil even if that soil is in need of improvement. Although their names are often linked they were not contemporaries.

Charles Townshend 1674–1738, Viscount Townshend of Raynham, made a study of soil improvement. He wanted increased yields to enable the over-wintering of cattle and sheep. The introduction of root crops (hence 'Turnip Townshend') was part of his 'Norfolk Four Course Rotation' strategy. Crops were to be grown in the order – wheat – roots – barley – clover (or grass) thereby abandoning the wasteful practice of leaving land fallow for a year.

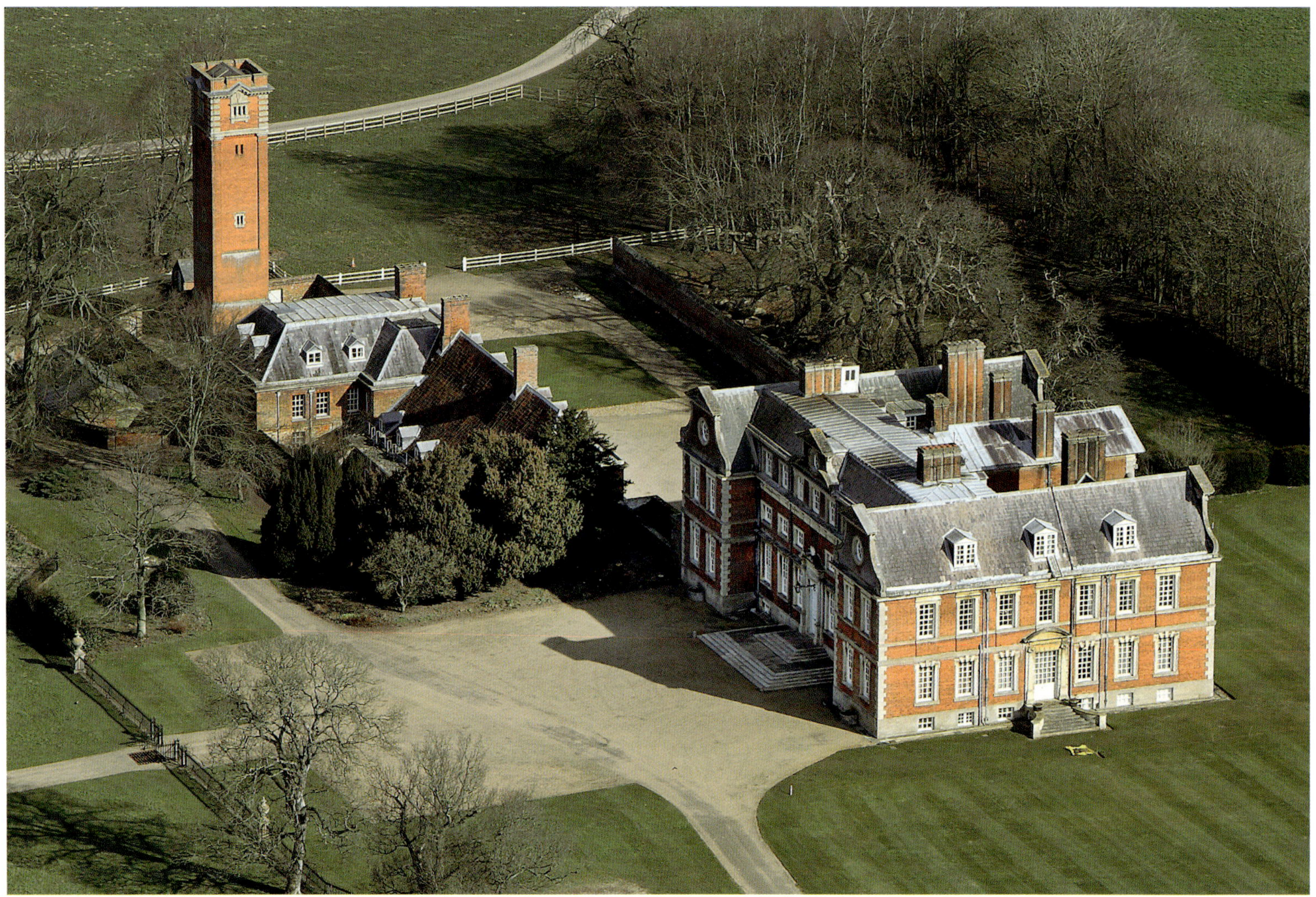

Raynham Hall – built by William Edge 1622 onwards.

Thomas Coke 1754–1842 (later Earl of Leicester) was the nephew of the builder of Holkham Hall. The difference he made to agriculture was far reaching. He improved the design of farm buildings, introduced different breeds of cattle (Devons) and sheep (Suffolks) onto the poor soil of coastal Norfolk, drilled new varieties of wheat, planted windbreaks (the Holkham pines) and reclaimed the salt marshes. Their 'doing different' improved farming especially during the period of the Napoleonic Wars when the need for increased food production was at its most acute.

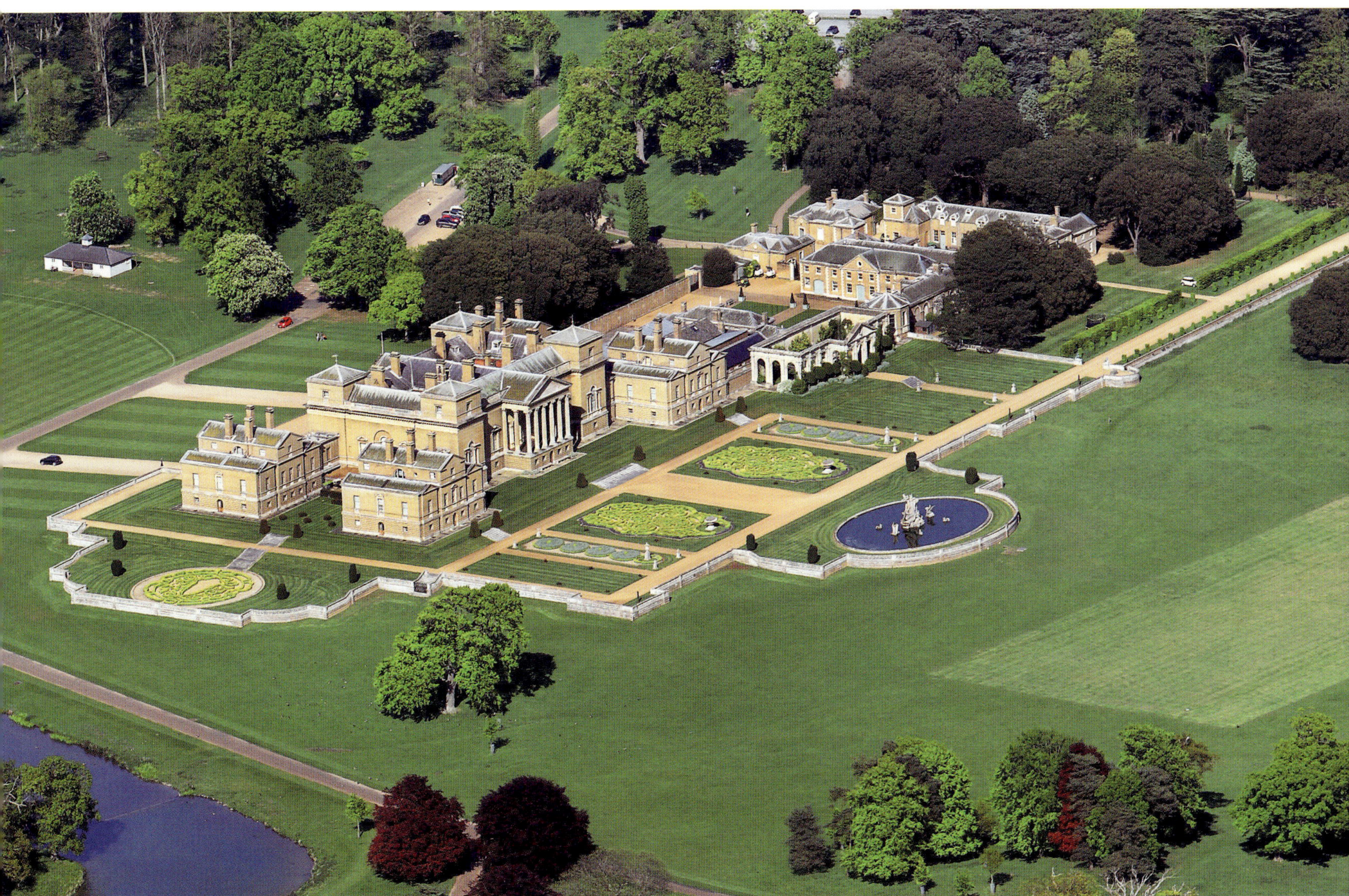

Holkham Hall – rebuilt 1734 by William Kent and Matthew Brettingham.

Horatio Nelson 1758–1805

'I am a Norfolk man and glory in being so'

Was England's greatest sailor clumsy, unlucky or deliberately wilful? He certainly qualifies as a 'do different' subject. He turned the loss of his right eye to good effect when disobeying the order to retreat at the (ultimately successful) Battle of Copenhagen. Wasn't being seasick every time he set sail a clue as to his unsuitability to be a sailor or a clue to his determination? Just as well he did different or the history of England might be different too.

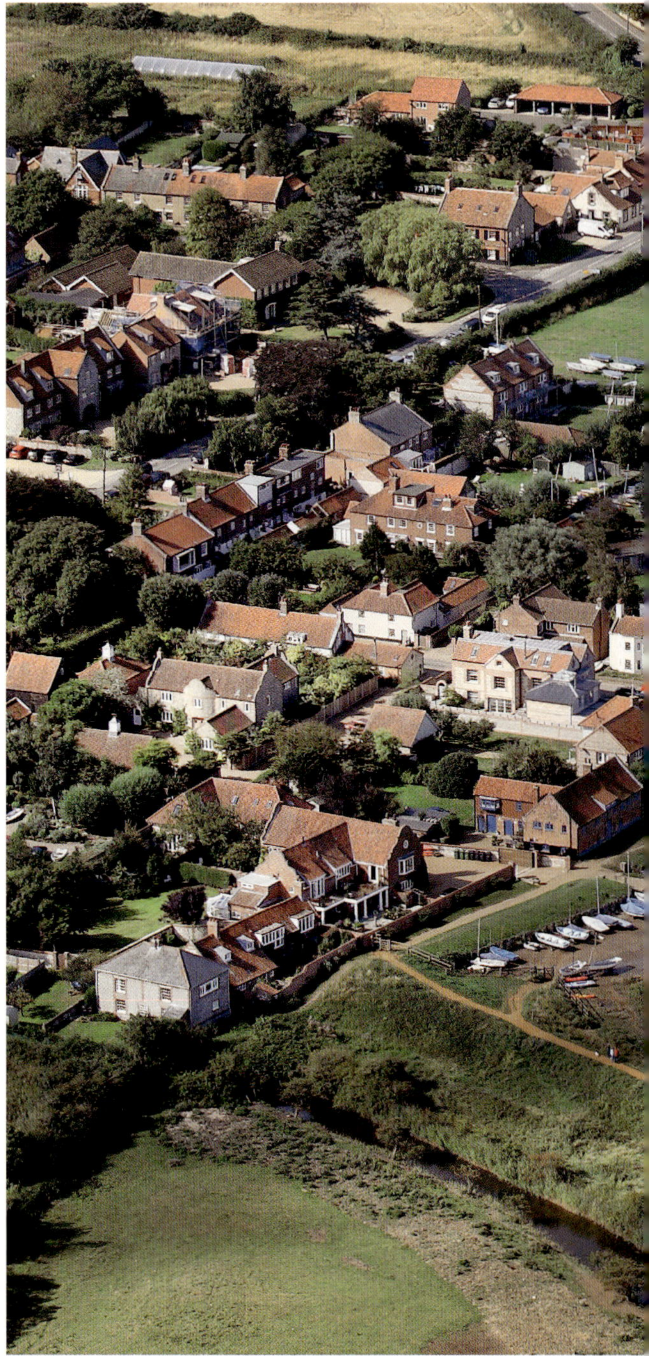

Burnham Overy Staithe, where Nelson probably learned to sail. But, when the sea is rough, what about the seasickness?

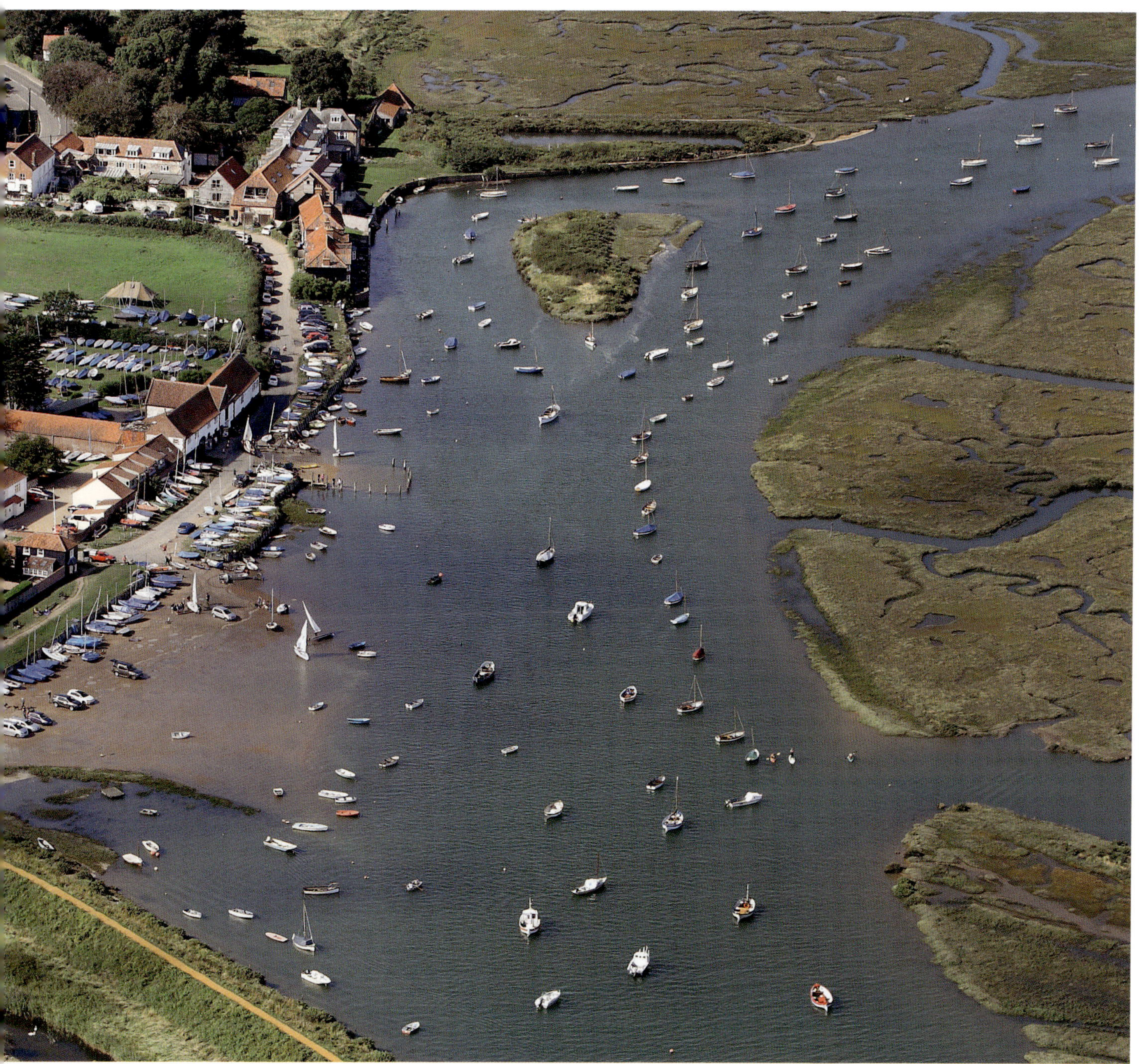

Bibliography

Anderson A   *The Captain & Norwich Parks*   Norfolk Society 2000
Barringer Chris   *A History of Norfolk*   Carnegie Publishing Ltd 2017
Chadwick Owen   *Victorian Miniature*   McDonald & Co 1960
Crane Nicholas   *The Making of the British Landscape*   Weidenfeld & Nicolson 2017
Dymond David   *The Norfolk Landscape*   Alastair Press 1985
Earwaker & Becker   *Literary Norfolk*   Chapter 6 Publishing 1998
Higgins David   *The Beachmen*   Terence Dalton 1987
Howe David   *Wandering in Norfolk*   Mousehold Press 2016
Kennett David   *Norfolk Villages*   Robert Hale 1980
Kent Peter   *Fortifications of E Anglia*   Terence Dalton 1988
Ketton-Cremer R W   *Norfolk in the Civil Wars*   Faber & Faber 1969
Loveday M   *Norwich Knowledge*   Loveday 2011
Malster R   *Wherries & Waterways*   Dalton 1971
Meeres F   *The Story of The Fens*   History Press 2019
Page M & Yardy A   *A-Z of Norfolk Windmills*   Halsgrove 2011
Pevsner N   *The Buildings of England:*   Penguin 1962
                      North-West and South Norfolk
                      North-East Norfolk and Norwich

Pryor F   *Seahenge*   Harper Collins 2001
Pocock T   *Norfolk*   Pimlico 1995
Wilson R & Lee P   *The Marshland World*   Blandford 1982
Yaxley D   *Portrait of Norfolk*   Robert Hale 1997

Acknowledgements

Mike Page would like to thank his co-pilots from Seething Airfield, Brian Barr, Dan Gay, Graham Wright and Greg Shepherd.
Also Norwich Air Traffic for their good-humoured help and cooperation as we have flown around the area.

Thanks also to Richard Adderson and Mike Gay for additional information and to Brian Cormack, Judy Speed and Carla Sutherland for proof reading.